Managing Staff in Schools
A Handbook

Managing Staff in Schools
A Handbook

Geoffrey Lyons and Ron Stenning

Hutchinson

London Melbourne Sydney Auckland Johannesburg

Hutchinson and Co. (Publishers) Ltd
An imprint of the Hutchinson Publishing Group
Brookmount House, 62–65 Chandos Place,
Covent Garden, London WC2N 4NW

Hutchinson Publishing Group (Australia) Pty Ltd
16–22 Church Street, Hawthorn, Melbourne, Victoria 3122

Hutchinson Group (N Z) Ltd
32–34 View Road, PO Box 40–086, Glenfield, Auckland 10

Hutchinson Group (S A) (Pty) Ltd
P O Box 337, Bergvlei 2012, South Africa

First published 1986
© Geoffrey Lyons and Ron Stenning 1986

Typeset in 10 on 12 pt Plantin Compugraphic by Colset Pte Ltd, Singapore

Printed and bound in Great Britain by
Anchor Brendon Ltd, Tiptree, Essex

British Library Cataloguing in Publication Data

Lyons, Geoffrey
  Managing staff in schools.
  A Handbook
  1. School personnel management——Great Britain
  I. Title II. Stenning, Ron
  371'.0068'3   LB2831.5

ISBN 0 09 159620 3

Contents

Acknowledgements

In the course of writing this book and the related volume of training materials, we became increasingly appreciative of the valuable assistance provided by the many individuals, agencies and schools who participated in the research which underpins our endeavour.

We particularly wish to record our gratitude to the Officers of the Local Education Authorities and to the headteachers and members of the teaching and support staff of the schools directly involved. We are also grateful to the Officers of the Teachers' Associations and their colleagues representing support staff who have given their unstinting support, together with the Officers of the Association of County Councils and the Association of Metropolitan Authorities. They freely afforded us their time and provided us with insights into some of the more subtle nuances of school life which greatly facilitated our study.

The need to preserve anonymity does not extend to Ron Webster, Professor Alan Brimer and Win Stenning, to whom we owe a great deal. Ron Webster inspired the original conception of this book. Alan Brimer and Win Stenning have sought to inject intellectual rigour into our work by challenging our ideas and assumptions, and accepting the onerous task of commenting on the draft manuscript.

We also welcome the opportunity to express our thanks to Elizabeth French and Susan Woods who suffered our idiosyncracies without complaint and shared in the typing and general presentation of the manuscript.

Finally, we gratefully acknowledge the support of the Department of Education and Science who sponsored the project which led to this book. The responsibility for the text, however, remains entirely with the authors and it does not purport to represent the views or policies of the Department of Education and Science.

Foreword

There is a widespread and growing recognition that the quality of educational leadership provided by the headteacher is a key factor in the success of a school. Such leadership is not just a matter of personality or style, important as these may be. Life in schools increasingly reflects the social, political and legal complexities of the world beyond the gates. The headteacher who is insensitive to these complexities, insufficiently knowledgeable about the legislative framework within which his or her responsibilities are exercised, unaware of weaknesses and breakdowns in communication, who does not know what to do about individual and collective grievances, is likely to have a hard time. Knowing about employment legislation, health and safety, staff development, appraisal and evaluation, communication and decision making, procedures for handling disputes and codes of conduct is not a *sufficient* condition for success as a headteacher – it is increasingly a *necessary* one.

In writing this book and its companion volume of training materials, Geoffrey Lyons and Ron Stenning have drawn extensively upon their research on school management and administration. The many examples and cases that enliven their treatment of management issues point up the demands that contemporary conditions impose on the knowledge, judgement and social and political skills of those who head our schools. Here as much as in other spheres, there will be those who regret the legal and bureaucratic constraints that surround employment relationships today, and the apparent absence of trust and goodwill they imply. Yet whatever the formal requirements, trust and goodwill remain conditions for real success. If they are to thrive, the formal requirements of good management have to be fulfilled effectively and expeditiously. This book is designed to help those who work in schools and other areas of the education service to be more aware of these aspects of their tasks and better equipped to carry them out. If it succeeds in these purposes, it will make a valuable contribution to the greater professionalism that remains an important aspiration for all those who care about the future of teaching.

Professor William Taylor
Vice Chancellor, University of Hull

Introduction

This book and the companion volume of training materials stem from research carried out by the authors between 1981 and 1985. The primary focus of the research was the conduct of employment relations in maintained secondary schools with particular reference to the headteacher.

The project was conceived in the belief that the day-to-day pressures and issues of employment relations were becoming as significant in the education service as they were in most other spheres of employment, but that the implications of this development were not altogether understood by many of the people with staff management responsibilities. In particular, it was felt that the effective management of individual schools could be assisted by providing headteachers with guidance and training in the processes and procedures of staff management.

Accordingly, the research methodology was inspired by a concern to determine the real, rather than the assumed, needs of headteachers and aspirant headteachers, in the sphere of employment relations. This was to ensure that the guidance and training materials, which represent the chief outcome of the research, were rooted in the realities of school life and thus credible and acceptable to both trainers and recipients.

The research highlighted some of the most important problem areas for headteachers and also indicated how many of these problems vary in size and nature from one LEA to another, and indeed from one school to another, within the same Authority. These variations arise in part from differences between LEAs in their overall policies, and in part from differences in the social and economic environment of the LEAs and the schools. These are complicated matters and in this book we have endeavoured to strike a balance between avoiding immersion in detail, which is the result of local idiosyncracy or accident of location, and ensuring that what is indicated as general good practice is realistic for the circumstances of all but the minority of secondary schools. We have generally erred on the side of providing guidance rather than tedious acknowledgement of why it is not always possible to follow the guidelines suggested.

Another feature of the research which merits attention here is that the awareness of headteachers of the volume and significance of employment relations problems varied as much from one headteacher to another as the problems themselves. At one end of the spectrum were headteachers who, through reading or personal experience, had a commendable grasp of the contribution that effective staff management could play in promoting and sustaining the wider operational requirements of the school. In contrast, there were headteachers who saw no personal scope for intervening in an unsatisfactory employment relation situation, and who looked almost exclusively to other agencies such as governors and/or LEA officers to provide the remedies that they believed were necessary.

In the light of such observations the purpose of this book is to present an integrated picture of staff management as a key activity in the management of the school. Staff management is not treated simply as something that headteachers do (though this has influenced the content) but rather on a contingency view of the processes involved. That is, what headteachers and senior staff do and how they conduct employment relations in the school is contingent upon the LEA context within which they operate, their own and staff attitudes and values and other societal pressures, such as demands for curriculum change, which to a greater or lesser extent impinge upon the life of the school.

Experienced and knowledgeable headteachers and other senior colleagures may find that some of the suggestions presented in the text are closely aligned with what they have been doing for many years. Equally, there will be some headteachers who will believe that the approach adopted in the text is inappropriate for a profession which sets great store on notions of peer relationships and commitment and loyalty to their chosen vocation.

While acknowledging the force of such views, the fact remains that in recent years the traditional goodwill and mutual accommodation among school staff and other parties involved is growing increasingly difficult to sustain. The rise in the incidence of individual and collective grievances is a manifestation of the problems which beset the education service. Irrespective of whether they have their roots in or outside the school, they serve to undermine the basis of trust which has been a characteristic feature of professional and employment relationships in the school.

It should also be noted that employment law does not discriminate between the education service and other occupations. The former is no less bound by the legislative provisions and associated codes of practice than the latter.

The relative decline in staff mobility and opportunities for career advancement is also not unique to the education service; though given the post-war circumstances of growth and attendant career progression, the impact of contraction is perhaps more severe among teachers than other occupational groups.

Frustrations consequent upon contraction and a relative decline in living standards have served to sharpen the criticism of the Burnham machinery and the associated teacher career structure, which has led to pressures for review and reform. The public debate about the assessment of teachers heralds a further challenge for existing practices, where informal assessment and the mentor system remain a feature of staff management in the school.

While some of the forces for change apply specifically to teaching staff others, including employment law and contraction, raise all sorts of implications for the management of non-teaching staff. These also pose a challenge to traditional relationships among the adult community and deep-rooted practices in the operation of the school.

Thus, the growth in employment law, and the consequent increase in the formalisation of procedures applying to recruitment through to dismissal of staff, inevitably impinges upon the processes of managing the entire adult community in the school.

The adoption of strategies designed to reduce costs (such as the privatisation of school meals services) are common. In many instances such actions have undermined hitherto harmonious relationships among and between support staff and teachers. Notions of 'togetherness' and mutual collaboration have, on occasion, been replaced by rigid adherence to 'work boundaries' and a lack of co-operation between members of various sections of support staff.

The book does not attempt to provide solutions to the sorts of issues and problems alluded to above, for it would be absurd to suggest that effective staff management can be conducted without reference to the particular circumstances of the school. The main endeavour is to offer guidelines that are essentially concerned with the processes of review and the adoption of staff management practices consistent with the needs of the school and staff. Many of the incidents cited in the text might have been avoided if attention had been addressed to some fundamental weaknesses in the practice of staff management as a matter of policy and planning.

The effective conduct of staff management demands foresight, stimulated by the motivation to engage in the processes of developing contingency plans which are born out of sound day-to-day practice. This requires a recognition by those responsible (especially the headteacher) of the implications arising from the dynamic changes in social values and economic policies. Among other things, this entails a degree of personal introspection to examine attitudes which were fostered and sustained in an era which bears little resemblance to contemporary society and attendant demands made on the headteacher. This is not to suggest that personal principles should be abandoned *per se*, but that the capacities of understanding and toleration in the stance of the headteacher, and an ability not to confront situations 'head on', especially in times of crisis, may be necessary to avoid exacerbating already difficult circumstances.

The text is organised around certain key elements of staff management. While the burden of the book is directed towards teaching staff, support staff are seen as an integral part of the school adult community. Accordingly, the contribution and management of non-teaching staff is acknowledged in the text.

For purposes of clarity the topics dealt with in the text are presented in a discrete form, but it must be stressed that they do not stand in isolation from one another and indeed from the general management of the school. The sequence of the text stems from the belief that ignorance of employment law together with inadequate staff planning and staff communications are at the root of many individual and collective grievances which, in some instances, result in disciplinary proceedings. Such manifestations of staff discontent invariably intrude into the day-to-day conduct of school affairs, with all that that implies for the health and vitality of the school.

Chapter 1 focuses on employment law and in particular deals with the legislative provision which the prudent headteacher will acknowledge in the day-to-day management of staff. It is written for the layman and is not intended to be a substitute for professional legal advice. The primary concern is to alert headteachers to the sorts of problems which can, and do, arise as a consequence of paying insufficient attention to the requirements of the law.

Chapter 2 is concerned with exploring the processes and techniques involved in staff planning and staff development. Models are included for purposes of illustration and to stimulate discussion in schools about the adoption of practices appropriate to the context and circumstances within which they operate.

In **Chapter 3** attention is addressed to staff communications and decision making in the school, with emphasis on the purposes and the chosen vehicles for communicating with staff including departmental meetings and noticeboards. The structures and processes of staff communication familiar to most secondary schools are reviewed in the light of comments received from members of school staff.

Individual and collective grievances are examined in **Chapter 4** with reference to their origins which may be self-evident or rooted in the human condition which does not allow for simplistic assessment. The coping strategies of a number of headteachers, who have been exposed to the full force of strikes and other forms of collective action by teachers and non-teaching staff, are reviewed with the aid of incidents. These are intended to provide insights that might alert headteachers to potential issues and problems which they may find difficult to contemplate in the absence of personal experience.

Chapter 5 is devoted to the processes involved in the maintenance of the staff code of conduct. Here guidance is offered about such matters as staff conduct and competence. Incidents are included to illustrate the sorts of problems which arise when inappropriate action is taken. These also serve to underline the significance of LEA disciplinary procedures and the headteacher's role in developing a code of conduct which is reasonable and capable of consistent application.

Apart from being a source of reference, the book lends itself readily to a variety of training forums including INSET and qualification programmes. In the former it is envisaged that the headteacher and LEA colleagues will be sufficiently stimulated by the presentation to develop and guide serving and aspirant headteachers through the labyrinth of managing staff in the school. Those engaged in studying for professional qualifications will find the book useful as a source of reference to underpin the more formal academic spheres of their studies.

The companion volume of training materials is an additional resource which ideally should be used in conjunction with the particular topic suggested in the text and which has been selected for review in a training programme. Some examples of training materials are included at the end of some chapters to indicate the sorts of issues embraced in the companion set of training materials.

In conclusion, we have been concerned to provide headteachers with the means of distinguishing between 'good' and 'bad' practice. We are aware that the use of such normative expressions begs many questions: whether something is regarded as good or bad depends on the standpoint of the observer and depends upon what is regarded as a satisfactory outcome of whatever phenomena it is which is under scrutiny. We have resisted the temptation to examine the ethical and political implications of such considerations, and have taken a stand on the need, which we believe to be self-evident, for the orderly and effective management of schools. What is meant by effective in this context will, we hope, become clear in this book and associated training materials.

The legal framework of employment

Introduction

As the manager of the school the headteacher is involved in:

- writing job advertisements
- staff appointments
- allocation of duties
- staff promotions
- maintenance of staff discipline
- staff dismissal
- health and safety.

This list is not exhaustive but it includes the key processes of staff management, and all of these functions have legal implications.

Consider these incidents taken from real life:

1 Shortly after she was appointed, a teacher told the pupils that they needed extra coaching in French and that she was willing to do this for a fee outside school hours.

Q What advice would you give this teacher with respect to her contractual obligations?

2 Two teachers refused to comply with the deputy headteacher's instruction that they go to their respective classrooms and take their classes.

Q What is the contractual significance of this incident?

3 A teacher could not account properly for the money given by the pupils towards a holiday trip.

Q Is the contract of employment relevant in this case?

4 A headteacher placed a note on the staff noticeboard which stated that he had promoted an existing member of staff. This was the first the staff had heard about the potential promotion opportunity and the LEA had not been informed.*

Q What are the contractual implications arising from the headteacher's action?

Headteachers who can confidently answer the questions posed in relation to these incidents may not wish to read any further. However, it may be prudent for them to check their answers against those provided at the end of this section. For less confident readers, the primary purpose of this section is to provide a *layman's* guide to matters which are of common concern to those with responsibility for the

---

* A commentary on the incidents presented in the text is provided on p. 34

conduct of staff management in schools. To this end, emphasis is given to what is usually termed employment law.

The following text proceeds from a brief discussion about recent developments in employment law. This provides the broad context for an examination of some relevant provisions of selected statutes. These have been identified with reference to the list of staff management functions indicated above, and are thereby what the effective headteacher needs to know.

Guidance is included at the end of the section for readers who wish to further their understanding about the different branches of the law and legal processes.

Examples of administrative documents used by different LEAs relating to different aspects of employment law may also be found in the Appendices. These are included for purposes of illustrating good staff management practice, and to stimulate discussion among headteachers who are seeking to improve their staff management practices.

Trends in employment law

There was relatively little statute law concerned with individual rights in employment until the early 1960s. This was because employers, unions and successive governments were agreed that workplace relationships were largely a matter for the parties directly involved and that the settlement of differences was best achieved by voluntary rather than legal means. There was, of course, the common law and disputes about breaches of contract were based on common law rights, though in the main employers and employees chose not to exercise these rights.

Over the past twenty years employment statutes have become the most significant feature of public policy concerned with employment relations. This reflects an important departure from the voluntary tradition since all sectors of employment, including education, are governed by a comprehensive legal framework.

The main themes of this legislation have been as follows:

- extension of individual rights
- anti-discrimination
- strengthening of trade union rights
- reduction in trade union power.

These strands of public policy may be identified to a greater or lesser extent with the following legislation:

Contract of Employment Acts 1963 and 1972*
Redundancy Payment Acts 1965 and 1969*
Equal Pay Act 1970
Trade Union and Labour Relations Act 1974 and 1976*
Health and Safety at Work Act 1974
Employment Protection Act 1975*
Sex Discrimination Act 1975

---

* The Employment Protection (Consolidation) Act 1978 brought together in one Act the provisions on individual employment rights previously contained in these earlier Acts. It was itself amended by the employment Acts of 1980 and 1982.

Race Relations Act 1976
Employment Protection (Consolidation) Act 1978
Employment Act 1980
Employment Act 1982

This legislation is extremely significant for the conduct of staff management in the school. The prudent headteacher will, therefore, keep abreast of the main points of the law and especially cases that occur in the education service.

Unions representing both teaching and non-teaching staff have long recognised the importance of briefing their lay representatives about the relevant provisions of the law, especially those relating to employment protection and the contract of employment.

The main concern here is to examine some major aspects of the legislation applying to individual employees, rather than the legal provisions relating to collective employment matters. To this end, the contract of employment is the first major point of reference.

Contract of employment

5 An assistant caretaker sold plants grown in the school greenhouse to the pupils.
Q Does the law of Contract offer any guidance in this case?

The contract of employment is the fulcrum of the employment relationship between individual members of school staff and the employer. In essence, a 'contract' means a bargain between two people which is legally enforceable. Thus the contract of employment is effectively a bargain whereby the parties to the contract agree to do something in exchange for an act or promise from the other side.

It should be noted that a contract of employment exists between the employer (either the LEA or governing body of the school) and an employee from the time the offer of employment is made and the employee's acceptance of the offer. Further, while the headteacher is not normally empowered initially to formulate the substance of the employment contract, as the person responsible for the conduct of staff management within the school, the headteacher inevitably influences the way(s) in which contractual relationship develops, such as the introduction of rules applying to staff.

Sources and elements of the contract of employment

- job advertisement
- selection interview
- letter of offer and acceptance of appointment
- job description
- custom and practice
- LEA rules
- school staff rules
- collective agreements between employers and unions
- Burnham regulations
- statutory minimum individual rights
- common law terms

These are the main sources of the employment contract and these are elaborated below. First consider these questions:

Can you give an example of an 'express term' in your contract of employment?

Can you give an example of what might be 'implied' in your contract of employment?

The two main elements of the contract are the terms which are *express* and those which may be *implied*. These can be a major source of difficulty where there is a difference over the interpretation of an employment contract.

The contract of employment reflects changes of procedure and substance over time. The terms of the contract include not only those expressly agreed between the individual teacher and the employer, but also those implied from other sources. Express terms can either be in writing or they may be verbally agreed between the parties to the contract. The letter of appointment, and a verbal explanation of the system of staff 'free' periods in the school, are two examples of what might constitute express terms of the contract.

Where a contract of employment is reasonably detailed the express terms usually pose few problems, at least in statute law, because the interpretations of the contract by the parties concerned are necessarily constrained by the governing legal provisions. However, it is not uncommon for differing opinions subsequently to emerge of what was said or promised at a selection interview, and great care should be taken by the participants to ensure that the contractual position is clarified before offering and accepting an appointment.

Consider this case:

6 A teacher was appointed as a full-time permanent teacher (with a standard contract of employment) in charge of the Resources Centre at the school. She was told at the time of her appointment that she would be required to apply herself almost full-time to the Centre's work. To begin with she had no regular teaching commitments, but after two years she was instructed by the headteacher to teach eighteen lessons a week. The teacher refused to comply with this instruction.

Q What advice would you give the headteacher in this case?

The Burnham machinery determines teachers' salaries subject to parliamentary assent, and these are an express element in the terms of the individual teacher's contract. However, other conditions of employment are subject to negotiation between the national employers' association (CLEA) and at the level of the LEA. The collective agreements which follow are not in themselves legally binding on the parties to the negotiation, but the various aspects of these agreements may be incorporated expressly or by implication into the individual teacher's contract of employment and thus have the force of law. For example, there may be an agreement between the LEA and the unions on the level of subsistence payable to teachers attending a parents' evening.

To this extent, therefore, elements of the collective agreement may become legally binding on the parties to the individual contract. Headteachers should make every effort to familiarise themselves with both national and local collective agreements and the associated provisions which are part of the individual teacher's contract of employment. A particular difficulty here is that apart from the School Meals Agreement of 1968, there is no existing national collective agreement on the 'teachers' day', duties and holiday entitlement.

The **implied terms** of the contract of employment are sometimes difficult to establish and may be drawn from common law, and custom and practice. Under common law it may be implied that a teacher is obliged to take reasonable care in the exercise of his/her duties; to obey a reasonable instruction within the scope of the contract; and to account for money entrusted to his/her care in the course of his/her employment.

For **custom and practice** to feature in a contract it must be 'reasonable, certain and notorious'. 'Reasonable' means it must be approved of by the judges; 'certain' means that it must be capable of being precisely defined; 'notorious' means that it must be well known. Generally speaking, unless a custom can fulfil these criteria, and be of long standing, it is not likely to be considered part of the contract.

Given the absence of national collective agreements concerning such matters as the 'teachers' day' and duties, the implied terms of the contract are a very important feature of employment relations in the school. In circumstances of mutual recognition of obligations and duties the implied terms of the contract of employment are rarely an issue.

However, teacher dissension is now more common and headteachers are frequently confronted with the problem of a member of staff refusing to carry out an instruction or declining an invitation to attend a parents' evening. While experienced headteachers will normally cope with these kinds of incidents, reference to what the individual contract states is an obvious starting point, followed by an investigation into the local and national agreements.

Changes in the contract

Consider these cases:

7 A typist in the school office was informed by the headteacher that her working hours were to be reduced from 18 hours to 12 hours a week.

Q Is this unilateral change in the terms of employment contract permissable in law?

8 The headteacher instructed the school caretaker to clean the windows on the second floor of the school. Previously they had been cleaned by 'contract' window cleaners 'employed' by the LEA. The caretaker refused to comply with the instruction.

Q What are the contractual implications here?

It was indicated above that the contract of employment is subject to change over time. For the contract to remain in being, however, there has to be agreement between employee and employer about any changes in its terms. Of course, if an existing term allows for a change by reference to a collective agreement, then this is permissible under the contract. It is not unusual for a headteacher (knowingly or otherwise) to attempt to change the terms of the contract.

If the member of staff concerned concurs and continues to carry out the assignment, then the courts usually find that the employee has agreed to the different arrangements or changes in the terms of the contract. There is the reservation that if the employer unilaterally changes the terms of employment and the employee works under the new terms, that is not sufficient evidence of agreement with the new terms. The employee can, during a 'reasonable period', try out the new terms before losing the right to resign and claim unfair dismissal or redundancy. A difficulty here is that a 'reasonable period' is not (except in the case of redundancy) defined in law. Thus it will be determined by the courts with reference to the particular circumstances.

An employee who is dismissed for not agreeing to a change in the terms of contract may, in certain circumstances, successfully claim that the dismissal was unfair. Thus the local Authority that dismissed seventeen school dinner ladies who refused to accept new contracts (which reduced their holiday entitlement and discontinued half-pay holiday retainers) were judged by an industrial tribunal to have been dismissed unfairly. The chairman of the tribunal declared that 'the county effectively tore up the national agreement which covered the employment of the ladies'. The decision of the tribunal was subsequently upheld by the Court of Appeal.

In accordance with the legal doctrine of 'freedom of contract', no court will normally order an employee to accept a contract, nor will an employer be ordered to employ a particular person. The courts' jurisdiction is with the award of compensation (damages) where one party to the contract breaches the rules mutually agreed.

Part-time employees

There is no legal definition of a 'part-time' worker, and under *common law*, whatever hours are worked, part-time workers have the same rights and obligations as full-time employees. However, under *statute law* employees whose contract of employment normally involves them working less than sixteen hours a week are excluded from certain rights; though those who are contracted to work at least eight hours a week gain similar protection to full-time workers if they have at least five years' continuous service with the same employer.

Temporary contracts may be fixed term or open-ended, but may terminate upon the occurrence of an anticipated event. Such contracts are extensively used in the following circumstances: to cover a member of staff who is ill over a long period; to stand in for a teacher on maternity leave; where there is a delay in filling a vacant post on a permanent basis; and to cover staff undertaking in-service training.

Thus, such contracts can, to some extent at least, relieve the headteacher of the burden of arranging for the permanent members of staff to cover for colleagues absent through illness or as a consequence of maternity leave. They facilitate the professional development of permanent staff because of the opportunity to engage in training activities outside the school or indeed within the school. Temporary contracts also provide a means of introducing 'new blood' into the school if only for a given period of time. These contracts may also relieve the pressure for making a permanent appointment from among an unsuitable list of candidates, for example, so that more time may be spent to ensure the school gets the person that it is seeking.

Temporary appointments are also made, however, in circumstances of school reorganisation, usually as a consequence of falling rolls and/or budgetary reasons. This can lead to staff tensions for a host of reasons including insecurity of teachers on temporary appointment and frustration by their permanent colleagues who believe their opportunities for career advancement may be reduced as a result of vacancies being filled by temporary appointments. The headteacher may thus be confronted with problems of staff motivation and poor morale with all that implies for innovative activities.

Consider this question:

9 Is it necessary to give notice to a teacher who is on a fixed term contract of employment?

Given the complexities of the contract of employment, effective staff management requires the headteacher to:

- take great care when writing job advertisements;
- be alert to the dangers of making injudicious statements when appointing staff;
- make sure they understand the contractual obligations of their staff;
- keep abreast with national and local collective agreements for both teaching and non-teaching staff;
- take heed of the LEA rules and notes of guidance relating to employment contracts of school staff;
- beware of the advice offered by other headteachers (they may have been lucky!);
- seek proper legal advice from the LEA where there is any doubt about the most appropriate form of action to take in respect of the contracts of staff.

Individual statutory minimum rights

The extension of the legislation concerned with the individual 'rights' of employees was identified earlier. These flow from a number of statutes but it is the contract of employment which, to a large extent, determines whether the 'rights' legislation applies.

The headteacher is involved in decisions about the following matters:

- staff dismissal
- time off for staff union representatives
- staff redundancy
- staff maternity leave.

What 'rights' does the law confer here, and in what circumstances?

Common law 'rights' apply irrespective of whether the contract of employment relates to full or part-time employees. However, the Employment Protection (Consolidation) Act 1978 and the Employment Act 1980 provide a wide range of individual statutory rights, most of which are allied to the length of continuous service of an employee. A selection of these 'rights' are summarised in the table below, together with the related continuous service requirements. While there are a number of other 'rights', they have been excluded because they are outside the headteacher's sphere of concern.

It will be noted that 'part-timers' as defined below do not enjoy some of the statutory rights which only apply to full-time employees. Further, statute law is concerned only with providing minimum employment rights to individuals. Employers may therefore provide better terms than those prescribed by law; here the headteacher needs to check on:

- *the local agreements between the LEA and union(s)*
- *the national agreements between the employers and union*
- *the individual staff contracts of service*
- *the related conditions of service documents.*

Having indicated the link between the individual rights legislation and the contract of employment, attention needs to be addressed to those aspects which have got many headteachers into 'hot water', beginning with employee dismissal.

Statutory rights	Minimum length of continuous service required
1 Protection from unfair dismissal	1 year
2 Written reasons of statement for dismissal	6 months
3 Protection against dismissal on the grounds of pregnancy	1 year
4 Protection against dismissal on the grounds of union membership activities	None
5 Time off for trade union duties or activities	None
6 Maternity pay entitlement	2 years
7 Pregnancy – pre-natal visits	None
8 Right to return to work after confinement	2 years
9 Entitlement to redundancy payment	2 years
10 Time off to look for work if under notice of dismissal for redundancy	2 years
11 Protection against sex or race discrimination	None

Dismissal of staff

Dismissal can take any of the following forms:

- termination of employment by the employer with or without notice
- termination of employment owing to redundancy
- constructive dismissal
- refusal by the employer to allow a woman to return to work following pregnancy
- refusal by the employer to renew a fixed term contract that has expired.

While the legislation details what constitutes unfair dismissal, it is for the tribunals to decided whether a particular case of dismissal was fair or unfair.

There have been many instances where the intention to dismiss a member of school staff has not resulted in the lawful termination of the employment contract, usually because of one or more of the following reasons:

- a failure of the headteacher to provide the evidence that would justify dismissal
- the headteacher did not observe the appropriate procedure
- the LEA did not observe the appropriate procedure
- the inadequacy of the procedure was recognised by the LEA or industrial tribunal
- the decision to dismiss was based on inadmissable reasons.

In circumstances of a dismissal of a member of school staff the headteacher is involved in:

- *the appropriate application of the disciplinary procedure*
- *the collating and submission of evidence to the governing body and LEA*
- *the recommendation that the individual concerned be dismissed.*

Here, the overriding aim is to part company with an individual who, in the view of the headteacher, has demonstrated a lack of suitability for employment in the school, though it must be stressed that the headteacher is not empowered to dismiss a member of the school adult community. But this should not impair the judgement and actions of the headteacher. There is plenty of scope for dismissing an employee fairly through the procedures laid down by the LEA.

However, potentially fair reasons for dismissal must relate to the following:

- conduct;
- capability, i.e. skill, aptitude, health, physical or mental abilities;
- qualifications relevant to the position held where continuing employment would contravene the law (either on the part of the employee or employer);
- redundancy;
- some other substantial reasons which could justify the dismissal in the light of the position held.

Potentially unfair reasons for dismissal include the following:

- trade union membership or activities
- pregnancy
- discrimination by race or sex.

The legislative criteria in respect of the grounds for fair dismissal reflect the difficulties inherent in the notion that employment relations matters of this sort can be rigidly prescribed for all situations and circumstances. The key questions which the tribunals invariably address is whether in the light of the known circumstances the employer acted *reasonably* in dismissing the employee with appropriate reference to the legal provisions.

Thus, conduct, capability and qualifications are an attempt to delineate specific matters that are an integral part of the contractual relationship. As the person responsible for the effective conduct of staff management within the school, the alert headteacher will monitor staff behaviour and be aware of their capability and qualifications. Nevertheless, problems may arise as a consequence of inappropriate action or reluctance to make an early decision where a member of staff is in breach of the staff code or has problems in the classroom.

Consider these incidents:

10 A newly appointed headteacher discovered that over the past year a teacher had persisted in disrupting staff meetings and was frequently abusive to colleagues, many of whom were so distressed that their teaching was adversely affected.

Q (a) What action should the previous headteacher have taken?
  (b) What advice would you give the present headteacher?

11 On the advice of the headteacher, the LEA dismissed a teacher for incompetent teaching. The teacher subsequently pursued a claim for unfair dismissal which was upheld by the industrial tribunal.

Q What questions need to be addressed here?

The remaining potentially fair reasons for dismissal range from the specific to a wide range of possibilities including:

- Contravention of a statute. This refers to a situation where retention of the employee in his job would involve a breach of statutory obligation by the employer or employee, for example employing a disqualified bus driver to drive the school bus.
- Dismissing an employee on the grounds of redundancy, because the need for the employee to carry out work of a particular kind has ceased or diminished thereby making the employee surplus to requirements.

Finally, other substantial reasons will be judged by the particular circumstances, but note:

- Long term illness and a criminal act commiteed in the course of employment are examples which may fall within the scope of fair dismissal.

It was noted earlier that a crucial factor in the consideration of dismissal cases is whether the employer acted reasonably in the circumstances. Here, the notions of equity and natural justice are important especially in relation to the way in which the dismissal was conducted. The headteacher's actions and the provision of evidence to the LEA can, therefore, exert a powerful influence on the outcome of an industrial tribunal hearing. Whether a dismissal was unfair is for the tribunal to decide. Certain legal provisions, however, give specific guidelines where a dismissal could be deemed to be unfair.

- Dismissing an employee for engaging in trade union activities may be considered *unfair*, if the activities took place outside normal working hours, or indeed during working hours where the employer had given consent.
- Selecting an employee from others to whom the circumstances of redundancy apply because of trade union activities, or where he/she was selected in contravention of an agreed procedure or a customary arrangement without good reason, may also be considered unfair.
- Dismissal for pregnancy is potentially unfair unless either the employee cannot or will not be able to undertake her work properly, or to continue to employ her would violate the law. For example, the employee may not be able to do work involving exposure to chemical substances that are known to be harmful to pregnant women and therefore constitute a breach of the Health and Safety at Work Act.
- Dismissal on the grounds of colour, race, ethnic origin or sex is inadmissable under the law and therefore unfair.

From the brief examination of the guidelines referring to potentially fair and unfair dismissal respectively, it would seem that the task of dismissing an employee fairly is not particularly difficult in the legal context. This observation is based on a number of assumptions:

- existence of carefully formulated policies and procedures
- observance of relevant procedures
- systematic collection of 'hard' evidence
- imposition of sanctions that are clearly articulated and understood

- standardisation of forms and letters dealing with such things as breaches of staff discipline and leave of absence
- a keen sense of judgement as to the appropriate action that should be taken in any given situation
- clear channels of communication between the school, governors and the LEA.

Staff 'time off'

Under the Employment Protection (Consolidation) Act 1978 (amended by the Employment Act 1980), there are four separate provisions which apply to staff engaged in any one or more of the following pursuits:

- public office
- looking for alternative employment as a consequence of redundancy
- trade union duties and activities
- ante-natal care for pregnant women.

Public office
Members of staff including non-teaching personnel are entitled to time off if they serve on:

- magistrates' bench
- industrial tribunal
- health authority board
- governing body of a maintained school
- local authority.

The duties are obviously various but include attending meetings of committees and other approved activities.

The amount of time off is that which is *reasonable* in all the circumstances, taking into consideration:

- the amount of time required generally to carry out the duties, and any particular duty on any given day
- the effect of the individual's absence on the school.

In the absence of any local agreement the LEA would not normally be liable to pay the individual concerned for the period(s) of absence to undertake public office.

Redundancy
Where a memeber of academic or non-teaching staff is to be made redundant, and providing they are entitled to redundancy pay, they may take time off from school to:

- look for alternative work
- seek to make arrangements for training.

For such absences the individual concerned receives normal pay, and the amount of time off is that which is *reasonable* in the light of the circumstances.

Trade union duties and activities

Here, an accredited union representative of an independent trade union, which is recognised by the L E A, may take *reasonable* time off for the purpose of:

- carrying out those *duties* which are concerned with employment relations between the L E A and school staffs
- undergoing training in matters of employment relations which is (a) relevant to the carrying out of those duties and (b) approved by their union.

Where the L E A permits a union representative to take time off from school for these purposes, it is required to pay him or her for the period of absence.

In addition, any member of the school staff who is a member of an appropriate trade union may take *reasonable* time off from school for the purpose of taking part in certain trade union *activities*. In this case the L E A is not liable to pay those concerned for the period of absence, unless there is a local agreement which provides for this.

While there is a long tradition in schools to give 'time off' to members of staff holding public office and to those heavily engaged in the professional activities of their union, it was also generally acknowledged that the school should not suffer undue disruption as a consequence. Inevitably problems do arise, particularly when, in the eyes of their colleagues, the same individuals seem to be taking advantage of their extracurricular role(s).

Consider this incident:

12   Members of the union, which was the dominant association in the school, held a meeting during the lunch break and by a narrow majority voted to send six of their colleagues to a demonstration in support of the health workers. The headteacher was besieged with complaints from other members of staff.

If local agreements between the L E A and relevant unions are silent about staff 'time off' the headteacher should endeavour to reach a clear agreement with his/her staff in the school.

The following guidelines have been adapted from the A C A S code of practice on this matter.

Union representative's duties are those duties pertaining to his or her role in the jointly agreed procedures or customary arrangements for consultation, collective bargaining and grievance handling. To perform these duties properly a representative should be permitted to take *reasonable* time off during working hours for such purposes as:

- negotiations with the L E A
- meetings with other representatives or with full-time union officers on matters which are concerned with employment relations between their members and the L E A
- interviews with and on behalf of members on grievance and discipline matters concerning them and the L E A
- appearing on behalf of a colleague before an official body such as the school governors or industrial tribunal
- initial basic training

- further training relevant to the carrying out of his/her duties such as changes in the structure or topics of negotiation, or legislative changes affecting employment relations.

Where possible the headteacher should received advance notice from the members of staff concerned together with details of the duty or training the representative wishes to undertake.

Union activities The general purpose of the statutory provisions on time off for union duties and activities is to aid and improve the conduct of employment relations. To this end it is suggested that members be given *reasonable* time off for the following activities:

- attending executive committee meetings
- attending the delegate conference
- voting in union elections
- attending union meetings during school hours where the matter to be discussed is urgent.

A representative in the case of union duties, and an ordinary member in the case of union activities, may complain to an industrial tribunal if they believe they have been unreasonably refused time off from school.

What is reasonable can only be judged in the light of the particular circumstances prevailing in the school, but the headteacher should consider the following matters when discussing the issue of time off with members of staff:

- *impact on pupils' tuition*
- *health and safety of all concerned*
- *number of staff seeking 'time off' in any one day*
- *number of requests for 'time off' by an individual in a given period of time*
- *the extra demands made on the remaining staff.*

Ante-natal leave
A pregnant employee, regardless of her length of service, is entitled to time off with pay to keep documented appointments for ante-natal care.

Staff appointments

A significant feature of the headteacher's role is the appointment of academic and non-teaching staff. The extent of involvement is determined by a whole range of factors including the procedures followed by the LEA; the part played by the school governors; and the headteacher's commitment to recruit staff of the calibre necessary to meet the current and future identified needs of the school.

While these aspects vary according to local circumstances and personal aspirations, a common aspect is the legal context, since employment law does not discriminate between schools and local authority boundaries. Here, there are four main areas that require early attention when the opportunity arises to appoint staff to the school, or when internal promotions are being considered. These are:

- *job advertisements*
- *candidate long and short lists*

- *selection interview*
- *appointment.*

The law intrudes on all of these processes, in particular the:

> Sex Discrimination Act 1975 (SDA)
> Race Relations Act 1976 (RRA)
> Defamation Act 1952

Job advertisements

With specific exceptions it is normally unlawful for anyone to publish, or cause to be published, any advertisement or notice which indicates an intention to discriminate on the grounds of:

- race
- sex
- marital status.

This includes internal circulars on staff vacancies, promotion and training opportunities and any other benefits. Further, qualifications or requirements applied to a job which would effectively restrict it to applicants from only one sex or racial group have to be justifiable under the law, otherwise they constitute indirect discrimination.

Discrimination is lawful where sex is a 'genuine occupational qualification' or where there is a need to 'preserve decency' in situations where close physical contact between the sexes is likely to occur, such as in physical education.

Checklist for guidance

When staff vacancies or promotion opportunities occur in the school, the headteacher should consider the checklist below before writing a job advertisement and/or internal circular:

- *Avoid using titles such as 'master' or 'mistress' unless the post falls within the specified legal provisions, i.e. 'genuine occupational qualification' or the need to 'preserve decency.'*
- *Make sure the advertisement for the job (e.g. school typist) could not be understood to indicate a preference for one sex.*
- *If you wish to use words like 'he, or 'she', make sure that they are used as alternatives, e.g. 'he or she', and are consistent throughout the advertisement.*

Selection for interview

The process of selecting applicants for interview usually entails the identification of those candidates who appear to be the most suitable. Whether a long list or short list is complied will depend largely on the number and quality of the candidates applying for the vacancies or promotion.

This can be a daunting task, but the law requires (with specific exceptions) that applicants are not excluded on the grounds of their race, sex or marital status.

Consider this case:

13 A headteacher, together with the LEA, advertised for a craft teacher. A short list was subsequently drawn up and the chosen candidates were invited to

attend an interview. Before the interview took place a redeployed teacher from within the Authority was appointed to the post. The headteacher advised the shortlisted candidates that the post had been filled and therefore the planned interview was cancelled. One of the applicants subsequently claimed that he had been discriminated against on the grounds of his race since he was more experienced and had better qualifications than the person who had been appointed.

Selection interview

The interview is the forum which is perhaps most prone to the pitfalls posed by the legal provisions applying to discrimination on the grounds of sex, marriage or racial/ethnic origin.

Experienced interviewers will be aware of this danger and forestall it by planning carefully their line of questioning and indeed the phrasing of questions in sensitive areas. This is not always easy where an interviewing panel is convened comprising school governors, LEA advisers and senior school staff. In these circumstances, it is not uncommon for some members of the panel to ask the cadidate questions which may give the interviewee the impression that his/her sex or racial origins are being taken into account in assessing their suitability for the post in question.

It is good practice, therefore, for the headteacher, together with the chairman of the interviewing panel, to remind members before interviewing commences that the questions they ask of candidates should relate to the qualifications, experience, and personal qualities previously identified as relevant to the post.

Below are some examples of the kinds of questions that are best avoided.

Of a woman:

When do you intend to start a family?
Who will look after your children if they are sick?

Of a man:

Most of the other staff here are women. How do you think you will fit in?
Do you plan to get married?

Of a candidate who belongs to an ethnic minority:

Have you ever suffered any prejudice in your previous posts because of your colour?
There are very few Asian families in this area. Do you think you could settle down here?

Such questions reflect simple prejudice.

Interviewers should ask themselves: 'Would I also ask that question of a male/ female, English candidate who was white?' Frequently, a question which appears to be discriminatory simply reflects a clumsy attempt to ascertain the relevant information.

Internal promotion

There are additional legal implications here which require careful consideration by the headteacher. Unless one of the exceptions applies, it is unlawful to discriminate on sex or racial grounds when opportunities for promotion or training arise.

The headteacher has a responsibility, therefore, to ensure the selection criteria for promotion and training remains within the law.

Consider this incident:

> 14   A member of staff successfully applied for promotion to a Scale 3 post, and a colleague who had also applied claimed she had been discriminated against because she had better qualifications and was more experienced than the successful candidate.

Staff references

The Defamation Act 1952 provides a legal remedy for a candidate who suffers as a consequence of a false characterisation. Under the terms of this Act a plaintiff may seek compensation through the civil courts. It is normal practice for the headteacher or a senior member of staff to give a reference to a member of staff seeking promotion or employment elsewhere, but as the employer, the LEA (governing body in the case of voluntary aided schools) may be vicariously liable for defamatory comments expressed in the reference. The statement need not be explicit to constitute a defamation. A legal action may be successfully pursued by a plaintiff if an innuendo could be drawn from the reference.

Guidelines for staff references

An employer is not under any *legal* obligation to provide a reference. The provider of a reference is not obliged to reveal its contents to the member of staff concerned. If the reference is substantially true and accurate then it may be justified on those grounds. No legal liability can result unless the plaintiff can establish malice.

Where an unintentional falsehood is included in the reference an apology should be conveyed to the wronged person and all other recipients of the libel should be informed it was untrue. Slander is also covered by the Act, but for obvious reasons it is very difficult for a plaintiff to substantiate that a false characterisation was made on the phone and/or during a private conversation.

The headteacher should take all reasonable steps to ensure a reference is accurate.

Health and safety

The modern school is an extremely complex institution and it is not the intention here to offer technical guidance covering the plethora of school activities and building environment. Readers are advised to consult the references included at the end of this chapter for information about specific health and safety matters.

The health, safety and general well-being of all those who participate in the life of the school is of obvious concern to the headteacher. While there has long since been a general duty under common law for reasonable care to be taken in the conduct of the school, the Health and Safety at Work Act 1974 places additional responsibilities on the LEA as the employer and on school staff.

The primary concern here, therefore, is with the Health and Safety at Work Act 1974, and the implications for staff management in the school.

Under the Act, the LEA as the employer is charged with the following general duties:

- provide and maintain plant and systems of work without risk to health, including a safe and healthy working environment;
- ensure that handling, storage and transport of articles and substances are carried out safely;
- provide information, instruction, training and supervision necessary to ensure the health and safety of employees at work;
- ensure that entry to and exit from the workplace is safe and without risk;
- ensure that the conduct of the school does not expose the public, or persons on the site who are not employees, to health or safety risks in so far as it is reasonably practicable.

For school staff the following general duties apply:

- take reasonable care for the health and safety of himself/herself and other persons who may be affected by his/her acts or omissions at school;
- co-operate with the employer so far as is necessary to perform any duty under the Act;
- not intentionally or recklessly interfere with or misuse any equipment, safety device etc. provided to keep up with the Act's requirements.

In keeping with the common law tradition, the Act places the responsibility for the 'management' of health and safety on the employing Authority. However, under the Act, an individual is liable to prosecution under criminal law as well as liable to be sued under civil law for errors and omissions having a detrimental effect on health and safety. Here the headteacher may be particularly exposed as the person responsible for the supervision of health and safety matters in the school.

A breach of the Act could lead to any of the following penalties:

- improvement notice
- prohibition notice
- up to £1000 fine for most offences in summary proceedings
- up to two years imprisonment coupled with an unlimited fine if there is a prosecution on indictment.

Improvement notice
If the inspector considers a law has been broken, or will be broken, he/she can issue a notice to the responsible person requiring that the contravention be remedied within a certain time.

Prohibition notice
If there is a risk of serious personal injury, the activity giving rise to the risk, e.g. a lathe in the woodwork room, can be closed down until the specified remedial action has been taken.

The other penalties may be imposed in the event that the two notices above were not observed, for example, or where some other breach of the law has been proven.

A defence may be offered against civil or criminal action where:

- the offence was committed by, or due to the neglect of, or negligence of another person;
- it was not known and could not have been reasonably ascertained that an offence was committed.

Role of school staff

The Act places emphasis on a system and procedures approach rather than prescribing minimum health and safety standards which must be complied with. The aim, therefore, is to get employers to introduce a method of organisation and system and procedures, that will become self-regulatory. The main burden of responsibility for developing the appropriate organisation structures and procedures is with the employing Authority.

Consider this incident:

15 The headteacher reported to the LEA that a piece of masonry had fallen from the lower school building. On this occasion nobody was injured. Three months later a piece of debris fell from the same building and a pupil was slightly injured and received first aid in the school.

Most members of staff will recognise the importance of supervising pupils, especially where dangerous substances are involved in craft rooms generally. They will also acknowledge the need to follow the manufacturer's instructions attached to bottles and items of equipment and any additional regulations supplied by the LEA. However, accidents do occur which sometimes might have been avoided, usually for any one of the following reasons:

- The member of staff responsible did not follow the manufacturer's instructions.
- The manufacturer's instructions were unclear.
- The injured person was grossly negligent.
- The buildings where dangerous chemicals were stored was unsuitable for the purpose.
- The activity was inadequately supervised.
- The people involved were genuinely unaware of the health and safety hazards associated with the particular activity.
- The external contractors were negligent.

From this list it is apparent that the responsibility for accidents is very wide-ranging and that it has to be acknowledged that it is impossible to legislate for all eventualities. Nor can codes and guidelines be sufficiently embracing to relieve the headteacher from having to make judgements and decisions about health and safety matters.

Consider this action:

The LEA safety regulations stated that the door leading from a classroom corridor to the back stairway should remain unlocked during school hours. The headteacher was concerned about the pupils' safety on the stairway and consequently kept the door locked.

To perhaps a lesser extent, all staff within the school are from time to time presented with such dilemmas. The Act implicitly, if not explicitly, recognises that a collective approach to the development and maintenance of effective procedures can ease the individual burden in making difficult decisions, while retaining responsibility for personal behaviour. Thus the regulations provide for the appointment of safety representatives from among the organisation's employees by recognised trade unions.

The Health and Safety Commission provides guidelines on the functions of safety representatives as follows:

Representation Represent the employees in consultation with the employer over arrangements for developing health and safety at the workplace.

Investigation Investigate complaints and make representations about health, safety or welfare to the employer on particular or general matters.

Inspection Carry out inspections of the workplace (normally quarterly) during which the employer may be present. Carry out inspections after a notifiable accident, dangerous occurrence or in the event of a notifiable disease. Inspect relevant statutory documents held by the employer, except personal medical records.

Safety committees Attend safety committee meetings.

Time off Time off with pay will be given to safety representatives in order to carry out their function and to receive training.

Legal liability No additional legal liability is attached to the functions of a safety representative beyond the general duties of employees.

It is common practice for schools to have safety representatives and safety committees which is in keeping with the notion of self-regulation and the participation of staff in the decision-making processes concerned with health and safety. Their presence can be of great assistance to the headteacher, especially in drawing early attention to potential health and safety hazards.

Nevertheless, while in matters of detail the practice varies between LEAs, it is normal procedure for the headteacher to be assigned the responsibility for general oversight of health and safety in the school. To this end the headteacher should:

- *give attention to the references at the end of this section;*
- *keep informed about relevant legal requirements;*
- *be familiar with the employing Authority's health and safety policy and its implementation;*
- *be alert to hazards associated with the life of the school;*
- *keep abreast with the documentation provided by the LEA;*
- *encourage the co-operation of staff in promoting measures to improve health and safety;*
- *identify the reporting channels to the LEA.*

Finally, a note of comfort for the hard-pressed headteacher. In the absence of specific legal requirements or other sources of guidance, subsequent judgements about particular decisions made by the headteacher in relation to health and safety will normally be based on whether, on balance, the headteacher's action, or indeed non-action, was reasonable in the prevailing circumstances. The same would apply to any other individual member of staff.

This brief survey of those aspects of employment law which are of most concern to the headteacher represents the legal dimension of the day-to-day practice of staff management in the school, which is the central concern of this book. Employment law intrudes to a greater or lesser extent on the themes and processes explored in the following chapters. Thus, reference should be made to the relevant sections above for guidance on the various elements reviewed in the main text.

Commentary on the incidents cited in the text

1   This matter was quickly resolved when the teacher gave an assurance to the headteacher that she would cease forthwith to offer pupils of the school private tuition for personal financial gain.

In the absence of an express term in the teacher's contract with the employing authority which excluded such activity, there remains the common law obligation which may be implied. Thus, by implication, no person in the employ of another should use their position for personal financial gain unless the contract of employment specifically allows for this. It is possible, therefore, that the teacher in this case was in breach of contract.

2   In this case the teachers concerned were refusing to carry out a *reasonable* instruction, which was to do the job they were paid for. They were, therefore, in breach of their contract. If the deputy headteacher had instructed the teachers to (say) empty the school litter bins, then the question to be addressed is whether the instruction was *reasonable* in the light of their contract of employment.

3   Here the teacher was expressly obliged under the terms of his contract to take proper care of any monies for which he was responsible in the school. Moreover, the teacher is obliged, under common law, to account for money entrusted to his care in the course of his employment. The teacher was therefore in breach of contract.

4   This offer of promotion was subsequently withdrawn with the teacher's agreement. However, the LEA view was that the headteacher had offered a new contract to a member of staff and had published this decision. The LEA, therefore, felt that they were bound to honour the new contract if the teacher concerned had insisted.

5   The assistant caretaker was dismissed for breach of contract. He had in fact used the school facilities for purposes of private financial gain.

6   The headteacher acted in good faith when he informed the teacher, on her

appointment, that she would be required to spend most of her time in the Resources Centre. The central issue is whether, in the light of the changed circumstances, the headteacher's instruction that the teacher teach eighteen lessons a week was reasonable. Matters to be considered here are: the competence of the teacher; the subject(s) she was instructed to teach; the level(s) of classes she was assigned to; and her future role with regard to the Resources Centre.

7   Providing the contract does not state to the contrary, there is nothing illegal in either party seeking to change its terms. However, if the typist refused to accept the reduction in her hours and was dismissed as a consequence, the Authority may have been liable to a claim for unfair dismissal. In this case, the question would focus on whether the Authority had acted reasonably in the light of all the circumstances.

8   No action was taken against the caretaker for refusing to obey the headteacher's instruction, but the incident raises a number of contractual implications that might be considered.

Since the windows had previously been cleaned by outside contractors it might be argued that as it was not the caretaker's customary task it was no part of his existing contract. If this is established, it is then chiefly a question of whether the headteacher's attempt to introduce a new term into the caretaker's contract, i.e. change it, was reasonable in the circumstances. Here such matters as: the medical condition of the caretaker; his age; and the degree of risk to the caretaker and others would almost certainly have a bearing on the outcome. Indeed, the headteacher's instruction may have been unlawful if the safety of the caretaker and/or others was clearly at risk.

9   This is a particularly murky area of law. Where people are on fixed term contracts, the law considers that they have been given notice at the outset of the contract, and this equals the length of the fixed term. However, in the celebrated case *Ford* v. *Warwickshire County Council*, the House of Lords ruled that a teacher employed for eight years under a succession of fixed term contracts was 'continuously employed' throughout that period for the purposes of the Employment Protection (Consolidation) Act 1978, since during the annual summer vacation between the expiry of one contract and the commencement of the next she was 'absent from work on account of a temporary cessation of work'. Ford could therefore claim to an industrial tribunal that she had been unfairly dismissed and that she had a similar right in relation to redundancy payments. It should be stressed that this case was decided on its own particular merits, and the legal position may be clarified in the light of future cases.

10 The previous headteacher should have acted immediately to ascertain that the possible causes for this teacher's behaviour were not attributable to his medical condition, domestic circumstances or unwarranted provocation by his colleagues. If these factors were inapplicable, the headteacher should have disciplined the teacher and if necessary recommended his dismissal. In this

case the problem was exacerbated because of the lack of a staff disciplinary procedure within the school and a breakdown in communication between the headteacher and the L E A.

The present headteacher must, therefore, monitor the behaviour of the teacher concerned, investigate the possible causes, compile a dossier, develop an appropriate staff disciplinary procedure and apply it, if necessary, to resolve this matter. Readers are advised to refer to the chapter on 'Code of Staff Conduct' for guidance on staff disciplinary procedures.

11 In this case, the industrial tribunal sought to establish the criteria used to assess the teacher's competence; the evidence of incompetence and the period of time the evaluation took place; whether the teacher had received the necessary training to teach the subject(s) he had been instructed to take, and any other appropriate support; the way in which the disciplinary procedures were applied.

The tribunal ruled in favour of the teacher because he was 'judged' in relation to the competence of his colleagues rather than against objective criteria.

12 This action by members of one teachers' union clearly did not fall within the guidelines on 'time off' for trade union activities. Furthermore, the absence of six members of staff in addition to those away on sick leave etc. was not considered reasonable. The teachers concerned were dismissed.

13 In this case the headteacher followed the L E A procedures relating to redeployment of teachers and appointments. While the headteacher was not aware that one of the candidates who had been shortlisted for interview was coloured, his position, and indeed that of the Authority, was extremely vulnerable, because they could not produce the criteria on which the selection and appointment was based.

14 The school and L E A were unable to provide an acceptable defence in this case because they could not produce the selection criteria used to promote the successful candidate and the unsuccessful teacher clearly had better qualifications and experience.

15 The maintenance of the fabric of school buildings falls within the general duties placed on the Authority by the Health and Safety at Work Act 1974. In this case, there was a clear breakdown in communication between the headteacher and the L E A. This explained the lack of action of the Authority in the intervening period between the first incident and the second occurrence. While the main responsibility for developing appropriate communication systems resides with the Authority, a quesion mark remains over the headteacher's position in not passing the matter to the L E A when no action followed from his report.

Appendix I: Law and the courts

Common Law

What distinguishes the English legal system from other legal systems is the extent to which decisions of judges may create binding precedents. This is known as the Common Law and has developed over the centuries. It remains largely uncodifed and is based on case law which judges have made by virtue of their decisions. Hence the term 'judge made law'. In dealing with cases, judges and tribunals are bound by decisions of judges in higher courts unless the facts of the cases can be 'distinguished'. This means that the judge does not follow the earlier case because he says the facts differ in kind from the case under review. Where the facts are of a similar kind, the principle of the earlier case is followed. Both Civil and Criminal Law have developed in this way. However, during the course of the twentieth century, the earlier supremacy of Common Law has largely given way to Statute Law created by Acts of Parliament.

Statute Law

Statute Law is the highest form of law in the land and it takes precedence over Common Law. Law courts cannot overrule Acts of Parliament, but judges interpret statutes and in this sense they continue to influence the development and application of statute law. The discretion of judges is limited, however, where Parliament passes enabling Acts. These are so called because Parliament grants the minister responsible authority for producing detailed regulations for the precise implementation of the legislation. In the context of Employment Law, the Health and Safety at Work Act 1974 is an enabling Act. Under this Act, the Secretary of State is authorised to draw up regulations which carry legal force without obtaining the assent of Parliament in the sense of amending the law or passing a new Act.

Civil Law

This branch of the law is concerned with the remedy for a civil wrong which has been committed and proven. In essence, Civil Law is concerned with settling disputes between individuals, and the courts may award damages and/or order that contractual obligations be fulfilled. The onus of proof is on the plaintiff to establish that the defendant has committed a civil wrong which entitles him/her to some form of compensation.

Criminal Law

Criminal Law is concerned with breaches of the 'rules' of society and to punish those found guilty of committing a criminal offence. The task of enforcement rests with the police who initiate prosecutions for minor crimes, and the Director of Public Prosecutions, who deals with serious crimes. Trade unions have strenuously resisted attempts by governments to introduce criminal law into the realm of collective employers/employee relationships. However, it should be noted that an individual and/or employer can be prosecuted for being in breach of the Health and Safety at Work Act.

The Courts

Statute and Common Law are administered through the civil and criminal courts. In the sphere of employment the county and high courts deal largely with Common Law actions such as breach of contract, while the industrial tribunals deal largely with Statute Law governing such matters as redundancy and unfair dismissal.

Appendix II: Letters of appointment

Model letter of appointment for established teaching Staff

Dear   ,

With reference to your application and interview. I am pleased to offer you an appointment as a qualified teacher on the teaching staff of the county's Education Committee commencing on   . You have been allocated in the first instance to the   School as a Scale   teacher responsible for

You will remain at the   School while there is a continuing need. However, it is a condition of your employment that you can be transferred to other school(s) within the county.

The appointment is subject to your having completed to the satisfaction of the Department of Education and Science an approved course of training and, where appropriate, the satisfactory completion of the period of probation, or to the possession of such special qualifications as the Department may approve, and to such terms and conditions determined by the Conditions of Employment as are adopted by the Council from time to time. If you are entering the teaching profession for the first time, or if this is your first appointment to a maintained primary or secondary school in England and Wales, you should send to this office satisfactory documentary evidence of your training and qualifications, together with your birth certificate.

The appointment is also subject to your satisfying the Authority and the Department of Education and Science as to your physical fitness for the post. If this is your first teaching post in a maintained primary or secondary school in England and Wales and you have not completed a course of professional training in these countries, you will be required to undergo medical examination. In this connection:

(i) An appointment for medical examination has been arranged with the Area Medical Officer as follows:

(ii) You should complete the attached medical enquiry form and return it to me as soon as possible.

A teacher's salary is liable to deduction under the Teacher's Superannuation Acts. Part-time teachers who have previously completed one year's full-time pensionable service may elect to pay superannuation contributions and Forms   are enclosed where appropriate.

Your salary will be determined according to orders made from time to time under the Remuneration of Teachers Act 1965, and as set out in the salaries document of the Burnham Primary and Secondary Committee and payable by the bank credit at the end of each month, will be assessed by the Director of Financial Services and you will be notified of this separately. The Committee, however, reserves the right to alter this, if it is subsequently found that this rate is not in accordance with the appropriate scales, and to recover the amount of any overpayment. A bank form is enclosed and you should complete this and return it will your income tax form P45 to this office before commencing duty.

Your other terms and conditions of employment (including certain provisions relating to your working conditions) are covered by national collective agreements negotiated between the Council of Local Education Authorities and the recognised unions of school-teachers (CLEA/ST), or of any successor body that may be set up by joint agreement to conduct such negotiations. And, local collective agreements negotiated by the LEA with a teachers' union or unions recognised by them for collective bargaining for the employment groups to which you belong.

These agreements are contained, respectively, in circulars issued from time to time by CLEA and in other documents available at your place of work on notice boards or in other documentary form. In addition, from time to time variations in your terms or conditions of employment will result from negotiations and agreements at national and/or local levels with the recognised union or unions; these will be separately notified to you or otherwise incorporated in documents available to you. In either case the effect will be that the changes are incorporated into your contract of employment. The Authority undertakes that changes to these terms will be entered in these documents, or otherwise notified to you, within 28 days of each change.

I enclose a Statement of Additional Employment Particulars and copies of the Articles of Government/Rules of Management, the Conditions of Employment, the
School's Teachers' Handbook and *an acknowledgement slip which should be signed and returned to this office* to signify that you are prepared to accept the appointment on the terms set out in this letter and to acknowledge receipt of the enclosures.

Yours truly,

Director of Education

I accept the appointment described in the letter on the terms and conditions indicated in the letter (and associated enclosures), of which the foregoing is a true copy.

Date .... Signature ....

Model letter of appointment for teachers appointed on fixed term contracts

Dear   ,

With reference to your application and interview I am pleased to offer you a fixed term appointment as a qualified teacher on the teaching staff of the Authority from
198 to   198 .

You will be employed as a Scale   teacher of   . The appointment is being made

and will therefore terminate without prior notice from the Authority.

The offer appointment is conditional upon your signing a waiver to your statutory rights against unfair dismissal and redundancy under the Employment Protection (Consolidation) Act 1978.

The appointment is subject to your having completed to the satisfaction of the Department of Education and Science an approved course of training and, where appropriate, the satisfactory completion of the period of probation, or to the possession of such special qualifications as the Department may approve, and to such terms and conditions determined by the Conditions of Employment as are adopted by the Council from time to time. If you are entering the teaching profession for the first time, or if this is your first appointment to a maintained primary or secondary school in England and Wales, you should send to this office satisfactory documentary evidence of your training and qualifications, together with your birth certificate.

The appointment is also subject to your satisfying the Authority and the Department of Education and Science as to your physical fitness for the post. If this is your first teaching post in a maintained primary or secondary school in England and Wales and you have not completed a course of professional training in these countries, you will be required to undergo medical examination. In this connection:

(i) An appointment for medical examination has been arranged with the Area Medical Officer as follows:
(ii) You should complete the attached medical enquiry form and return it to me as soon as possible.

A teacher's salary is liable to deduction under the Teacher's Superannuation Acts.

Part-time teachers who have previously completed one year's full-time pensionable service may elect to pay superannuation contributions and Forms   are enclosed where appropriate.

Your salary will be determined according to Orders made from time to time under the Remuneration of Teachers Act 1965, and as set out in the salaries document of the Burnham Primary and Secondary Committee and payable by the bank credit at the end of each month, will be assessed by the Director of Financial Services and you will be notified of this separately. The Committee, however, reserves the right to alter this, if it is subsequently found that this rate is not in accordance with the appropriate scales, and to recover the amount of any overpayment. A bank form is enclosed and you should complete this and return it with your income tax form P45 to this office before commencing duty.

Your other terms and conditions of employment (including certain provisions relating to your working conditions) are covered by national collective agreements negotiated between the Council of Local Education Authorities and the recognised unions of school-teachers (CLEA/ST) or of any successor body that may be set up by joint agreement to conduct such negotiations. And, local collective agreements negotiated by the LEA with a teachers' union or unions recognised by them for collective bargaining for the employment groups to which you belong.

These agreements are contained, respectively, in circulars issued from time to time by CLEA and in other documents available at your place of work on notice boards or in other documentary form. In addition, from time to time variations in your terms or conditions of employment will result from negotiations and agreements at national and/or local levels with the recognised union or unions; these will be separately notified to you or otherwise incorporated in documents available to you. In either case the effect will be that the changes are incorporated into your contract of employment. The Authority undertakes that changes to these terms will be entered in these documents, or otherwise notified to you, within 28 days of each change.

I enclose a Statement of Additional Employment Particulars and copies of the Articles of Government/Rules of Management, the Conditions of Employment, the School's Teachers' Handbook and *an acknowledgement slip which should be signed and returned to this office* to signify that you are prepared to accept the appointment on the terms set out in this letter and to acknowledge receipt of the enclosures.

Yours truly,

Director of Education

I accept the appointment described in the letter on the terms and conditions indicated in the letter (and associated enclosures), of which the foregoing is a true copy.

Date .... Signature ....

Appendix III: An example of one LEA's practice

Conditions of employment of teachers employed in Primary, Secondary, Nursery and Special Schools maintained by the Council of the

PART I – FULL TIME AND REGULAR PART-TIME TEACHERS
(Excluding teachers employed on temporary Contracts covered by Part II)

1. The teacher shall be appointed to the service of the Council in the post indicated but may subsequently be transferred to any school maintained by the Council in a

capacity appropriate to his or her qualifications and Salary Scale provided that no teacher shall be allocated as a reserved teacher without his/her consent. There shall be prior consultation with the teacher concerned before he/she is transferred to another school, in accordance with the Council's scheme of redeployment.

2. (a) The Regulations of the Secretary of State for Education and Science;
    (b) The financial regulations of the Council so far as relevant and not inconsistent with these Conditions;
    (c) The Articles of Government made under Section 17 of the Education Act 1944;
    (d) The national collective agreements negotiated between the Council of Local Education Authorities and the recognised unions of schoolteachers (CLEA/ST) or of any successor body that may be set up by joint agreement to conduct such negotiations, copies of which are available for inspection at each school and/or establishment;
    (e) Local collective agreements negotiated by the Council with teachers' unions recognised by the Council for collective bargaining purposes; and
    (f) Such other benefits adopted by the Council for all officers in the employment of the Council and which appear on notice boards or in other documentary form, shall apply to the employment of the teacher, insofar as they shall respectively be in force from time to time.

3. The teacher shall be employed exclusively in the capacity of a teacher and shall not be required to perform any duties except those which are connected with the work of the school or to abstain outside school hours from any occupations which do not interfere with the due performance of his/her duty.

4. The appointment shall be subject to such evidence of medical fitness as the Council may require.

SALARY AND NOTIFICATION OF APPOINTMENT

5. Salary will be paid in accordance with the Scale of Salaries of the Burnham Primary and Secondary Committee and other provisions approved by the Council as in force for the time being and as governed by the Orders of the Secretary of State for Education and Science under Section 2(4) (b) of the Remuneration of Teachers Act, 1965.

6. (a) The salary of the teacher will be payable by equal instalments at the end of each calendar month (normally by credit to his/her personal banking account) but so that subject to the following provisions, the teacher shall receive not less than one-third of a year's salary for each full term's service with the Council. For this purpose the three terms in each year shall be constituted as follows:-

    The Summer Term, 1st May to 31st August.
    The Autumn Term, 1st September to 31st December.
    The Spring Term, 1st January to 30th April.

    (b) Newly appointed teachers taking up work:-
    (i) at the beginning of the Autumn Term will be paid salary from 1st September or from the first school day of the Autumn Term, whichever is earlier;
    (ii) at the beginning of the Spring Term will be paid salary from 1st January;
    (iii) at the beginning of the Summer Term will be paid salary from 1st May or from the first school day of the Summer Term, whichever is earlier;
    (iv) during the school term will be paid salary from the first school day worked by the teacher, provided that at the discretion of the Council, salary may be paid from such earlier date as may be necessary to avoid a break in service and superannuation rights in a period during which the school was closed prior to such first day of teaching duty.

    (c) All teachers resigning their appointment:-
    (i) at the end of the Summer Term will be paid salary to 31st August or, in the case of a teacher resigning to take up an appointment with another Authority, to the day preceding the day on which the school under the new Authority opens for the Autumn Term if this is earlier than 1st September;
    (ii) at the end of the Autumn Term will be paid salary to 31st December;

      (iii) at the end of the Spring Term will be paid salary to 30th April or, in the case of a teacher resigning to take up an appointment will another Authority, to the day preceding the day on which the school under the new Authority opens for the Summer Term if this is earlier than 1st May. Unless the teacher is taking up an appointment with another Authority, the Council will have the right to call upon the teacher's services until the 30th April.

7. A teacher appointed to the service of the Council shall receive from the Director of Educational Services wherever practicable before taking up duty
   (i) written notification of appointment indicating the scale of remuneration
   (ii) a copy of these Conditions of Employment and appropriate Articles of Government.

PERIOD OF NOTICE AND TERMINATION OF CONTRACT

8. (a) The appointment of a Head Teacher shall be determinable upon written notice on either side of three months' notice expiring on 31st December or 30th April, or four months' notice expiring on 31st August in any year, without prejudice to the right of the Council to dismiss the Head Teacher summarily for misconduct or for any other urgent cause. (See Condition 10 below).
   (b) Except in the case of summary dismissal for misconduct or any other urgent cause, the appointment of all other teachers shall in all cases be determinable by written notice on either side of two months, expiring on 31st December or 30th April, or three months, expiring on 31st August in any year. (See Condition 11 below).
   (c) All teachers with 9 years' or more continuous employment with the Council shall receive from the Council one additional week's notice for each full year of employment in excess of eight years, with a maximum of 12 weeks' notice for teachers with 12 years' or more service.

9. The employment of a teacher will terminate automatically at the end of the term during which he/she reaches his/her 65th birthday. Service may be extended by mutual agreement beyond the end of that term, such extension to be subject to annual review at least one term before the expiry of the period of extension on the written application of the teacher concerned.

10. (a) The Education Committee or Governors may by resolution suspend the Head Teacher from his/her office for misconduct or any other urgent cause according to the agreed procedures.
    (b) The Governors may resolve to recommend to the Council that the Head Teacher should be summarily dismissed for misconduct or any other urgent cause or should be given notice under the provision of Condition 8(a). Such a resolution shall not take effect until it has been confirmed at a meeting of the Governors held not less than fourteen days after the date of the meeting at which the resolution was passed.
    (c) The Council shall have the right, after consultation with the Governors, to dismiss the Head Teacher without such recommendation as aforesaid having been made.
    (d) The Head Teacher shall be entitled to appear accompanied by a friend, at any meeting of the Governors or of any Committee or Sub-Committee of the Council at which the termination of his/her employment is to be considered and shall be given at least seven days' notice of such meeting. Where dismissal is determined by such Committee or Sub-Committee to which power has been delegated the Head Teacher shall have a similar right of appeal from such decision to that afforded to established officers in the general service of the Council.
    (e) When a Head Teacher is given notice of a meeting at which his/her dismissal or termination of appointment is to be considered on the grounds of some charge, complaint or adverse report affecting his/her capacity, he/she shall at the same time be supplied with a statement in writing of such charge, complaint or adverse report. Proceedings at such a meeting shall be confidential until the decision of the Council has been made and thereafter any publication shall be restricted to the operative decision.

11. (a) The Director of Educational Services or the Head Teacher may suspend a teacher from office for misconduct or any other urgent cause according to the agreed procedures.

    (b) The procedure for terminating the employment of or suspending a teacher shall, subject to paragraph (a) hereof, be the same as in the case of a Head Teacher, except that only one meeting of the Governers shall be required.

12. Where the appointment of a Head Teacher or teacher is determined by notice of dismissal as aforesaid, salary shall be paid to the date on which the notice expires, even though such date may fall within a school holiday.

13. Salary shall be payable for any period during which the teacher has been suspended unless the Council for some compelling reason decides otherwise.

DISCIPLINARY PROCEDURES

14. The disciplinary procedures applicable to a teacher shall be as set out in the Articles of Government.

    A teacher who is dissatisfied with any disciplinary decision relating to the termination of his/her employment, shall have the right of appeal to the Council's Appeals Committee, details of which shall be made known to him/her at the time of appointment. If a teacher is dissatisfied with any other disciplinary decision relating to his/her employment, reference shall be made to the appropriate grievance procedure.

GRIEVANCE PROCEDURE

15. The grievance procedure relating to the employment of a teacher shall be made known to him/her at the time of appointment.

ABSENCE ON ACCOUNT OF PERSONAL ILLNESS

16. (a) Subject to the following Conditions, full salary during absence on account of personal illness, injury or other disability, shall be paid in any period of one year in accordance with the following scale:

    (A part-time teacher shall be paid the appropriate proportion).

    During the first year of service 25 working days and after the completion of 4 calendar months' actual service, 50 working days.

During the second year of service	75 working days.
During the third year of service	115 working days.
During the fourth and subsequent years of service	150 working days.

    The Council has discretion to make other payments.

    (b) For the purpose of ascertaining the number of working days for which salary shall be paid, all periods of service with any local or public Authority shall be aggregated provided that, if the teacher was not in such service during the 12 months immediately preceding the date on which his/her present employment commenced, service prior to that date shall normally be disregarded. The Council has discretion to make other payments.

    (c) For the purposes of calculating the period during which salary shall be paid in respect of any period of absence due to illness, the year shall be deemed to begin on   of each year and end on   of the following year. Where a teacher commences service on a date other than   such service shall be deemed, for the purpose of this scheme, to have commenced on the preceding   . A teacher who is absent owing to illness on   of any year shall not be entitled to a fresh allowance in respect of the following year until he/she has resumed teaching duties; the period from   until the return to duty being deemed to be part of the preceding year for the purpose of this scheme. Where a teacher transfers from the service of another Authority, any sick pay paid during the current year by the previous Authority shall be taken into account in calculating the remaining sick leave entitlement.

    (d) Sickness during a school closure will not affect the period of a teacher's entitlement to sick pay.

    (e) For the purpose of these Conditions, two half school-days shall be deemed to be equivalent to one working day.

    (f) When a teacher is ill immediately preceding a closure of the school and has exhausted his/her sick-pay allowances and recovers during the period of the closure, such teacher shall be deemed, for the purpose of calculating the amount of salary due, to have returned to duty on the day he/she is authorised medically fit to do so by means of a doctor's statement obtained for that purpose, provided he/she actually returns to school on the first day after the period of closure.

(g) A teacher is required to submit a medical certificate to cover any period of sick leave in excess of seven calendar days.

Further certificates shall be forwarded after the date of the first certificate at intervals not exceeding one month, except that a teacher entering a hospital or similar institution as an in-patient, shall submit a medical certificate on entry and on discharge in substitution for periodical certificates during that time.

A teacher who has been absent for a period exceeding fourteen days must, not later than the day of return, forward to the Director of Educational Services a medical certificate as to his/her fitness to resume duties.

A teacher who is absent for more than three working days and less than eight calendar days shall on return to duties be required to sign a statement detailing the reason for absence.

(h) Where the absence is attested to be due to pulmonary tuberculosis and the teacher carries out an approved course of treatment, full salary shall be paid in respect of the first twelve calendar months of the period of absence after attestation. The Council shall have discretion to make further payments.

EXAMINATION BY THE COUNCIL'S MEDICAL OFFICER OF HEALTH

17. After a prolonged or repeated absence or in other exceptional circumstances, a teacher may be required to submit to examination by the approved Medical Officer. The Medical Attendant of the teacher may be present at such an examination, at the teacher's request and expense.

SUSPENSION FROM DUTY OR TERMINATION OF CONTRACT ON MEDICAL GROUNDS

18. A teacher who is found by the approved Medical Officer, acting in accordance with Condition 17, to be incapable of carrying out his/her duties through ill-health or who is found to be suffering from diseases such as pulmonary tuberculosis, epilepsy or mental illness (including nervous disorders) may have his/her employment terminated or be suspended from duty on medical grounds until the Authority is satisfied that he/she is fit to resume duty. There shall be the right of appeal as set out in Condition 14.

ABSENCE DUE TO CONTACTS, ACCIDENTS OR ILLNESS CONTRACTED IN THE COURSE OF DUTY

19. Periods of absence due to the following causes shall not be counted in calculating any period during which salary will be paid in accordance with Condition 16(a):-

(a) Any period during which a teacher is, on the advice of the Council's approved Medical Officer, absent from school in order to prevent the spreading of an infectious disease with which the teacher has been in contact.

(b) Any period during which a teacher is absent owing to an infectious or contagious illness which the approved Medical Officer is satisfied was probably contracted in the course of employment as a teacher.

(c) A period not exceeding six months in the case of absence due to an accident or illness which the Council is satisfied was sustained or suffered in the course of employment as a teacher, including approved attendance at Teachers' Courses or participation in any extra curricular or voluntary activity connected with the school.

(d) Any periods of absence set out above shall be extended at the discretion of the Council in exceptional circumstances.

DEDUCTIONS FROM PAYMENT DURING SICK LEAVE

20. (a) The following deductions shall be made from all payments under Condition 16(a):-

(i) The amount of sickness benefit including earnings related supplement receivable under the National Insurance Acts.

(ii) The amount of injury benefit, including earnings related supplement but not disablement benefit, under the National Insurance (Industrial Injuries) Acts.

(iii) The dependancy element of any treatment allowance received from the Department of Health and Social Security.

(b) A teacher shall be under an obligation to declare to the Council his/her entitlement to benefit under the foregoing Acts and any subsequent alteration in the circumstances on which such entitlement is based, in default of which the Council shall be entitled to determine the benefit by reference to the maximum benefit obtainable.

(c) If the absence of a teacher is occasioned by the actionable negligence of a third party in respect of which damages are recoverable, he/she shall advice the Council forthwith. Any sick pay given for such absence shall be deemed to have been given by the way of a loan and it shall be competent to the Council to require the teacher to refund a sum equal to the aggregate of the allowances paid to him/her during a period of disability or such part thereof as is deemed appropriate but not exceeding the amount of the damages recovered. In the event of the claim for damages being settled on a proportionate basis, the Council will require full details and will determine the actual proportion of the salary to be refunded by the teacher.

(d) Married women and widows exercising their right to be excepted from payment of flat rate National Insurance contributions shall be deemed to be insured in their own right and in their case deductions will be made from pay in accordance with Condition 20(a) (i) to (iii) above of an amount equal to sickness benefit that would have been receivable had full National Insurance contributions been paid.

(e) If, during closure of a school, a teacher becomes or would, but for election to be excepted from liability to pay contributions, become entitled to claim any of the benefits referred to in these Conditions, it shall be his/her duty to notify the Council thereof and of the period of such entitlement, so that the Council may make the deductions provided for in (a) above.

(f) (i) Where a teacher is absent from work because of injury in respect of which a claim will lie to the Criminal Injuries Compensation Board and the teacher is otherwise qualified to receive sick pay, such sick pay shall be disbursed to him/her without his/her being required to refund any proportion of it from any sum which the Compensation Board may award.

(ii) Where an award has been made by the Compensation Board the Council shall discount the period of sick leave occasioned by the injury, in calculating the teacher's entitlement to pay.

(g) In the event of a teacher exhausting in part or full his/her entitlements under Condition 16(a) and being given notice of the termination of his/her contract in accordance with Condition 18, without returning to work, on the ground of permanent incapacity or for some other reason, he/she shall be paid full salary for the notice period with normal deductions only.

CONDUCT PREJUDICIAL TO RECOVERY

21. A teacher absent owing to illness or injury must not undertake any duties or conduct himself/herself during such absence in any way which may in the opinion of the Council, tend to delay his/her recovery.

ABSENCE DUE TO PARTICIPATION IN SPORT AS A PROFESSION OR THE TEACHER'S OWN MISCONDUCT

22. The Council reserves the right to withhold sick pay in the case of an accident due to active participation in sport as a profession, or in a case in which absence arises from or is attributable to a teacher's own misconduct.

ABSENCE DUE TO OTHER CAUSES

23. (a) Except in cases of serious urgency, no teacher may, without previous permission,

be absent from duty for any reason other than personal illness.

(b) Leave of absence may be granted to teachers for reasons other than personal illness for such reasons and on such conditions as are set out in Appendix I and as the Council may from time to time determine.

(c) Where unpaid leave of absence occurs, either with the permission of the Council or without such permission, deduction of salary shall be made at a daily or part-daily rate based on the day's salary being 1/365th of a year for each day of the period of absence. A morning shall be regarded as 6/11ths and an afternoon as 5/11ths of a day's salary.

CONFINEMENT OF WOMEN TEACHERS

24. (a) Payment of salary during a period of maternity leave will be made in accordance with the scheme set out in Appendix II.

(b) A woman teacher expecting the birth of a child shall give the Council at least 14 weeks' prior notification of the expected date of confinement. Where a teacher does not intend to apply for maternity leave, her appointment shall terminate: EITHER: at date 11 weeks prior to the expected date of confinement (with the agreement of the teacher, or if because of her pregnancy she is incapable of doing her own or some other suitable work) –
OR: at some other date less than 11 weeks as the teacher wishes, provided she is fit to continue.

DEFINITION OF A TEACHER'S DAY, DUTIES AND HOLIDAY ENTITLEMENT

25. There are no prescribed hours of work and holiday periods for teaching staff, and the working week may vary from school to school subject to the appropriate general requirements of the Schools Regulations. A teacher is required to be present for duty during the normal school hours of the school in which he or she is employed. There are no existing national collective agreements on teachers' duties, beyond that affecting the school midday break (see Appendix VII of the Codified Conditions of Service).

PROBATION

26. (a) Unless satisfactorily completed in previous employment, a teacher's appointment shall be subject to the satisfactory completion of a period of probationary service in accordance with the Regulations of the Department of Education and Science. During the probationary period of service, a teacher will be expected to establish his/her suitability for continued employment as a qualified teacher.

(b) If a teacher is unable to demonstrate his/her practical proficiency after an extended period of probation and the Secretary of State determines that the teacher is unsuitable for further employment in that capacity, his/her service shall terminate with appropriate notice and the teacher shall cease to work as a teacher immediately.

TRAVELLING ALLOWANCES FOR TEACHERS

27. A teacher may claim travelling allowances in respect of approved journeys necessary to faciliate the discharge of his/her duties, in accordance with the Council's scheme, a copy of which is available at every school.

INSURANCE

28. The following are among matters covered by the Council's general regulations on the conditions of service of officers, which also apply to teachers:-

(a) Indemnity against death or disablement caused by violence or criminal assault suffered in the course of or as a consequence of their employment.

(b) In the case of loss or damage to the personal property of teachers incurred during the course of their duties at school or during out of school activities the Council, while accepting no legal liability may consider making an ex gratia payment providing that such loss or damage is not attributable to negligence on the part of the teacher.

(c) In addition to the above, a teacher or his/her dependants shall in certain circumstances be entitled to compensation for death, personal loss or injury sustained during activities voluntarily taken out of school but during a school activity which is outside the scope of the contract of service.

TEACHERS IN SPECIAL SCHOOLS AND UNITS

29. A teacher who is appointed to teach in a residential Special School, may be required, as part of his/her contract, to undertake additional duties for which additional allowances are payable in accordance with national agreements. A teacher may also be liable to pay certain charges as a result of national agreements.

DATE OF APPLICATION

30. These Conditions shall apply from 1st September 1982 to teachers who are in the service of the Council   and to teachers employed in Voluntary Aided Schools maintained by the Council

PART II: TEMPORARY TEACHERS

A temporary teacher, as defined in the Codified Conditions of Service, shall be covered by all Conditions in Part I of this document except the following:-

i) Condition 8   – period of notice.
ii) Condition 10   – unless the dismissal is on the grounds of conduct or capability.
iii) Condition 24(a)   – maternity leave.

APPENDIX I

Provisions for special leave of absence with pay approved under Condition 23(b).
(A part-time teacher shall be paid the appropriate proportion).

(i)	Serious illness of husband, wife, child, near relative or dependant	Up to 5 working days, depending on circumstances.
(ii)	Death of husband, wife, child, near relative or dependant	Up to 5 working days, depending on circumstances.
(iii)	Attendance at funeral in approved representative capacity	1–3 working days, according to distance and circumstances.
(iv)	Wedding of near relative	1 working day, where the ceremony does not take place at a weekend.
(v)	Removal of household effects	1 working day.
(vi)	Attendance at interview for other appointment	1–3 working days, according to distance and circumstances.
(vii)	Examination, if one that would improve the educational qualifications of the teacher	Period necessary to sit for the examination.
(viii)	External Examinations	Leave for Moderators and Examiners in accordance with national recommendations.
(ix)	Jewish or other religious festivals	Not more than 3 days in calendar year, as required for observance of Jewish or other religious festivals.
(x)	Justice of the Peace duties	12 days or 24 half-days in any year.
(xi)	Jury Service	In accordance with the regulations relating to Officers.
(xii)	Other Public duties	In accordance with the regulations of the Council relating to Officers.
(xiii)	Attendance at Conferences	In accordance with the regulations of the Council relating to Officers.
(xiv)	Facilities for Representatives of Recognised Teachers' Organisations	In accordance with the local facilities agreement.
(xv)	Other urgent reasons	At the discretion of the Director of Educationl Services.

APPENDIX II
SCHEME OF MATERNITY LEAVE for full time and regular part-time teachers employed in schools and educational units maintained by the Council

QUALIFYING SERVICE

1. (a) The teacher shall have had at least one year's full time, or equivalent part-time service as a teacher, whether with one or more Local Education Authorities, immediately preceding the commencement of maternity leave.

    (b) A teacher who has two years' continuous employment as defined in the Employment Protection (Consolidation) Act, 1978, or any statutory re-enactment thereof, whether with one or more Local Education Authorities, by the beginning of the eleventh week before the expected week of confinement, shall be eligible for additional rights and conditions as detailed in paragraphs 4(b), 4(c), 5(iv) and 6(a).

    (c) These provisions are without prejudice to statutory rights and obligations.

NOTIFICATION OF ABSENCE

2. (a) The teacher shall notify the Council, in writing, as soon as practicable and, unless she can show good cause, not less than fourteen weeks before the date of her expected confinement, that she will be absent from work because of her pregnancy. At the same time, she shall state her intention to return to work in the post in which she was employed, at the conclusion of her absence for maternity.

    (d) The teacher shall give at least three weeks' notice of the date on which she intends to stop work prior to her pregnancy.

COMMENCEMENT OF ABSENCE

3. The teacher may absent herself from duty not earlier than the beginning of the eleventh week before the week of expected confinement. She may continue at work, if she so wishes, until a date later than the beginning of the eleventh week before the week of expected confinement, but she shall not remain at work if certified medically unfit to do so.

DURATION OF ABSENCE

4. (a) The teacher may remain absent for a period of eighteen weeks from the beginning of her absence for maternity, save that, in the event of a stillbirth, she may remain absent for up to six weeks after the week of confinement.

    (b) A teacher with at least two years' continuous service as a teacher as defined in 1(b) may remain absent for up to 29 weeks beginning with the wek in which the date of confinement falls. The teacher shall give to the Council at least seven days' notice in writing, of the date on which it is her intention to resume teaching duty after the confinement.

    (c) In such a case, the Council may, by notice in writing, postpone the teacher's return to work by not more than 4 weeks after the notified day of return. Such notice shall specify the reason for postponement.

SALARY ENTITLEMENT DURING MATERNITY LEAVE

5. (a) The teacher shall be entitled to pay during the period of maternity leave as follows, without prejudice to entitlement in respect of other periods under the Sick Pay Regulations:-

    (i) For the first four weeks of the period of maternity leave – full pay with deduction of maternity allowance and any other additions which may accrue but not less than 9/10ths of a week's salary with deduction of flat rate maternity allowance.

    (ii) For each of the next two weeks of absence – 9/10ths of a week's salary with deduction of flat rate maternity allowance.

    (iii) For the remainder of the 18 week period of absence – half pay without deduction of maternity allowance except to the extent to which the combined pay and allowance may exceed full pay.

    (iv) For any remaining period of absence up to the date of return to duty – absence without pay.

Teachers who do not pay contributions shall be deemed to be insured and the appropriate weekly allowance shall be deducted from full pay.

(b) It shall be at the discretion of the Council to postpone payment of the twelve weeks' half-pay entitlement until the teacher has returned to duty.

CONDITIONS GOVERNING SALARY ENTITLEMENT

6. (a) Payment of salary to the teacher in accordance with these provisions shall be made on the condition that the teacher will be available for full time duty for a period of at least thirteen weeks – (or equivalent part-time duty in the case of a part-time teacher). Should she fail to comply with this understanding, the Council, at their discretion, may require a refund of such proportion of the monies paid in respect of the period of maternity leave as they may determine. A teacher with two years' continuous service as in 1(b), however, shall be entitled to retain the first six weeks' payment. The period of thirteen weeks (inclusive of school holidays and dates of school closure) shall run from the date on which the teacher returns to duty or the date during a school holiday on which, having been certified medically fit, she is deemed to be available for duty under paragraph (b).

   (b) Where the date when maternity leave terminates occurs during a school holiday, she shall be deemed to be available for full time duty and on full salary from such date, though the salary may be withheld until such time as the teacher has returned to duty.

   (c) Following the return to work, the normal conditions for termination of appointment upon notice shall apply.

   (d) In special circumstances and with the prior agreement of the Council at the commencement of the maternity leave, a full time teacher may be permitted to return to duty on a part-time basis. In such cases, the teacher shall be required to work a minimum period of part-time duty which shall equate to thirteen weeks' full time service.

OTHER ABSENCE RELATED TO MATERNITY

7. (a) Absence on account of illness due or attributable to the pregnancy which occurs outside the period of maternity leave or absence on account of miscarriage shall be treated as ordinary absence on sick leave, provided it is covered by a medical certificate, and shall be subject to the conditions normally governing such leave.

   (b) If in the early months of pregnancy, a teacher is advised by the Council's Medical Officer to absent herself from school because of the risk of rubella, she shall be granted leave with full pay, provided that she does not unreasonably refuse to serve in another school where there is no such undue risk.

Further reading and information

Contract of Employment Acts 1963–1972
Employment Protection (Consolidation) Act 1978
Sex Discrimination Act 1975
Employment Protection Act 1975
Race Relations Act 1976
Trade Union and Labour Relations Acts 1974/76
Health and Safety at Work Act 1974
Employment Act 1980
Employment Act 1982
Defamation Act 1952
ACAS Code of Practice (1)   Discipline Practice and Procedures in Employment
ACAS Code of Practice (3)   Time Off for Trade Union Duties and Activities

Further information may be obtained from:

Local Department of Employment

Local Advisory, Conciliation and Arbitration Service (ACAS) Head Office: Cleland House, Page Street, London SW1P 4ND

Equal Opportunities Commission, Overseas House, Quay Street, Manchester M3 3MN

Commission for Racial Equality, Elliot House, 10/12 Allington Street, London SW1E 5EH

Health and Safety Executive, Baynards House, Chepstow Place, Westbourne Grove, London W2 4NJ

Local Factory Inspector or Environmental Health Officer

Further reading

DES Safety Series	First published
No. 1 Safety in Outdoor Pursuits	1972
No. 2 Safety in Science Laboratories	1973
No. 3 Safety in Practical Departments	1973
No. 4 Safety in Physical Education	1975
No. 5 Safety in Further Education	1976
No. 6 Safety at School: General Advice	1979 (2nd ed.)

Barrell, G R, *Teachers and the Law*, 5th edition, Methuen, London, 1978.

Harrison, G, and Bloy, D, *Essential Law for Teachers*, Oyez, London, 1980.

Hepple, B A, and O'Higgins, P, *Encyclopaedia of Labour Relations Law*, Sweet and Maxwell, London, 1972 (loose-leaf, updatings issued 6 times a year).

Ireland, K, *Teachers' Guide to the Health and Safety at Work Act*, Schoolmaster Publishing Co, Kettering, 1979.

Case Law

Industrial Cases Reports, Published by the Incorporated Council of Law Reporting for England and Wales, 3 Stone Buildings, Lincoln's Inn, London WC2A 3XN.

Industrial Relations Review and Report, Published by Industrial Relations Services, 67 Maygrove Road, London NW6 2EJ.

Staff planning and staff development

Introduction

It is not so many years since the headteacher managed a school where issues and problems relating to change and development were neither intrusive nor dominant. In that previous age, a shared concern regarding the nature of professional roles and obligations was a principal regulatory mechanism in the management of staff. In fact, a professional obligation existed on the member of staff's own part to be responsible for his/her own development. The headteacher would have met with the member of staff at the time of appointment, but subsequent to appointment, regulatory responsibility was devolved at a day-to-day level to department and to individual. The need for *formal* contact between the member of staff and the headteacher, up to the time at which the staff member chose to leave, unless a disciplinary issue had arisen, was minimal.

Should a change of direction in school organisation or curriculum have become necessary, then the headteacher, having identified skills or experience in an individual which were of relevance to future development, may have appropriately approached an individual member of staff, but these circumstances would by no means apply to all staff in a school. Similarly, should a member of staff have expressed interest in promotion, then the headteacher may have directed him/her towards promotion opportunities. Occurrences of this sort may well have been the extent of the responsibilities headteachers practised in staff development.

Change and renewal of the school usually took place through external appointments and correspondingly members of staff sought progression and increased job satisfaction through moves to other schools. The arrival and expansion of the secondary comprehensive system has begun a process of change which has continued to this day.

Initially the organisational and curriculum complexity of the school, and the enhanced opportunity for promotion in an expanding system, caused some headteachers to reappraise the existing patterns and philosophies of the management of staff. As one headteacher pointed out:

> In the days of high turnover when staff were constantly on the move for promotion, people used to be persuaded to stay by offering them a promoted post and this was done in the interest of giving some stability to the structure. [Now however,] staff can see that the opportunities for promotion are decreasing and that the work they do correspondingly increases. Exams and pastoral work have to be undertaken, the weight of communication is still there, the school still has to be run. Morale is the problem now. Staff have not been promoted who should have been, redeployment and redundancy are with us and staff know this. The Head is faced with maximum pressure to bring about change and denied the traditional way of satisfying such

need through promotion and external recruitment, (yesterdays 'carrots' for motivating staff are no longer available), the Head has to face up to the fact that this group of staff will probably have to work together for many years.

It is quite apparent that a totally new approach to the management of staff is necessary.

In these circumstances, job satisfaction and developmental opportunities have to be sought and created. They will not occur by chance. The headteacher has to adopt a purposive and visible role in the planning of staff use and to the development of staff. He/She has to respond to challenge and pressures to change by creating opportunities. The principal method by which this may be accomplished is by ensuring that the development of both the organisation of the school and its staff is integrated and is directed towards a common purpose and a common goal. The headteacher must be fully conversant with the techniques and processes of staff management which are available, build the contacts with resource providers, determine existing skills and experience amongst staff and identify those which may be useable by the school in future school development, establish staff's own preferences for development, establish what training or developmental opportunities are actually offered or available locally etc. The headteacher therefore must turn to sources of information which will yield this information and do so in a constructive and consistent manner. That is, the information to be useable should be collected in a *purpose-specific manner* to satisfy questions related to these issues.

The philosophy associated with this perception has proved in many circumstances to pose a substantial barrier to many headteachers, who may have felt reluctant to intervene in matters which they considered to have a strongly professional basis. If teaching is seen as a craft, then tasks can be rationally planned and programatically organised, the teacher expected to implement a prescribed programme and a supervisor to carry out direct inspection of a teacher's work. The worth of a teacher may be measured by reference to a product or outcome of the work. However, if teaching is viewed as an art, of course knowledge specific to the situation is necessary, but equally important is the determination of when and how 'professional' judgements are to be applied in the teaching act. Here the duty of the 'manager' is restricted to providing the environment in which the art can be practised: the teacher is functionally autonomous.*

The conventional modes of collecting and acting on this information in other employment sectors is by undertaking, for example, a staff survey, a review of job descriptions, careers counselling, staff appraisal, succession planning etc. From this information, and with the school's identified priorities and goals in mind, an institutional led staff development programme can be constructed which sets priorities for staff training and which will lead to the achievement of the school's goals in the most effective way available.

There is currently one other important staff development role for the headteacher to enact. That is, firstly, for the headteacher to help staff to adjust to and understand the dimensions of the changes in professional relationships which

---

* For an exploration of these issues see Darling-Hammond, L, Wise, A E, and Pease, S R, 'Teacher evaluation in the organisational context: a review of the literature'. *Review of Educational Research*, Vol. 53.3, 1983.

schools are daily witnessing and, secondly, that the headteacher should work with staff particularly through the school communication/consultative procedures, to develop and implement anticipatory policies to cope with the new style professional relationships which are now occurring in schools. This latter issue is explored in the following chapters of the book.

The emphasis found here upon institution led staff development, that is the focusing upon the development of staff principally to help the school achieve identified organisational goals rather than assuming the primacy of individual development, is not necessarily widely adopted in the schools sector. Often the issue of the development of the organisation or the development of the individual has been masked by notions of professional development.

Here we put forward one particular view point and we do this to give coherence and consistency to our discussion. We do so acknowledging that many headteachers, due to circumstances and the culture prevailing in their schools, will adopt different styles and philosophies of managing staff, and that the procedures and policies existing or being developed in L E As will depart in many different ways from the ones outlined here. We offer these as examples to sustain discussion not as models or exemplars to be copied. We are aware that deeply held views about the nature of teaching as a profession exist and that these views in turn will influence attitudes brought to the management of staff. Our concern is with the headteacher's responsibilities in the management of staff planning and staff development in the school.

The headteacher should use this chapter to re-examine and appraise the policies and practices of staff planning and staff development currently adopted in the school. The individual sections provide a framework against which action can be constructed. If it proves practical to the circumstances of a school, then the headteacher should collect and analyse the information identified as a means of re-creating or regenerating any aspect of staff planning and development which it is felt would benefit, or to design and initiate an aspect of the process presently not occurring in the school but which it is now felt could be usefully implemented.

The headteacher should also be prepared to draw upon the additional materials appearing in the accompanying volume of training materials. The substance of this chapter is also intimately related to other chapters of the book – to the legal framework of employment, staff communication and decision making, individual and collective grievances and the staff code of conduct. Any proposed action should be planned taking into account the substance of these chapters.

Constraints on the headteacher's freedom of action in staff planning and staff development

A headteacher's personal viewpoint

The principal difficulty is that the L E As do not have managerial policies. All they seem to have is single issue strategies, e.g. what do we do this year about staffing, support staff, deployment of staff etc. This, in turn, implies that there are no frameworks for headteachers to work in and against which their actions may be judged. No wonder headteachers are becoming stressed: it is not resources they are short of, it is policies. Consequently, the morale of teachers suffers because they cannot perceive any rhyme or reason in what is occurring and the system guarantees the misuse of resources, e.g. staff teaching their second or third subject. In the absence of policies, the freedom of Heads to manage their school is limited by their terms of employment and by the LEA in which they work, as well as the school and its staffing composition.

The context in which the headteacher operates

Traditionally, LEAs may be thought of as providing a framework of procedures, constraints and controls related to overt aspects of staff employment, e.g. recruitment and selection, salaries and pensions. Additionally, the LEA may be thought of as providing a set of bargaining opportunities. Through these opportunities the headteacher may seek to negotiate access to points distribution and allocation, and in doing so test the firmness with which formulae are applied.

In earlier years it was uncommon to find codified policies and procedures regarding the development and assessment of staff amongst LEAs, or policies for promotion and succession planning being systematically developed and applied. Because of current pressures on the school from within and without, the trend now is towards the formalisation of agreements and effectively, therefore, of the policies which follow in train. However, as school and LEA begin to move in this direction, a number of other substantial issues are currently encountered:

- the impact of resource and financial diminution and of falling pupil rolls
- increased uncertainty about the future (employment/technology etc.)
- increasing shift of authority and control from the school to LEA, local Authority and national levels (though this can involve devolution of financial responsibility to school level)
- an enhanced awareness of the impact of labour law
- a lack of sanctions to apply against staff
- an increasing involvement of trade unions and/or professional associations in both the day-to-day management of the school and its longer term action.

All of these factors have, in one way or another, been drawn to the attention of a wider public and given exposure by national media as well as by the educational press. Less well documented are other matters of longer term impact on the management of staff, but nevertheless of substantial importance to the headteacher's sphere of operation, some of which may in fact be a result of issues identified above, such as:

- the changing nature of professional relationships in the school
- the complexity, the ambivalence and the changes in the headteacher's own authority and responsibility
- the extent to which LEA and headteacher perceive staff management as a central aspect of their management thinking.

Additionally, it seems that the role in staff planning and staff development matters of a middle management structure has rarely been sufficiently articulated. In many schools it is unclear whether, other than tacitly, deputy heads and heads of departments accept or discharge such responsibilities.

In the absence of policies then, the freedom of the headteacher to manage his/her school is likely to be limited by the terms of his employment, the actions of the LEA in which he/she works, as well as the school and its staffing composition. Considerable variation exists between LEAs, and also within the LEA between different schools, as to the degree of authority and autonomy afforded to the individual headteacher. The first act of a headteacher who wishes to establish the limits of his/her managerial action in staff management matters is thus to mark out the responsibilities and duties *vis-à-vis* the LEA and the school of which he/she has charge. One formal way of doing this is by an annual review of the school and it is to an example of this used for staff planning purposes that we turn to first.

The LEA annual review

This is the first of the major purpose-specific processes of staff management we shall consider. Here information of direct relevance to staff planning and staff development is generated. The example is provided by the scheme adopted and operated in one particular LEA.*

The LEA annual review with each secondary school: three-year staffing policy for secondary schools

Each year the headteacher meets with the Deputy Director and Chief Inspector who use the opportunity, firstly, to review how the school performed over the previous year and, secondly, within the overall policies of the LEA, to agree pupil numbers and staffing levels over the next three-year period based upon an agreed curriculum: a projection updated annually.

Certain educational assumptions have to be made explicit in such analysis, as a means of obtaining a fair, balanced and equitable distribution of the teaching resources available within the LEA between the varying schools. The assumptions are not intended, nor should they be interpreted, as pre-empting the managerial responsibilities of individual headteachers in setting priorities for the utilisation of available teacher expertise across the differing age and ability range of pupils within any specific school.

The timing of the activities is as follows:

September Secondary schools are asked to give details of their current and projected rolls and are also asked to summarise their current and projected curriculum plans.

September–October The information collected as described above is analysed centrally and liaison occurs with individual education districts on an agreed pupil projection for the coming three years. The Authority's thinking on how its secondary schools should be staffed is made available to schools and reference is made to this thinking for the preparation of the three-year staff/pupil projection for each school.

October–January Each secondary school is visited by a team led by the Deputy Director and comprising the Chief Adviser and at least one of the following: Pastoral Adviser, Assistant Director (Schools), District Education

---

* For details of this scheme the reader should contact the Director of Education (ref. I T P), West Glamorgan County Council, County Hall, Swansea SA1 3SN.

Officer, AEO (Schools) and Professional Assistant (Schools). The needs of the curriculum are discussed with the headteacher and his senior staff and the LEA's policy is compared with (a) the school's expressed needs, and (b) the previous year's allocation.

Should there be a known change in the school roll of greater than 50 pupils, then the existing three-year allocation would be altered. Otherwise every effort is made to adhere to it in the interests of continuity. As a complementary aspect of the curriculum/staffing talks, the Authority seeks, on these visits, to highlight a particular aspect of curriculum planning.

February   The allocation for the next three years is completed centrally and, as far as possible, takes account of any changes that have emerged during the school visits. The allocation is sent to the DEO and thence to individual schools allowing them sufficient time to proceed with timetable plans in the knowledge of a firm staffing roll.

One headteacher who had participated in the review commented as follows:

> This is based upon the 'Sheffield' system of curriculum notation and has clear implications for staff planning. . . . It's a subtle review and I find it a very useful mechanism – to review the school and plan changes from year to year. Once you have done it the information is at hand. It helps you to formulate your own ideas of what goes on in the building.

The headteacher has agreed with the LEA and has its commitment over a three-year period to known staffing levels related to the overall shape of the curriculum. One major step in staff planning has now been undertaken. Having established this framework of policy and action with the LEA, it is now possible for the school to create coherent plans for staff use, development and training against this framework. We now turn to the next stage of this process – the school staff survey.

School staff survey

A regularly updated staff survey will identify the range of professional expertise, the skills and experience held by staff, the distribution of posts by age and sex . . . and also, by identifying any likely staff movement, indicate to the headteacher areas where opportunity for change, development, training etc. could forseeably take place amongst staff.

The information upon which a staff survey is based is available from a number of sources. These would include staffing returns, the member of staff's personal file, information from previous staff appraisal interviews etc., though occasionally it may be necessary to collect some information with staff survey purposes in mind. The information may not have previously been codified for staff survey purposes, or have been collected to provide answers to specific 'staff survey' questions, and initially a certain amount of clerical work may be necessary.

Examples of these questions, which would be posed by a staff survey, are:

- What are the qualifications of staff, their current deployment, their special-isms, their administrative or other competencies, and training undertaken?

- What kind of staff replacement am I likely to be seeking, what freedom of staff appointment might arise in the next few years?

The purpose of undertaking a staffing survey is to help the headteacher answer the fundamental question, 'What do I need, what haven't I got, therefore what steps do I take to overcome any identified deficiencies?

In an ideal situation, maximum use of the information provided by the survey is made if it is possible for the headteacher to compare the information collected over a time scale of three or even five years, and if it is at all possible, to compare the information provided by the school staff survey against similar information on staff provided from other *comparable* schools. The headteacher, were he/she to identify changes in trends, or discrepancies between schools, should always be prepared to ask why this is the case, if this is as it should be, if this is what I want to occur, and always the basic question at the back of his/her mind should be, 'What possibilities of organisational renewal does this situation offer?'

The headteacher should collect information in answer to the following questions. (Sometimes the information is easier to use if it is tabulated or expressed in a diagrammatic form.)

- What is the distribution by age, ethnic background and sex for each level of post?
- What is the distribution of qualifications and subjects offered, including second/third specialities, by age, ethnic background and sex and the subject to which staff are currently deployed for teaching purposes?
- Are there administrative or other competencies amongst staff which the school may use, e.g. first aid skills, PSV licence etc?
- Have staff undertaken additional training, that is, both post experience and in-service training which give skills or experience the school may use?

The headteacher should identify:

- the number of years to retirement of the different members of staff
- the members of staff actively seeking other posts
- the members of staff who may seek other posts
- the average length of service according to post held
- the level of post that shows the greatest movement in,
  or flow out, consequently;
- where there is the greatest/least movement etc.

By identifying skills and experience amongst staff upon which the school may draw and also, should there be any, by identifying deficiencies in skills and experience which may emerge as the school accommodates to changes in direction or initiates development, information is generated which will contribute to more effective planning of staff use and which will therefore help in achieving the identified goals of the schools.

Invariably other issues are identified in a staff survey and the headteacher may choose to direct attention to them subsequently. For example, it may be found that the majority of movement into or out of the school is at probationer teacher level, or that it is a considerable number of years since some groups of staff have undertaken any form of in-service training, or that there are levels of post in the school failing to provide any movement other than through retirement etc.

In determining the beginnings of answers to the basic questions 'what I need, what I have got and what I haven't got', significant implication for the school's staff development and training and replacement policies arise. We shall turn to staff development later in this chapter, but next we turn to other contributory information to the staff planning and development process, that is information provided through an examination of staffing and organisational structures and their operation.*

Staffing structures and organisational charts

The headteacher must ensure that the existing staffing structure facilitates the pursuit of the school's goals, or would facilitate change, or would cope with a new direction that it may be necessary for the school to take. A succinct way of displaying information on which a judgement can be made is by means of a chart.

Such charts, merely a means to an end, can be constructed to reflect different aspects of the organisation, including salary structures, responsibility structures and decision-making structures. (Most school handbooks would contain a chart that diagramatically sets out lines of authority and responsibility in the school. The reader should see the next chapter 'Staff communication and decision making in the school' for a fuller discussion of staff handbooks.) The opportunity therefore arises, that by making a comparison between charts, discrepancies and dysfunctions within present staffing structures may be identified.

For example, an important aspect of the staffing structure is the distribution of promoted posts, and whilst the headteacher cannot change the 'pyramid' of salary distribution, the assumption that salary levels are necessarily tied to responsibility levels is worth examining. Comparable salary holders/post holders may be undertaking duties of different responsibility levels; members of staff may be performing tasks for restricted periods without salary increase to gain additional experience, and many schools have staff who carry protected salaries.

Let us consider some of these charts and then examine the staff planning and staff development implication from their comparison.

A chart reflecting salary distribution inevitably is in the form of a pyramid and reflects the fact that the volume of monies paid in salaries is at the lower level of the salary scales. Because of national and local agreements on staff salaries, the headteacher's capacity to vary the shape of this pyramid is limited.

Additionally, pressures from staff and unions further constrain the head-teacher's already limited freedom in the choice as to when and how 'surplus' points may be allocated.

Minimal scope is available to the headteacher to negotiate an increase over formulae levels through which such points are conventionally allocated to schools by the LEA. However, it is important that the school can compare its profile to, firstly, what would be an acceptable norm within the LEA and, secondly, to other comparable schools within the LEA.

---

* For other sources of information which may be considered in the initial stages of the staff planning process, the reader is referred to the information check list in the accompanying volume of training materials.

A decision-making chart should identify the position, the terms of reference and responsibilities of, for example, the management team, standing committees (heads of faculties, houses, departments, sections . . .), as well as curriculum committees of an academic board should there be one, and joint consultative committees involving the various staff unions and associations.

A chart of the school's decision-making structure ought to match closely the salary distribution chart, or at least indicate to the headteacher how differences reflect the *actual* philosophy of the school. Where a mismatch occurs, then this is of concern and an explanation should be sought.

The most conventionally adopted chart is the one which **outlines the lines of authority and responsibility** within the school. Inevitably it reflects a hierarchy of responsibility and invariably is in the shape of a pyramid – the greater the responsibilities then the fewer are the post holders. (The conventional way of making such responsibilities more specific is by job descriptions – see below.)

The headteacher now has information to hand to help in identifying discrepancies and dysfunctions within the staffing structure, particularly with reference to the major decision-making areas in the school and the major carriers of responsibility, and can determine whether or not this reflects the school's philosophy and is a preferred pattern. The opportunity of identifying potential areas where change may be implemented (duplication or overlap of areas of responsibility, post holders reflecting responsibilities no longer of relevance to the school's present or future goals) is now more realistic, and the perception of a staffing structure, to reflect more closely the goals the school pursues, becomes possible. However, there are other sources of information to consider before action can be taken and here job descriptions are extremely useful. It is to these that we turn next.

Job descriptions

Many headteachers may feel that a job description represents an impossibly precise attempt to encapsulate in writing the nature of a member of staff's duties, trivialising and excluding important areas of professional responsibility, judgement and action.

Some headteachers attempt to overcome these difficulties by focusing attention onto a member of staff's role and find it more useful in their schools to talk of role guidelines rather than job descriptions. Role being seen as more general and permitting interpretation and initiative, whereas job is seen to be more specific, more easily defined and evaluated, a list of tasks in fact.

An example of one headteacher's view of this is presented below.

The teacher's position in the school and the teacher's role: a headteacher's personal view

When defining roles it is important to lay down guidelines which express the policies of the school. The policies of departments are written within that context. When departments produce role guidelines, they have to incorporate the following elements: administrative, pastoral, curriculum and teaching method and staff management responsibilities.

Generic role guidelines deliberately focus on roles rather than job descriptions. All guidelines are written by the head of department and brought to the deputy head. Their *raison d'être* is for all individuals and members of departments to get a clear view of their own and each other's responsibilities. The exercise is not done by the head of department in isolation but emerges from discussions and consultations at departmental level. . . .

Heads of department write the generic role guidelines of their own responsibilities and the issues and problems that they would deal with.

If teachers in a school are to participate fully, exercise responsibility and gain expertise as managers, they have to have a clearly defined position. They should not have to test the structure to find out what policies are. They should know what is policy and what is not and how policy is formulated. All policies are written down and are either referred to or included in the staff handbook. This is necessary to identify the boundaries and the strategy that goes with them. This applies as much to me as to them. The principles define the limits of our freedom and the boundaries of commitment.

The problem in attempting to operate with role guidelines only is, for example, in differentiating the duties of the respective heads of departments, in dealing with changes in staff when tasks and responsibilities may have to be re-allocated, or to ensure equality of status and expectation etc. It is here that the 'conventional' job description provides a framework which helps the school.

The job description

A job description is a means to an end. It provides, firstly, a written statement of exactly what the job involves, what the jobholder is expected to do and the responsibilities involved in the job, thereby providing a basic framework for the discharging of professional and management responsibilities. It also provides a framework whereby both jobholder and the person assuming responsibility for the jobholder can mutually discuss the nature of that job. Secondly, it allows others in the school to perceive what the job is about, particularly since job descriptions are often published, e.g. in the staff handbook. Inevitably, job descriptions rapidly become out-of-date unless they are regularly reviewed.

A job description should record the facts about a job, that is it should:

- give the title of the job
- indicate to whom the jobholder reports
- indicate who reports to the jobholder.

Further, it should give a brief and succinct summary of

- the overall purpose of the job
- each of the main functions to be carried out by the jobholder.

As a consequence, and following from the description of the job that is made, although some overlap of function between posts inevitably occurs, it should be possible to distinguish this job from other jobs in the school, and indicate clearly to others the limits of the jobholder's authority. It should also be possible to tell whether the jobholder has done the job or not. Succinctness of description is the watchword and statements should be limited to one (or two) sentences at the most.

The job description is concerned with the job not with the person who does the job. A job description is different to and separate from a personal specification.

The personnel specification identifies the personal attributes and skills necessary for a jobholder to perform that job effectively and is most profitably used in the recruitment and selection process.

The use of a job description can be extended in two main ways. Firstly, it is possible to identify from the job description major elements which can be used as 'performance indicators'. That is, the identification of certain aspects of the job by which an assessment of the effectiveness with which the jobholder performs these functions may be made. This is of particular relevance to staff appraisal (see below). Secondly, it is possible to indicate in the job those elements regarded as fundamental to the performance of the job, e.g. a teacher of French should speak the language, a PE teacher should have competence in a number of sports etc. These can be separated from other aspects of the job which, although necessary to successful performance, may be subsequently acquired. This latter perspective is most useful when recruitment to a post is taking place. For example, a preferred candidate does not possess negotiating skills considered as necessary to a post of, for example, head of faculty, but a judgement is made that he/she may be trained to become competent in this area.

Providing the job description is up-to-date, then the headteacher has to hand basic information regarding the duties performed by staff and, through the management structure of the school and the staff appraisal programme, can obtain agreement with a member of staff as to what constitutes his/her current duties.

An example of a job description is given below.

Sample job description: head of faculty

Title: Head of faculty of . . .

Reporting to: Headteacher and management team, Academic Board

Direct involvement with: Heads of other faculties, Heads of departments, Academic Board, Curriculum Working Parties

Scope: Primarily curricular, faculty finance and administration, staff performance, assessment and development, pupil records system, quality of work, behaviour standards, progression

Purpose: To give overall leadership within the disciplinary area of departments falling within the faculty, and to provide an administrative framework within which the activities of staff members can contribute to curriculum and related matters

Functions:

(1) Responsibility to headteacher or management team for overall performance of faculty

(2) Define policy for faculty: values, objectives, aims, staff development and appraisal, curriculum development, resources

(3) Plan development, phasing, access to resources

(4) Consult with Heads of faculties, pastoral heads on co-ordination of policies, plans, assessment and records

(5) Consultation and policy making with heads of subject departments within faculty

(6) Responsibility for staff/teacher performance, assessment and development within faculty, appointments, probationers

(7) Estimates co-ordination

(8) Control of standards: examinations/assessments, records, progression
(9) Organisation of functions overall within faculty, implementation of plans.

Job descriptions are an essential element in staff appraisal to which we now turn.

Staff appraisal

Introduction

A headteacher's personal view:

> Appraisal if it is worth anything at all needs to be continuous and needs to be interactive. Will it tell me that teacher A is better than teacher B, will it unerringly discern the good from the indifferent teacher? If it won't, or you can do that already, then why bother?

We have up to this point considered specific processes central to staff planning and staff development, and now turn to staff appraisal, which is certainly the key element in the staff planning and development process. The school cannot become involved in institution led staff development without having first appraised itself of training and development needs mutually shared by itself and its staff.

Appraisal of any member of staff inevitably takes place on a daily basis. A word of encouragement, a thank you for a job well done, a rebuke for a mistake, are at least explicit indicators. Comments from a parent, a late attendance, a noisy class or enthusiastic participation in a working party etc. noted in someone's memory are more nebulous. So often staff complain that they never know how they are doing. A head of department made this point forcefully when he remarked, 'In this school it's all nudges, winks and innuendo. You've got to guess where you are by comparing yourself to others.'

Staff appraisal is a critical element in the responsibilities of any manager. In exercising responsibility for people, minimally at least, he/she must check and monitor that work is being done and is being done properly. Whether or not these responsibilities for staff are openly admitted or recognised and assessments passed on to staff in a regular, constructive and helpful way, appear up to now to have been ambivalently handled in the schools' sector.

The pressure for staff appraisal to occur in a formal systematic and open way within schools is steadily increasing, and a movement towards bringing the management of the education sector in line with the management of other large, complex, bureaucratic service organisations is discernible. One other point is worthy of note: if staff are assessed informally and the information **not** passed on to them, then they may as well become involved in an official and formal staff appraisal system. At least the opportunity arises to negotiate about criteria, and to appeal against a damaging assessment should one be made against them.

Various terminologies are in use. Amongst these are staff appraisal, assessment, inspection, review . . . , and the reasons for their adoption reflect the different philosophies likely to be found. A desire not to appear judgemental, critical or damaging but constructive and developmental appear, or at least appear to evoke a sense of collaboration and partnership and to play down the managerial function of control.

Staff appraisal provides basic information upon which policies for change and development of the school, and for the development and growth of the individual, are constructed. Staff appraisal is an integral part of the responsibility of any 'manager' who has staff working for him/her. Staff appraisal forms part of the managerial processes adopted in other employment sectors. Whilst acknowledging that the culture, philosophies and goals of these sectors are different to those found in schools, let us briefly consider some of the issues which arise from the practice of staff appraisal there, to see if anything might be derived from the experience and applied to the school.

Staff appraisal in other employment sectors
Appraisal is found throughout other employment sectors: the armed services, commerce, manufacturing industry, the Civil Service, other public sector organisations etc. They all have their respective schemes. These satisfy different managerial functions:*

- A 'control function' – with the emphasis on relaying management information about individual performance so that effective action may be taken where appropriate.
- A 'communication function' – with the emphasis on letting people know where they stand, enabling them to see how they are doing and how the organisation regards them as employees.
- A 'corporate function' – here concern with an individual's performance and potential are subsumed under a superordinate concern for planning, growth and development of the organisation and its dependent and allied future manpower requirements.

The objectives of appraisal may also differ. Appraisal may be concerned with a 'reward review'. Here an assessment is made of the relative worth of individual members of staff as the basis for awarding salary increases or 'bonuses'. Appraisal may also be concerned with 'performance review'. Here the appraisal is designed to identify standards of performance, to praise work well done, rectify weaknesses and to set further targets. A third commonly occurring objective is 'potential review'. Here the principal purpose is to identify an individual's capacity to do different kinds or levels of work, and then to ensure that a developmental programme is set in train to realise this potential to a timetable of the organisation's requirements.

Such reviews necessarily form an integral part of career planning, succession planning and of training and development programmes. *In practice it has proved critical to distinguish and separate these functions and objectives. There seems to be no more self-evident way to guarantee the failure of an appraisal scheme than, for example, to attempt to conduct a 'reward review' and a 'performance review' simultaneously.* The school, therefore, must be sure of what precisely it intends to derive from a staff appraisal programme.

---

* Derived from Stenning, W and Stenning, R, 'The assessment of teachers' performance: some practical considerations'. School Organisation and Management Abstracts, **3**, No. 2, 1984.

Deciding on the objectives*

If staff are to commit themselves to an appraisal scheme, it is necessary that all involved know exactly what the scheme seeks to achieve: the consequences to them of the various roles and responsibilities involved in operating and participating in it; the obligations which will follow from their participation. They must also be given the opportunity of playing a meaningful role in shaping, implementing and operating the scheme. It is also necessary that all are offered the opportunity of training for appraisal, both as potential appraisers and potential appraisees.

Any of the following objectives are likely to be given prominence by a school in assessing a member of staff against the job they perform:

• the assessment, development and improvement of the individual's effectiveness in major task areas;
• to provide a record of that individual's work, and of any special circumstances relating to that work;
• to compare that individual with others;
• to provide a commitment to action from both school and individual's point of view and certainly if improvement of performance is involved.†

The appraisal will provide information to the school regarding the disposition of:

• skills;
• individual career aspirations;
• development and training needs amongst staff; and will further enable the school:
• to give to the individual the school's view regarding their performance;
• establish the basis for *subsequent* discussions of an individual's future; and when appropriate:
• to afford the opportunity of careers advice or careers counselling should such skills be available in the school.

Appraisal is essentially an interactive process and the headteacher should anticipate the generation of information which will help in the identification of, and clarification of, promotion requirements, or of alternative development opportunities where promotion opportunities are restricted. These are likely to surface in many different ways and the school must be prepared at least to listen to any proposals made. By entering into appraisal the headteacher along with staff is entering into a 'contract' where obligations are mutually owned.

What should the headteacher do to operate a programme of staff appraisal? Here are some points for consideration.

---

* An example of a staff appraisal scheme in operation in a secondary comprehensive school can be found as a case study in the accompanying volume of training materials.
† Adapted from D I T B handbook, *Appraisal and Appraisal Interviewing*.

Staff appraisal: A check list

The system
Who appraises whom, when and how frequently?
How are the appraisals conducted?
Are the matters appraised/evaluated, those intended?
Is the documentation being produced, and is the information useable and being used?
Is the 'interview' a genuine two-way exchange?
Is feedback to the member of staff taking place?

Managing the system
Are the appraisals being conducted on schedule?
Are standard approaches being maintained?
Is there uniformity throughout the school?
Are there any reluctant participants? If there are, then:
Are training needs of appraisers anticipated and met?

Using the material
Are we analysing the material assembled?
Identifying training needs for staff?
Addressing training needs?
Identifying potential?
Associating the results with the future development of the school?
Using results to identify succession problems?

Staff attitudes
What are the attitudes of appraisers?
Attitudes of members of staff under review?

Estimate of success
Does it contribute to more effective use of staff?
Do staff show greater involvement and commitment to the work of the school?

Is the context right?
Where do teachers' unions come into the scheme?
What is the role of the LEA in the appraisal system?

Let us use this check list as a way to examine salient issues which consistently arise and cause substantial problems in the adoption and operation of staff appraisal schemes. In fact, without sufficiently thinking through difficulties and anticipating problems, many staff appraisal programmes simply fail to survive. Most appraisal schemes focus upon the appraisal of the individual *per se* and are conceived to view this as sufficient in itself. Here consideration is given to staff appraisal occurring as part of everyday managerial processes, particularly those which form an integral part of the management of the department. We turn to this, firstly, through quotations from a headteacher and a head of department who work in a school where this style of appraisal is adopted.

*The form appraisal will take**

A departmental approach, a headteacher's personal view:

> The task is not to look at the evaluation of the individual teacher *per se*, but to be concerned with the departmental context and the structure of support offered to the teacher. That is the whole management structure, the generation of staff development and personnel policies. Staff appraisal is part of the wider process of evaluation, the cycle of planning, teaching, assessment and development and it is based upon the department.
>
> Staff evaluation in the context of the development of the curriculum is considered a dialogue between senior and departmental management. It is structured so that all members of staff are involved. If this is not managed well then many appraisals would be unjust. Staff appraisal, at the end of the day, depends upon in what esteem you hold your assessor – whether they carry the position or not. You cannot simply set up a scheme and have it happily accepted, especially if there is not a strong residue of trust and confidence. In the end it comes down to trust and integrity. If these do not exist then you are on a hiding to nothing. The purpose of the scheme is not whether I ask them questions but whether they ask the questions of themselves. The purpose of staff appraisal is to get them to ask the questions of themselves.

A head of department's view (first year in post):

> I have relied very much on the headteacher to set the structure and to tell me what had to be done and when. We work very much as a department here, to agree the policies and to sort out problems, usually in meetings. This has taken some getting used to, since I carry the responsibility for what happens.
>
> This year there has been an evaluation of classroom management in which we have discussed different procedures, i.e. discipline, team teaching, sharing of expertise etc. It was useful to develop a department policy and this will help a number of people, such as supply teachers, to identify the key elements, work content and approach. The second major evaluation this year was in response to the headteacher's initiative on the development of the curriculum. I conducted the departmental response which was sent to the headteacher.
>
> The headteacher had asked all teachers in the school to make an appointment for discussion with their head of department, so over a five-week period, as part of the annual review of the curriculum, I talked to each member of the department about our respective roles and responsibilities. To let them know my expectations of them and vice versa, also to see if we could avoid unnecessary duplications of effort and expertise and, at the same time, to give them as much freedom as possible to develop their own interests. The focus of the evaluation is the department. However, we do reviews as individuals as well as departments, i.e. setting goals and objectives. There are seven members of the department. We discuss things corporately and then, if necessary, on an individual basis. All documents on role guidelines etc. are circulated to everyone concerned and discussed mutually. The documents are kept together in a single file and passed round to avoid unnecessary duplication. There are no secrets, it is an exercise in negotiation. If, however, there were classroom discipline problems then I would link up with the pastoral people.
>
> I found it very useful to see, as head of department, how the people in the department see me as a manager. I felt it was a bit of a gamble – you feel very exposed – but overall it was good for the department and the people. It raised questions relating to people's knowledge of policy and how they are implementing it. It was a very open discussion. It is a matter of mutual expectations and how far they are fulfilled. No one person has all the answers. We reach decisions through consultation, mainly discussion.
>
> I also have responsibilities for technicians and meet with them at least once a term

---

* For an example of an appraisal process, see accompanying volume of training materials.

to have a general discussion about the way their job is going. It also provides an opportunity of establishing what they expect of me. We have job descriptions for technicians.

The school may consider self-reporting, it may opt for peer appraisal where classroom teachers choose colleagues to observe their lessons and comment on them, it may determine that a formal interview take place between subordinate and superordinate, or that documentation on an agreed pro-forma becomes the basis of the appraisal. Such documentation may involve preparatory work by appraiser and appraisee who separately score performance on a rating scale. These ratings have then to be mutually agreed at an interview, which in turn may have to be further approved by a panel, or the headteacher, or any combination of these methods. The school will also need to determine whether or not one mode of appraisal is to be used for all staff in the school or separate modes for teaching and non-teaching staff, or even for senior staff, middle management and main grade staff. Staff appraisal for non-teaching members of staff must also be accommodated. It might also be viewed as desirable in some schools to use different forms of appraisal at different stages of a member of staff's development, at different stages of their career, or according to length of service in a particular post. Some form of interview conducted by a more senior to a more junior member of staff is the basis of most appraisal schemes.

Who will be appraised?   Will appraisal apply equally to teaching and non-teaching staff in the school? Will the headteacher, deputies and other senior staff be appraised, or is appraisal only to be for main grade staff of teachers and for non-teaching staff? Who will have responsibilities for appraising non-teaching members of staff?

Who will do the appraising?   Will the school use the hierarchical responsibility structure as the basis for conducting appraisal? Thus heads of department will appraise the staff in their departments and those who work to them, deputies appraise heads of department, and so on. However, the school should not initially assume that heads of department or pastoral units are able and willing to appraise staff who are in their charge. Pressures are likely to arise for a deputy or the headteacher to assume this responsibility and if this is the case, then responsibility for the monitoring and the development of the appraisal scheme as a whole needs careful consideration. A clear onus of responsibility exists on the school's part to train both appraisers and appraisees for their potential roles.

Training of staff for appraisal   It must not be assumed that staff will be fully attuned to the procedure involved in the mode of appraisal adopted, or will have the necessary skills to operate the scheme. For example, it is not a self-evident fact that each member of staff who should conduct an appraisal will be skilled at all aspects of appraisal. They may lack confidence to manage a stressful situation which may necessitate delivering to colleagues formal judgements about their performance, and particularly where such action should take place face to face. Training programmes to acquire or to rehearse these skills will probably be required. The school might also propose a policy that no member of staff conducts an appraisal who has not himself/herself been appraised. Probably the most important need is to train and make ready staff themselves to be appraised. An orientation to thinking about their job in a way which was not previously the case, and to projecting certain information about themselves, might not come easily to all staff. The ability to participate freely and constructively in departmentally based reviews also requires skills which may take some time to acquire.

The recognition that most staff would need to acquire appraisal skills, and for staff to recognise this themselves, is an important issue. It is acknowledged that training is most likely to be acquired through on the job experience, although the personnel department of the LEA ought to be capable of giving considerable training assistance.

How often will appraisal occur?   The staff time involved in a staff appraisal scheme is very considerable. If, for each member of staff in the school, both appraiser and appraisee undertake preparatory work (including classroom visits), meet for a formal interview, produce and agree a summary of the appraisal and of the action stage (training/performance outcomes) which are then ratified by the person who has overall control, the hours collectively involved are the equivalent of many weeks' work. Many appraisal schemes are designed around an annual interview and formal updating of documentary information subsequently placed in a member of staff's file.

It might be more practical for the formal appraisal (interview) to take place less frequently, but for the action stages, checking on the follow-up or action plan agreed at the formal stage, to take place far more frequently, and as part of the normal, daily, managerial responsibilities.

Appraisal pro-formas and written records   If an appraisal document is to be produced which includes a written record for the staff file, or from which a written record will be made, then the school has to give consideration to several issues. Who will see the record? Who will have access to it? Where will it be stored and to whom does it belong? Will the member of staff have his/her personal copy? Is a policy agreed that, for example, any reference provided for a member of staff will rely entirely on information produced from appraisal?

Careers counselling   The dialogue between appraiser and appraisee may provide the basis for a discussion about a member of staff's future. Whilst this will not occur for all members of staff, where it does occur it may become obvious that certain members of staff would benefit from careers counselling. The school needs to consider carefully what it should do in these circumstances.* Does a member of staff exist in the school with sufficient experience and personal status, and with the requisite skills, to offer this service? Since the school is obviously not in a position to guarantee future promotion or even mobility to a member of staff, then anyone who offers careers advice will need sufficient seniority in the school to have insight into overall policies, and in particular, access to its training policies and identified priorities.

---

* A guide to help the teacher think about his/her future career and development is included as Appendix I. The school should carefully consider to whom it would give the guide. It is the intention that the member of staff concerned would themselves decide whether or not to discuss any of the issues arising upon completion of the guide with any other member of the school.

Performance review Not all schools will incorporate into their appraisal scheme objectives which relate to performance review. (See the earlier discussion of objectives.) An example where this is adopted and based upon the job description for the post of head of faculty given earlier is set out below.

Here the job description is used as an enabling device. Both appraiser and appraisee must agree on the nature of the post and duties currently undertaken. Once this agreement is obtained then this provides a basis for a discussion of current performance and, automatically therefore, of future performance. In effect, an action plan can be introduced concerning the assessment or development of the individual.

An example of such 'performance indicators', as they are usually known, which might have been put forward for the job description of the head of faculty post is given below. Performance indicators might be general in nature or specific to a task that is current or a goal to be achieved by the end of the term, of the year, etc.

Head of faculty: sample performance indicators

- Organisation of functions overall within faculty: This will be demonstrated by evidence showing the degree of acceptance of faculty aims and goals by staff, clear plans agreed, resources adequate for task in hand, as shown by minutes of departmental meetings, actions of departments, formal agreement of management team to proposals, and so forth.
- Responsibility for staff development within the faculty: This will be demonstrated by evidence showing, for example, a scheme for staff training, guidance and development agreed and in operation, departmental agreement on INSET plans existing, resource commitment for individual members of staff agreed. Any ongoing programme and staff training are in harmony with school policy and agreed with management team.
- Control of standards: Standards of work, performance in the classroom being reviewed as shown by minutes of departmental meetings, programme of classroom visits for faculty/department staff within and between departments agreed and timetabled, programme of individual classroom visits by heads of department taking place etc.

Performance indicators may also relate to an item where it has been agreed that the development and training of that member of staff should occur, perhaps because of an identified weakness or the need to acquire additional experience has been identified. The intention is that a review and monitoring of any individual's performance should take place on a regular basis as an integral function of, either the individual manager's responsibilities or as part of the function of the department's work, or both.

Oversight of the programme

An important role exists for one person to have overall responsibility for the different stages of the programme. At implementation, the school policy on staff appraisal has to be conveyed to staff, their backing and commitment sought and given, training requirements or resource requirements identified, and the co-operation of the unions gained. Overall responsibility for the day-to-day monitoring of the scheme is also necessary to ensure that standards are equitably applied across the school, to assess the effectiveness with which the objectives of the scheme are met, and to develop the scheme in order that future challenges can be accommodated. Identified training needs, either at group or individual level, have to be followed through and liaison with staff training and development carried out. It is also necessary that a **right of appeal** against a damaging assessment may be heard, and if the appeal is upheld, to amend any records which may exist. Whether or not this right is contained within the school or forms a part of LEA procedure will ultimately depend upon policy developed in practice by individual LEAs.

The question of standards

Any well-conducted staff appraisal scheme must be based upon:

- standards of performance that are derived from the job that teacher does, and are seen to be relevant, realistic and reasonable
- the method of appraisal used being acceptable to staff and applied consistently across the school
- the keeping of a written and agreed record of any appraisal
- the mutual agreement of appraiser and appraisee to any action plan involving the training and/or development of the member of staff. (Where a member of staff fails to improve performance all have agreed is necessary, then recourse may ultimately be made to the LEA's disciplinary procedure.)
- senior and middle management in the school giving their full backing and commitment to the staff appraisal programme.

To be effective, staff appraisal must be based upon standards which are derived from:

- the objectives of the appraisal scheme, which in turn are derived from
- the overall policies and objectives of the school.

One immediate and fundamental problem, of course, is the known difficulty of assessing the long term impact of the educational process on any child and, therefore, of the part that any individual member of staff may play in this. In admitting these difficulties, there is a danger that only those aspects which are more immediately amenable to appraisal will ever be appraised to the disadvantage of the educational process as a whole. However, to deny that any part of a member of staff's responsibilities and performance can be appraised is to imply that the educational process itself is not amenable to assessment and this is transparently not the case.

Sample criteria

For most members of the teaching staff of the school, the assessment process would most likely focus upon at least some of the following:*

- their work with individual pupils and groups of pupils which would include at

---

* For further examples of criteria and a scheme of appraisal, see the accompanying volume of training materials.

least their classroom activities, teaching methods, schemes of work and the teaching materials they would use;

- that they maintain control over the pupils in their charge;
- that they mark and record pupils' work;
- that they participate in the school's pastoral activities and arrangements;
- that they consult with and inform parents and other agencies;
- that they participate with other members of staff in planning relevant department, curriculum and welfare activities and those associated administrative activities;
- that they participate in in-service training;
- that they undertake collective responsibilities;
- that they supervise other members of staff as appropriate.

The list of responsibilities would vary somewhat according to experience and to the level of responsibility held. It would also vary between the different sectors of staff the school employs. For example, in some local Authorities, responsibilities of non-teaching staff are documented by the relevant personnel departments or sections.

Maintenance of standards

The question regarding how well members of staff perform on the sample criteria outlined above relates specifically to how well those occupying management positions perform their responsibilities. The assessment of, for example, a teacher's performance in the classroom must be based upon clearly agreed schemes of work and open access to classrooms by heads of both teaching and pastoral departments who must regularly make such visits. For non-teaching members of staff, assessment must be based upon agreed duties, as published by the LEA, or job descriptions provided by the school and to which members of the non-teaching staff have signified their approval.

Maintenance of the standards of 'appraisals' across departments must be a key function of the person in overall control of the appraisal programme. He/she must regularly review appraisal methods with those who do the appraising. The key to the whole operation is that appraiser and appraisee would regularly have informal contact in the course of their working relationship, where the work and development of staff can be constantly monitored.

The headteacher will need to consider the objectives of staff appraisal in the school, its form and timing, the training of staff, to anticipate the difficulties in implementation and development etc. He/she will need to ensure that they manage the staff appraisal programme satisfying the points identified in the check list on page 65. In the absence of a systematic approach to staff appraisal, the 'grooming' of staff for other roles must remain an arbitrary activity and stands some chance of being so perceived in the staff room. We shall give further consideration to these matters in the next section, 'Succession Planning'. However, before we do so, as a final statement on staff appraisal let us consider the comments of a deputy head appended below.

Staff appraisal, a programme in operation. Learning the hard way: a deputy head's personal view

To get appraisal working you need to approach it very cautiously and carefully over a number of years and with the clear knowledge that it will take time to change attitudes, roles, and in fact, get people used to new roles.

I worked for five years gaining trust with individuals and found that 50% of what I said had had no impact. If staff think you are manipulating them, then it will immediately show. Initially, I was like a bull in a china shop. I thought I knew how to evaluate classroom teaching but I didn't. It proved a painful lesson to me. If you try to be a single evaluator you can't do an effective job on more than 12 teachers, and you will *never* have credibility with them all. You have to be evaluated yourself. You have to find things which you can personally improve – it's important to learn what a shattering experience appraisal can be and how it can undermine your confidence. It is most important to check that the original aims are being fulfilled and are not being distorted. For example, if you were to try to develop a system of appraisal that is based on promotion then you have to have some position to promote people to, if it is going to be based upon self help or mutual growth, then say so, if your evaluation is only to identify weak teachers then you are going to be awfully frustrated when you try to put it into practice. However, if you can get people to accept criticism or a positive offer of help then you can go a long way towards improving people. It shouldn't be threatening. You should work with people as sensitively as possible. Most people know where their weaknesses are and need help in working towards overcoming them.

It should be about helping people to do their jobs better, but in practice it so often comes out to be about managerial control. Unless institutions are made more accountable they will deal with staff appraisal in the way they have dealt with everything else in the last two decades, i.e. it stands a high chance of being distorted by attitudes and managerial incompetence.

What you are trying to improve must fit into the overall philosophy and objectives of the school. We are trying to move the school to cope with the issues we anticipate facing over the next five years. Although we do have an evaluation pro-forma, the most important thing is how you actually communicate with people – it is the quality of the relationship between appraiser and the person being appraised that is the outstandingly important fact.

Job descriptions, if you use them, must be embedded in the classroom teaching situation. You should be concerned with what a classroom teacher *per se* should do, not with the specifics of a 'science' or 'humanities' teacher, and you would look at what you expect a child to have derived from the experience. The intention is to go some way towards issues/events which can be observed or evaluated in the classroom, and you must constantly ask the fundamental questions:

What *is* the difference in learning now?

What *were* that group of children like when they *arrived*?

What *were* they like when they *left*?

Can the teaching in the school be shown to have improved in some way?

The main focus must be on the delivery of classroom instruction, but there are other aspects of the job which are important, for example commitment to the total school, what do they contribute, professional growth etc.

At the time of an evaluation it is very easy to slip into a routine of attempting to evaluate the extent to which previous job targets are met and to set up the new ones, but this can be too mechanistic in a school. However, your experience might prove to be like ours if you fall into that trap and it will make you think very carefully about what you are doing.

You cannot really go it alone in making an appraisal on any individual member of staff. You really need to have a number of different colleagues all homing in on what is happening in this particular classroom. It should at least involve the deputy, the head of department and a colleague of the teacher's own choosing.

It will be rare for the deputy head to have a final say in the appraisal, so that opportunity is there for him/her to talk to any teacher in what is a less threatening way about what goes on in the classroom. One word of warning. In practice everyone has to be clear as to what it means if staff fail to meet their job target. Since there can be such horrendous consequences following from a poor evaluation you need to ensure that staff are set realistic targets. Give them a target they can meet. At least allow them this way out. Are they capable of meeting the (simple) targets set? These should be within the individual's compass and he/she should be able to work on these issues himself/herself. If this isn't the case then here are the teachers that you help.

Succession planning, promotion policy, redeployment and redundancy

To achieve the school's goals staff use should be planned purposively through a framework of 'succession planning' and a 'promotion policy'. These in turn must be allied to the framework of policies set by the LEA, certainly as regards recruitment, redundancy and redeployment.

Headteachers have always identified and developed members of staff who appear to be ready for development. The classroom teacher given a key role in a working party to gain experience of working with other staff, the head of department placed in a position to extend his/her skills, secretaries/clerks systematically moved round the school office in order to acquire skills in all office routines, are common place examples. Such action on the headteacher's part may have been allied to school development needs, e.g. to replace Mr X when he retires, or to take responsibility for a new curriculum initiative, but it is more likely that the development would have been offered with solely professional motives in mind and not have been tied to a specific development in the school.

We are concerned with the purposive development of the school itself and with development of staff now conceived with these goals in view and identified from the staff planning process.

By this stage of the staff planning process, the headteacher has amassed a considerable volume of information upon staff. What is now necessary is a simple system for organising information such that future organisational requirements can be closely attuned to potential development of staff. The construction of 'potential profiles' is one way in which this information may be presented and we shall look at this below. However, before we do let us first briefly consider one headteacher's view on succession planning.

Succession planning: a headteacher's personal view

I do not invite people in here and offer them posts. It is not good enough for me to act as patron and sponsor. I advertise the post on the staffroom noticeboard and then publish the list of candidates and applicants. Everyone has to put in a letter of application. It is essential that staff understand and can see that every attempt is made to operate in terms of their own development. My responsibility is to continuously offer and make opportunities for them. How they respond is up to them. I should never have to make a judgement as to how someone should operate. Just to provide opportunities. Staff know the total number of scale posts and the range of points available to each curriculum area, so that applicants for promotion know which curriculum areas are open for development.

Potential profiles

In other employment sectors many ways are used to enable comparison of staff 'potential profiles' to be made. One of the simplest is to put the information on to cards, one to each member of staff, and either to use numerical rating or colour coding to allow an immediate rating of staff to occur against whichever variable is of interest. The cards usually would hold the following information:

- job title
- name
- age
- qualifications
- years of service in present school
- years of service in present post
- previous posts
- training received
- information from most recent appraisal, to include performance in present post and career aspirations of member of staff.

A card could be laid out as follows:

Job Title _____			Date _____		
Name _____					
Age	Qualifications (degree (D) diploma(Da) etc.)	Years in school	Years in present post	Training	Previous posts
APPRAISAL INFORMATION Strengths Training recommended					
PRESENT PERFORMANCE O Outstanding A Above average B Below average W Weak		Readiness for increased responsibility now/ 1 – 2 years / 2 – 3 years etc.			

It must be stressed that such a card would only enable an initial assessment to take place. The readiness of a member of staff to benefit from additional or different responsibilities calls for considerable sophistication of judgement and it is unlikely that the decision of one member of staff would solely prevail.

Redeployment and redundancy. Criteria for choosing people for redeployment

A headteacher's personal view:

Undoubtedly, maintenance of the curriculum would be the highest priority. The first thing I would do is try and up group size, cut back on option sizes whilst maintaining curriculum. Then it would have to be on an individual negotiating basis because I don't see how you could do it without taking personalities into account. For instance, it is difficult to see how you could redeploy someone, say, with two years to go, and it would be the grossest cruelty to expect them to adjust to a new school in these hard times . . . it's always been arranged by a combination of gentlemen's agreements and what have you.

The headteacher will largely be constrained by agreements negotiated between LEA and unions and in consultation with governors. He/she might not have to select members of staff for redeployment or redundancy, or to decide whether or not for a particular post to accept a redeployed member of staff, for such decisions might be made within the LEA. However, if this is a responsibility of the head-teacher, then the information from earlier staff planning stages and particularly from staff appraisal are the key elements in determining future need and therefore the member(s) of staff whose services the school could most afford to lose whilst preserving the integrity of its objectives, organisation and curricular processes.

However, other issues may arise. Staff themselves may determine whether or not they would choose to go. Their age, their health, the availability of (enhanced) premature retirement compensation are factors which may persuade members of staff to leave whose services the school would otherwise wish to retain.

In the absence of overall LEA policies, it is difficult for the school to do other than to adopt an *ad hoc* response and this usually works against curricular integrity and for staff security.

Institution-led staff development

Creating opportunities for staff development

A headteacher's approach:

> I try to create an increasing range of opportunities for teachers to respond to. I restructured the responsibilities among senior staff because many had been in post for five or six years and needed a change of direction, for the school and for personal development.
>
> It was necessary because the pace of the school needed lifting. It needed rejuvenation in terms of developing policies and strategies in information technology, multicultural education, special needs provision etc. It follows on from our policy of providing access to the curriculum.
>
> There was also the need to tap the range of the juniors underneath to keep them motivated and involved. Since [September] I have changed 34 people's jobs to give them different challenges. For example, the ex-head of Maths still teaches Maths but now someone else is head of department. The head of Science is taking over responsibility for professional development and the assistant head of Science is taking over as head of Science. In doing this the delicacies are the length of time you spend talking to people and, more important, the order in which you talk to them. To do this you have to know your people well. In this exercise no one has gained financially – there are no points available. When a member of staff is approached with a proposition, they have to know that you are, and they will be, concerned with the overall welfare of the school.
>
> Are we building up a problem – an expectation of additional remuneration when posts become available? However, is it right to leave the junior staff frustrated? Is not the decision, in the final analysis, theirs not ours? When doing this it is important that the policy applied is consistent.
>
> Professional development is currently a designated responsibility of one of the deputy heads.

The deputy head's view:

> Professional development is necessary to improve the work of the school, to respond to needs of pupils as well as teachers. Responding to curriculum needs requires both. My general rule is to identify areas for courses, publications etc. and to fill in the gaps not already met by initial training, LEA provision etc. but which we have identified that the school needs to do something about.

Staff development and training   Having previously ascertained the organisational goals which the school is now being directed towards, the headteacher, through earlier staff planning stages, will have identified training and development needs for both groups of staff and individual members of staff. The school's staff development programme provides the way in which these identified/anticipated needs can be met. The programme will have to have a realistic time scale, be constructed with regard to wider LEA policies for staff and INSET, be within the resource capacities of the school and take note of individual feeling and career ambition of members of staff.

What is necessary is to establish the practicalities of that programme and to anticipate difficulties which may arise in trying to make it operational. The earlier staff planning phases will have established several major strands of development and training requirements. Briefly these are likely to concern, firstly:

- the development of staff to enable the school to reach or achieve identified (new) goals

and once these are achieved, then

- to have staff trained and developed sufficiently in advance for them to maintain the school in its new pursuits.

This is likely to require the training of groups of staff, or even in some circumstances of the whole of the staff, and will certainly encompass substantial areas of what is often separately identified as professional development. It may involve staff participating in, for example, staff conferences, working parties, school review, in-service training provision organised by the LEA, and so forth.

Also, in identifying new goals or directions for the school to take, it is likely that needs are identified which may be satisfied by the development of one individual, e.g. an individual who is seen as capable of fulfilling a specific requirement. For example, teaching computer studies, or an individual whose classroom performance is falling below par and who would certainly be placed under additional pressure by the changes it is anticipated making. Here we are likely to be looking at training programmes tailored to the needs of one individual if they are school based, or to identify an external programme if the individual is to obtain the requisite training from outside the school. These two types of training needs are likely to account for the bulk of the school's training and development resources over a definable time span. However, it is likely that individuals will separately present themselves for development, often under the premise of professional development. Additionally, there will always be individuals who identify themselves for development because of their perception of their personal need, possibly a career need. This is an important aspect to take into consideration because it is never possible for the school to perceive all of that which is necessary and here may be a potential source of new ideas. In addition, morale and ambition are likely to be factors to take into account in making staff development decisions.

In formulating a staff development and training programme, the headteacher must always find a balance between the following:

- *ad hoc* staff development which depends on the initiatives and aspirations of individual teachers
- planned development in which the school is able to place sufficient balance upon both (a) the identified development needs of the school or sections of it, and also upon (b) the identified needs of individual teachers.

The reconciling of individual and institutional need is always likely to be a source of tension.

What modes of development and training are available to the school?

A headteacher's policy:

> Here the question is not whether I release them but whether they release themselves. Each department has a programme linked to departmental needs which the departments themselves identify. The departments themselves decide who goes on what course. The department makes recommendations to me and it is the department that releases them. The results of the training have to be fed back to the department.
>
> The school INSET programme is maintained through recommendations from departments and new initiatives from management *re* the development of school policies. The annual staff conference, which takes place over a week towards the end of the summer term, also considers the INSET implications of new school policies and initiatives and will work out a strategy for covering the training needs identified.
>
> There is an in-school in-service programme (which includes a yearly residential programme) that tackles the development needs of staff. This is carefully supplemented by use of external in-service programmes. All members of staff have access to one external course per year.

Types of training available   A bewildering variety of terms are available to describe the different types of training/development initiatives available to a school. Such training may be 'on the job', 'off the job', 'school based within school', or 'out of school', and so on. External consultants from colleges, polytechnics, universities, as well as LEA-based consortia, are all available to run programmes. The school may rely entirely on its own resources, it may make use of LEA in-service training provision, or even of training opportunities which have a national base.

Staff within the school should all anticipate at some time adopting the leadership of a particular in-service initiative. This role is a particularly acute one for the headteacher to adopt, and also for middle management in the school, who may not necessarily agree that they in fact should fulfill such a role. In some schools a staff tutor may be found. Amongst their duties are likely to be the receipt and circulation of information about in-service training courses, usually external to the school and, more problematically, the offering of careers advice to staff.

Schools have adopted at least some of the following training/development formats:

- Whole school training, based upon school self-review or self-evaluation, and for which school staff may take up residence at an LEA residential centre. Many variations of this format exist in terms of duration and sub-groupings of staff involved. The initiative may also involve staff from contributory feeder schools, pupils, parents, governors etc.

- Staff may be given an increased breadth of perspective into the work of the school through work related development. One form of this was identified earlier under 'staff appraisal' as performance review and target setting.

- Staff membership of working parties, chairing of committees, membership of moderating panels may, in appropriate circumstances, all give breadth of insight and expertise, as may mentoring (particularly useful to the induction of probationers, providing the probationer has the capability and is in a position to exercise some choice in the selection of a mentor), team teaching, classroom observation etc.

- Adding to the breadth of an individual's skills and experience through addition to the functions performed whilst retaining the same level of post is also possible (usually known as job enrichment).

- A variety of other training methods exist where both individual and school can mutually benefit. Amongst these are the traditional modes of participation in in-service training and courses which may vary in level from one day to award bearing levels. Staff may undertake consultancies, research, study visits, participate in effecting curriculum or organisation development and renewal, or be seconded, or receive visits from staff in other schools and colleges.

- A more problematic but rewarding way to give additional experience is through job rotation. The problems associated with this are self-evidently allied to status and salary payments, but can be negotiated within a school by an adroit senior management team.

- Even more problematic is transference of staff between schools to acquire experience additional to that which any one school could normally be expected to provide. The mechanism of redeployment provides the example that where the goodwill exists, then such schemes, operating on an LEA-wide basis, could be brought into existence.

The purposive nature of the developments described above must be allied to an articulated policy of succession planning. This must be rooted in LEA-based policy which takes into account the need existing for both development of classroom teacher expertise, and for the allied development of managerial competence.

Assuming that the school is clear about the purpose of any particular training/development initiative, then the school should ensure that:

- the proposed initiative is appropriate to that individual (group of staff), in the circumstances at this time;
- that the headteacher is keenly aware of his/her own role in training and development of staff;
- that the proposed initiatives can be met either within the resource and policy framework of the LEA or from the school's own resources.

Where this is not the case then the school should negotiate with the LEA to make such provision; consider joining forces with other schools to satisfy this identified need; or perhaps with the LEA approach external trainers who can provide the training required.

The special problems of induction and of probationary teachers

Induction: the integration of the individual into the school: a headteacher's personal view:

> Professional development here is in terms of integration into the school, into the school structure, especially at department level to make it difficult for the teacher to become isolated. In order to absorb him or her into the principles and policies of the school, we run a special course for all new staff coming into the school. We also try to encourage a group feeling through the annual staff conference, and provide a documentary history of the school etc. Staff tend to become well inducted into their departments but not so well inducted into the aims and principles of the school. This is why we have to develop structures, meetings, information, to engender a feeling of the school. This transcends but is reinforced by departmental meetings. . . .
>
> This is why we tell the story of the school as part of the pastoral programme to promote a feeling of identification and belonging. Generally, it is much more difficult to integrate the new teacher than the new pupil. The teacher must identify, not with the class, but with the community. The two week induction programme is held at the end of July, when new teachers come into school – not to teach but to find out about the school. Also the attendance at the end of year staff conference helps them to become acclimatised socially with the staff in a working environment. This helps induction and initiation.

Probationary teachers: a headteacher's personal view:

> The key feature in the development of probationary teachers is the day-to-day consultation with the head of department. In this school it is the head of department who is generally recognised as having responsibility for probationary teachers. Then there are twice weekly meetings with myself. The heads of department identify a problem and the matter is then passed to me to identify the resources, and sometimes – nearly always – to develop a strategy based on finding support in the classroom.
>
> Increasingly here, departments now recognise that the need is theirs and the individual's. So we develop programmes of team teaching, observation, meetings etc. It is getting the departments to recognise the richness of their own resources. Other things, like courses, personal interviews, etc. can be (mistakenly) used as a substitute for departmental support.
>
> I have developed the view that where probationers have the greatest difficulty is where the support for them is weakest. The staff handbook includes a section on the 'Professional Development of Staff' and a variety of structures and strategies are engaged to encourage the probationary teacher to evaluate his or her own performance. The departmental meeting ensures that a wider context for such evaluation is borne in mind.
>
> A senior teacher has overall responsibility for probationers. He has the responsibility to identify good teachers teaching across the curriculum. He also encourages form teachers to observe their form being taught by other teachers. When a teacher is not teaching he or she is free to go round the school, find the form group and ask the teacher if he or she can go into the classroom. This is essential so that teachers as well as the pupils have an awareness of the school as a whole.
>
> In this school we have access to classrooms because all the doors are open. People feel more secure if the doors are open. I walk into classrooms, so do heads of department. Here it is not an issue.

Where a probationary teacher is involved in more than one department the senior tutor would rely on the deputy head to liaise with the different heads of department.

Check list for the induction of probationary teachers: a school based approach

1. Is there a school policy and an LEA policy for the probationary period?
   Is this concerned more with protecting the employer against an unsatisfactory employee than with helping the individual teacher?
   Does the approach adopted by the school fit into existing approaches to staff appraisal, staff training and staff development at both school and LEA levels, and to school and LEA policies for staffing and recruitment?
   Does the policy adopted by the school cover the relevant stages of the probationary period, namely recruitment, assignment of duties, reception, guidance (including professional and academic development) and evaluation?
   Has the school the capacity and flexibility to resource its approach or to work with others when additional resources are required?
   Is the probationer familiarised with the purposes of the probationary period and is he/she sympathetic to the intention?
   Do staff involved understand the roles and responsibilities entailed by the induction of probationers and are they trained and sufficiently skilled to carry them out?
   Does a procedure exist for evaluating the effectiveness of the experience offered to the probationer?
   Does the induction of the probationer allow him/her to fulfill their own expectations of themselves as teachers?

2. Is the approach conceived as a planned sequential experience?
   Is it planned so that difficulties probationers regularly encounter can be anticipated and alleviated, especially those relating to:
   induction into the school
   induction into the profession of teaching?
   Is the programme conceived around the normal functioning of departments and responsibilities of heads of departments?
   Is the person with overall responsibility for probationers the same person that the head of department reports to in the course of his/her departmental duties?
   Is he/she able to co-ordinate the experience offered to the probationer(s)?

3. Is the approach individualised and relevant to the probationer's own teaching circumstances, particularly:
   does the school encourage the probationer to visit prior to the start of the new school year to meet the classes they will teach and the colleagues they will work with?
   is the probationer provided with a copy of the staff handbook and the opportunity of seeking clarification on issues which they may subsequently raise?
   does the school provide an appropriate timetable and duties load?
   is the probationer provided with information on the children and their backgrounds?

prior to the start of the school year has the probationer received their timetable, a syllabus, and information regarding living accommodation (if relevant)?

Is the probationer shown round the school, acquainted with the resources available, introduced to staff, inducted into the community of the school?

at the start of the school year are any problems regarding salary rapidly rectified?

is interaction with staff (particularly probationers) from other schools facilitated?

is the opportunity made available to observe other members of staff teaching classes forming part of the probationer's own timetable?

is additional support to the probationer offered through a mentor who has himself/herself recently completed the probationary period?

does the programme offered by the school take place with reference to training organised by the LEA for probationers, and programmes offered by the local teachers centre?

4.   The assessment of the probationer raises separate issues. How does the school enable the probationer to clearly understand that he/she must work with staff who are both colleagues and assessors?

Is the probationer informed in writing of the conditions of the probationary period and the mode of assessment to be made and its timing?

At what stage(s) of the probationary period is the LEA (officer or inspectorate) involved?

What is the role of heads of departments in the assessment process? Do they understand and discharge responsibilities effectively?

Who in the school has the final say as to whether or not the probationer has successfully completed the probationary period?

Who informs the probationer of the decision?

Does the school operate the principle of 'if in doubt fail'?

Why institution led staff development might fail

Some points for consideration   Any or all of the following are likely at some time to be encountered by schools as they set up, and attempt to run, staff development and training programmes aimed at satisfying diagnosed development needs:

- The perception of teaching as a profession and the views of the nature of professionalism held by some teachers. When the development of the individual would be seen as the right, and the subordination of individual to institutional need would not be tolerated.

There are many issues related to the levels of trust existing between staff:

- The nature of leadership and authority in the school and, dependent upon the leadership style, the willingness of ambitious staff to take on unfashionable and unprofitable causes.

- The perceptions held of the school as an organisation, and the unstated 'value' premises upon which much proposed action is predicated – the development of whom, by whom, for whose purposes and benefit readily come to mind.

- That staff development may well be perceived as a tool of management and hence concerned with managerial control and therefore in conflict with the concept of professionalism and of collegiate behaviour.

- In some institutional contexts the circumstances in which staff development is likely to arise would make it difficult for an individual to refuse development. If they did then their action could be seen at least as irrational and at worst selfish.

- Consequently the possibility emerges that those most likely to be developed are those showing the greatest degree of ideological purity, thus turning purported school development into actual individual development.

Questions of resources and prioritisation inevitably arise:

- Has the headteacher sufficient power and authority delegated to him by the LEA and governors to bring about an effective development programme for the staff of his school?

If this is not the case then planned staff development directed towards identified goals in the school suffers a considerable handicap.

Additionally, staff development encompasses, in an inter-related way, change or development of the organisational structure and of the curricular and pedagogic processes by which the school serves its 'clients'. That is, staff development cannot exist in isolation; it is affected by and in turn affects the wider process of change in the school – curriculum development, organisational development and staff development are inextricably linked.

In order to have staff development programmes based upon goal identification, affecting (as they will) the careers of individuals, then choices about the organisation's future most appropriately need to be based upon some style of open decision making, or open discussion about the goals to be achieved by the school and the strategies to be adopted to achieve these goals. This, in turn, raises a further issue of who has access to what kinds of information to inform debate. Here, restated, is the nature of contract or consensus existing between individual and institution, and the extent to which congruence towards the pursuit of common goals exists.

Briefly then, some of the assumptions which underpin approaches to the development of staff are likely to be beset by problems. The school should anticipate these and declare the position it holds. For example:

- That a shared view about the nature of the school as an organisation and of the objectives it seeks to achieve, can exist.
  Is a school ready and able to act without this congruence? How many and which staff must it take with it?

- That individuals within the organisation can comfortably have separate but inter-related career goals. Dilution or distortion of institutional needs for individual need is always likely to be present.
  What level of dilution will the school tolerate?

- That school and LEA 'manpower' assumptions are not antithetical and that sufficient authority is delegated to the headteacher to implement meaningfully a staff development programme, and that education committee members, LEA officers, advisers/inspectors, school governors, all share a framework of policies and a context into which any one school's development programmes are located.

  Is the school prepared to discuss its future in a forum where these key decision makers are present?

- That those staff responsible for the staff development programme are trained for their staff development tasks, and that agreement exists upon a time scale upon which the effectiveness of the staff development programme can be evaluated.

  Are the middle management of the school really committed to staff development and do they see this as a key part of their responsibilities?

- That an individual member of staff can establish sufficient information about the 'real' goals of the institution, and of the real intentions of its senior staff to forge a meaningful developmental contract, that is, that 'trust bonds' of sufficient worth can be established in the school.

  Is the leadership style likely to bring about a sharing of goals and ambitions?

What should a well conducted staff development programme do?

The programme would be planned, based upon the identified developmental needs of the school, and also take note of the developmental needs of individuals, their career tracks and career timetables.

The programme would be related to wider developmental programmes set up by the LEA and particularly to their succession planning policies and resource policies.

It would have an agreed evaluation strategy to assess its effectiveness and a person responsible for ensuring this evaluation takes place would be identified. Such a person would be a focal or reference point for all matters concerned with staff development, e.g. deputy head, or senior member of staff planning/co-ordinating committee, to which departments or faculties, groups, individuals can turn. They should be of sufficient seniority to have real insight into the developmental policies of the school.

Mechanism or procedures would exist whereby:

- conflicting claims can be reconciled and consensus explored
- staff co-operation and agreement can be obtained
- long and short term needs can be distinguished
- priorities can be established and agreed, and a balance obtained.

The staff development programme would include both teaching and non-teaching staff, and inter-department needs of all staff would be ascertained, e.g. use of the school office, use of micro-computers/word processors for school administration.

All training/development opportunities would be investigated, e.g. attendance at out-LEA/in-LEA courses, school-based courses, visits to other schools, reference to and help from advisory staff, observation of and involvement in the work of other colleagues in the school; team teaching, staff discussion groups/working parties, the use of project work, research; talks/demonstrations for other staff. The role of the department in all of this would be fully articulated.

The aim of any development/training would be made clear to the individuals(s) involved. For example:

- to provide new expertise – knowledge and skills for the school;
- to add to breadth of personal experience and expertise;
- to develop leadership skills;
- to improve ability to administer and organise;
- to provide effective induction procedures for new teachers and probationers.

The programme would:

- allow for more than one item at one time;
- allow for an effective balance to be obtained;
- determine what kind of commitment is necessary – short term (one day, one weekend), longer term (secondment), part or full-time, in school/out of school/vacation;
- take account of existing teaching programmes/timetables and, where gaps occur, ensure that they are met, and replacement staff found if necessary;
- make clear to staff participating in them the function of, for example, internal working parties/committees etc.

The school would ensure that experience exists to ascertain the relevance or quality of any training or of available courses/materials, and where doubt exists about the availability of resources, then advice would be sought from, for example, LEA in-service education centres (inspectors, advisers, teachers' centre leaders).

Organised feedback from staff development would take place:

- the teacher involved is briefed to report back;
- the manner of reporting back is defined and understood;
- deliberate attempts are made to assess the value of the feedback and to absorb that which is of benefit into the system;
- responsibility for doing this and assessing its usefulness is clearly ascertained.

The staff development and training programme should above anything else:

- enable existing staff to develop, to adjust to and to cope with new demands;
- provide individual members of staff with help or opportunity, where this need is identified.

We have examined the major elements of staff planning and institution led staff development as a means to enable the headteacher to plan staff use and development more effectively. However, in putting into operation any aspect of the process, the headteacher must take careful account of other manifestations of staff management which are of equal importance – the legal implications of action, the grievance procedures through which staff may complain, the staff code of conduct to cope with unacceptable departures from professional standards and how he/she would communicate with staff regarding staff planning and development processes. It is to this, staff communication and decision making, that we turn in the next chapter.

To demonstrate the complexity of these inter-relationships we ask the reader to consider the simple incident below. This recently occurred in a secondary comprehensive school and initially concerned a letter from the AEO schools regarding reduction of points for ancillary staff.

Incident: Reduction of points for ancillary staff

You have received a letter from the LEA informing you that by September, in line with cuts being made in other secondary schools, you are to lose 25% of the points allocated to your school for ancillary staff. You have considered the information arising from the staff planning process, particularly the staff appraisal programme, in relation to the overall goals you seek for the school and the curriculum you will maintain, and have decided that two courses of action are open to you: firstly, to ask all ancillary staff to take a pro-rata reduction in their hours; secondly, to make some members of staff redundant. If you were to follow this latter course of action then you have determined that you must lose two part-time laboratory staff, and one part-time member of the clerical staff: all are married women. You are also aware that only one lady would go voluntarily.

Decide the strategy, a timetable of activities and identify any other action you would need to take, firstly to adopt course of action number one, and then, course of action number two.

The following points are put forward to help you plan your action.

- Who is the employer, is it yourself?
- If you act as the agent of the employer, then do you do so by carrying out their instructions, or do you advise them of the course of action you wish them to take on your behalf?
- Who would you turn to for advice anticipating that problems may arise? They may be individual officers of the LEA, of your own professional association, or a union to which ancillary staff may belong, other headteachers, members of the Board of Governors etc.
- Do you know if policies are in existence, agreed between LEA and unions, regarding terms and conditions of service of non-teaching staff and, is there a no redundancy clause?
- Would you consult with members of the teaching staff, particularly the heads of departments and the staff in those departments most likely to be affected by the cuts?
- How would you announce your proposed action to members of the teaching staff?
- Consider how you would announce your proposed action to the members of staff concerned. Firstly, if you were to ask all members of non-teaching staff to take a pro-rata reduction in their hours and, secondly, to the actual members of staff who are to be made redundant. In each case you should determine how members of teaching staff would be informed of your proposed actions.
- What advice would you give to those staff who are to be made redundant, e.g. would you advise them to join a union, would you offer to help them find another job?

- Who would write a letter of redundancy, and who would sign it? Is a 'model' letter available in your files?

In producing a timetable for your actions, indicate particularly who you would speak to and the order in which you would speak to them. In proposing your action you should refer to the previous chapter, and to the subsequent chapters.

Appendix I: A guide to help the teacher think about his/her future career and development

A note for the headteacher's consideration

It is not intended that this guide in the form of a series of questions should be made widely available to all teachers in a school. The teachers who might complete it should be chosen with care, and it should be suggested to them that they will probably derive personal benefit from completing it.

It is designed with different groups of teachers in mind. For example, it might be used by the teacher who has reached a career stage where several alternative goals might be possible, or by the teacher who has perhaps reached a plateau in his/her career. The intention is to help the individual teacher think about his/her career and for them to develop some strategies as to what they might do next to achieve their goals.

Although the answers to individual questions in the guide must remain the property of the teacher, it would form a very useful part of a wider career discussion that the head-teacher is holding with the teacher. Once the teacher is more certain about his/her overall goals, then it is important to ascertain that the strategies for achieving them are realistic and within the resource capabilities of the school. Here the experience of the headteacher would be invaluable in offering staff careers advice, in commenting on the realism of their strategies, and in commenting on the practical and realistic likelihood of a member of staff achieving certain goals within a forseeable time span. The difficulty in steering a path between raising false expectations for the member of staff concerned, or dampening off enthusiasm and commitment, need not be elaborated to the experienced headteacher.

Introduction*

This exercise is designed to focus the individual teacher's attention onto certain aspects of his/her career. In doing this it is assumed that this exercise forms part of a wider process of thinking about aspects of a career and turning certain issues over in one's mind. Whilst some teachers will find the emphasis and focus of questions given here of benefit to themselves, others may well feel that a less structured and directed approach is more in tune with their own philosophy and style. Even in the case of these latter teachers, the identification of certain personal issues and priorities would be valuable. It is suggested that to think purposefully and constructively once in a while about one's career and development is not necessarily to be seen as calculating and clinical.

Objectives

The objectives of the exercise are:

- to help you clarify your future career goals, through considering your present situation in relation to other goals that you might have;
- to help you identify ways of obtaining greater satisfaction and achievement in your present job if you do not wish to move to another post;
- to help you develop action plans to achieve these goals through considering your present strengths and areas in which you have yet to gain experience, thereby

---

* This guide forms a considerably modified and extended version of an earlier questionnaire of unknown source.

capitalising on your strengths and minimising as far as possible your weaknesses, or identifying how to correct them or add to your experience through development or training;

- to help you improve your ability to present yourself both verbally and in written form when applying for a new position.

What you should do

The exercise is conducted via paper and pencil and is confidential to you. You should find somewhere where you can guarantee a quiet and uninterrupted period of time to complete it. You need not reveal to anyone else what you write or what your reactions are, if that is your wish. However, when you have completed the exercise and possibly produced goals and priorities, you may wish to share your thoughts with someone else. This may be with the headteacher or deputy headteacher, with another person in the school, in the LEA, or someone outside the educational sector who you feel could be of assistance to you and to whom you can easily relate. It may be that you will only wish to discuss particular aspects of the exercise, e.g. Section D. This must be left entirely to your discretion. You may at certain stages want to seek additional information. You can do this without in any way revealing the sorts of answers you might make.

The exercise is likely to be most useful to someone who has reached a 'mid-career' post. It is not likely to be particularly helpful to the young or inexperienced teacher at the beginning of his or her career.

A   Where am I now?

Life and Career Lines   We want you to draw a line(s) which represents your life and your career to date.

You may, if you wish, construct a 'graph', putting the jobs or positions you have held chronologically along one axis and salary earned along the other axis, an example of which is provided overleaf if you wish to use it.

Superimpose over this career line another line or series of lines which represents the satisfaction, fulfilments and the frustrations which you may have experienced at different stages of your life: identify them by writing on them what they are. However, try to keep within the framework of dates as set out on the horizontal axis.

The lines you have drawn may be straight, slanted, curved, jagged or any shape that seems right to you. Be as creative as you can . . . it represents something about how you think of your life.

Look at what you have drawn. What is the shape of any individual line(s)? What is the overall shape of your 'graph(s)'? Can you decide? What are the moments, moves, circumstances, events, which stand out as being most important to you? What are some of the things you would like to avoid repeating in the future? What are some of the things you would like to happen again? Make a list of these things.

B   How satisfied am I?

Before you go on to plan for the future, you need to examine how satisfied you are with your present life.

The following is offered as a list of aspects of your life you might like to think about. You can add items to this list or subtract items from it as you wish. They are offered as examples of aspects of your life you might wish to think about.

For each category, rate the degree to which you are satisfied with your current position. Use a 5-point scale with '1'(one) being low and '5'(five) meaning completely satisfied.

Rate each category as a whole, not each question separately. The questions are meant as a guide to help you clarify your thoughts.

Contacts with family and relatives   Do my job and job-related duties: enable me to spend as much time with my family and my relatives as I would like; constrain how we actually spend our time together; allow sufficient time to become aware of each other's different needs and wishes?

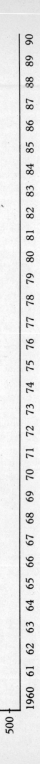

Friends and other social activities Do my job and job-related duties: enable me to form the friendships I would like to have; enable me to spend as much time with friends as I would like; enable me to develop the social skills and social activities I would like to have?

Financial aspects of my life Does my salary: enable me to get by on a week-by-week basis; live the life style I really would like to lead?

Leisure time activities Do my job and job-related duties: enable me to have adequate leisure time; enable me to develop or become involved in the hobbies or other leisure pursuits in which I am interested?

Professional development Do my job and job-related duties: enable me to spend as much time as I ought in keeping up with current developments in the educational world, e.g. subject, teaching methods, matters of wider educational concern. . . ? Do I find my work intellectually satisfying? Do I enjoy my work?

Where you have rated any item *less* than completely satisfactory, take a few moments to jot down some notes as to how you would like them to change.

C *Where do I want to go?*

This exercise is private to you. What it has done so far is to allow you to think creatively about your life to date. We want you to use this as an orientation, as a basis, to thinking about your future.

Look back at the career and life lines you drew at the start of this exercise. Extend the career line you drew to the job(s) that you would really like to do in the future, and the life line(s) to the level of satisfaction and fulfilment you would like to achieve. Once you have done this use it as an orientation to think about the following questions.

1   Am I content to remain where I am in the same job or, at least, in the same school?
   If I imagine myself ten years older and with my family making either increasing, or lessened, demands on me, will the job I presently occupy still be satisfying?
   If I contemplate a career move, what is the furthest point ahead I can personally and realistically foresee, both in terms of level of aspiration and distance, into the future?

2   How does this career goal relate to your:
   (a) social goals
   (b) financial goals
   (c) personal goals regarding family and relatives
   (d) leisure goals
   and so forth?
   Does it conflict in any way with other types of success and fulfilment that you may be seeking in other parts of your life? Are you and your family willing to tolerate the 'discomfort' which the single-minded pursuit of a career goal might entail?

3   Is it possible for you to rank the most important thing(s) you want to achieve? What are they?

4   Have you considered a career outside teaching in another educational related sector, or into a completely different employment sector? Would this be a viable proposition for you? Who have you turned to for advice on a move of this magnitude.

5   Remaining within the framework of schools and professions related to education, what job can you see yourself doing three to five years from now? Is this a stepping stone or is it likely to prove a 'terminal' post.

What we have done so far is to allow you to review different aspects of your own career and your life, as a way of helping you identify more clearly those career or life goals you value most highly. What we shall now do in Section D is to concentrate your attention on achieving the *career* goals you have identified.

D   How do I get there?

1 The strategies open to me to reach my chosen goal(s)* It might prove useful in determining and choosing strategies to talk to some other people. Firstly, you might choose 'significant others', that is colleagues perhaps in other schools, L E As, H E or F E, known personally to you, who started their career at the same time as yourself and whose career you might think of measuring your own progress against. Secondly, you should discuss, with someone who has achieved, or is promoted beyond, the post to which you might aspire (the Head or a Deputy would be obvious examples here, providing you think you could speak to them sufficiently openly), questions of the following kinds: What are the requirements for post X? What sort of person do they look for to fill these posts at appointment: firstly, in terms of skills and experience, and secondly in terms of personal attributes and attitudes? How might I acquire the 'relevant' training and experience? What was their strategy for achieving their goals and how would they adapt such strategies today if placed in your present circumstances? What steps should I take to achieve my ultimate goal?

2 The resources I have which will be a help to me in making my present post more satisfying or in achieving new career goals
(a) List the qualities about yourself that you value highly and which you think will help you achieve your goals.
(b) List five areas of work experience you have had which you value highly and which you think will help you achieve your goals.
(c) List up to five major achievements during your career which you value highly and which you think will help you achieve your goals.

3 The qualities I have which will be a hindrance to me in making my present post more satisfying or in achieving new career goals
(a) List the qualities about yourself which you think may hinder you in achieving your goals.
(b) Identify any areas of work experience you have had or which you have not had which may hinder you in achieving your goals.
(c) Identify any extra or additional achievements which might be necessary to help in achieving your goals.

It might help you to represent these impressions diagramatically by drawing horizontal lines to express the extent to which any item helps or hinders you in attaining your goals, and note some items might both help and hinder you. You might even wish to represent the strength of the helping or hindering factors by a number on a numerical scale, and then to add up the total, for helping or hindering factors.

The finished diagram might look like this:

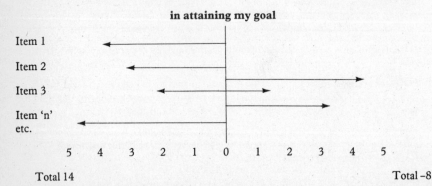

* For further ideas you might like to consider looking at Chapters 3, 4 and 5 of Lyons, G, *Teacher Careers and Career Perceptions*, NFER, Windsor, 1982.

Draw a diagram like this one to show which the helping and hindering factors are in your career. In the hypothetical case above, helping factors outweigh the hindering factors. On balance are the strengths greater than the hindering forces or vice versa? How would you sum up your position? If the disposition is towards the strengths then you ought to consider how to offset or mitigate any hindering forces before you proceed to the next section. If the hindering forces seem to outweigh the strengths then you ought to consider training or other developmental initiatives to offset these forces – you will very probably need to take advice on this from a person whose views you would respect.

4 What action do I need to take now?
(a) What is your immediate goal?
     What is your ultimate goal? Are they the same?
     If your ultimate goal necessitates intermediate steps or stages make a list of what these are.
(b) Whether your goal is to develop your present job and make it more satisfying, or to attempt to take the next step in your career, think of a date one year from today. Draw up a list of the steps you would need to have undertaken by the end of the year in order to achieve this goal, the additional accomplishments and experience to be gained, and so forth.
(c) Think of the year ahead in terms of the dates by which you must have taken each of the steps necessary to achieve your goal. Do dates bunch up at certain times? Is this realistic?
(d) Consider the points above again carefully. Pick out the major characteristics of the next position you need to apply for, or the major change necessary in your present job to bring about the satisfaction you seek. Does this now represent a critical list of things for you to aim at?
(e) Can your present school offer you the satisfaction you seek, do you think? If not, then what are the characteristics of a different school which might satisfy these ambitions and needs?
(f) List the people you see as resources for improving yourself and accomplishing your career goals. How available are these people as resources? What can you do to improve their availability?
(g) If your aim is to attempt to move to another school:
     (i) Write a curriculum vitae suitable to send to a prospective employer. You should discuss this with a person in a more senior position to yourself, whose views you would trust.
     (ii) Find an advertisement for a job which you might apply for. Write out a letter of application that presents you in the best light for this job. You should discuss this with a person in a more senior position to yourself, whose views you would trust.
     (iii) If possible, discuss a completed application form for this post with the same person.

Perhaps you would like to discuss with the headteacher or the deputy any of the points above which you are unsure about, or on which you have insufficient information to answer the questions adequately. Certainly, if training is identified as one of your needs, then the opportunity of undertaking this would best be discussed at least departmentally, or with the headteacher or deputy.

Is there anyone else you know, a colleague in your own school or another school, the LEA Adviser, perhaps, who could help you with the information you require? It is likely to be someone who has held the post which you are interested in.

It might prove a very good idea to discuss your completed form with your wife or husband, girlfriend or boyfriend, and let them give you advice about any sections which you have particular difficulties with, or hear their advice if they think or feel your views might be incomplete or insufficiently expressed in some way. However, the intention of the exercise is that the answers are private to you. If you feel you would benefit by sharing your ideas or difficulties with someone else, you should think carefully about who the best person would be for you to approach. The decison is your own to make.

Further reading

The list below refers firstly to texts which relate specifically to the educational sector, and secondly to texts, usually pamphlet length, which have been produced for other employment sectors. These are offered to provide different but related perspectives to those usually found in the school.

For a general introduction to staff planning and staff development

Lyons, G, *Heads Tasks: A Handbook of School Administration*, NFER, Windsor, 1976. (Particularly the section on 'Staff Development', and also the section 'the School Office'.)

Management of Staff, E232, Block 6, Management and the School, The Open University, Milton Keynes, 1981.

Staff development

Trotter, W, and Willsher, S, *Staff Development*, Scottish Centre for Studies in School Administration, Occasional Paper, No. 10 Moray House, Holyrood Road, Edinburgh, 1978.

Oldroyd, D, Smith, K, and Lee, J, *School-Based Staff Development Activities: A Handbook for Secondary Schools*, Longman, Harlow, 1984.

The personnel function

See booklets published by ACAS (Advisory, Conciliation and Arbitration Service), Cleland House, Page Street, London SW1, e.g. '*Job Evaluation*', '*Personnel Records*', '*Absence*', '*Induction of New Employees*', . . . etc.

Information for planning

McMahon, A, Bolam, R, Abbott, R, and Holly, P, *Guidelines for Review and Internal Development in Schools*, secondary school handbook, Longman, Harlow, 1984.

Promotion and career development

Promotion, A new look at appointments and staff development, SHA (Secondary Heads Association), Occasional Paper No. 1, Gordon House, 29 Gordon Square, London WC1, 1983.

A Fair Way Forward, A memorandum on appointment, promotion and career development, NUT (National Union of Teachers), Hamilton House, London, 1981.

Lyons, G, *Teacher Careers and Career Perceptions*, NFER-NELSON, Windsor, 1981.

Job descriptions

Armstrong, M, and Hackett, P, *The Daily Telegraph Recruitment Handbook*, Kogan Page, London, 1981.

Staff appraisal

Appraisal and Appraisal Interviewing, DITB (Distributive Industry Training Board) Training Guide, The Distributive Industry Training Board, Maclaren House, Talbot Road, Stretford, Manchester. (N.B. Although DITB no longer exists, their publications are still for sale.)

Darling-Hammond, L, Wise, A E, and Pease, R, *Teacher Evaluation in the Organisational Context: A Review of the Literature*, Review of Educational Research, Vol. 53.3, 1983.

Warwick, D, *Staff Appraisal: Education for Industrial Society* (Management in Schools), Robert Hyde House, 48 Bryanston Square, London W1, 1983.

Naismith, D, *A System of Professional Performance Appraisal*, Local Education Authority, London Borough of Croydon, 1984.

Stenning, W, & Stenning, R, 'The assessment of teachers' performance: some practical considerations', *School Organisation and Management Abstracts*, **3**, No. 2, 1984.

Staff communication and decision making in the school

Introduction

The main focus of this chapter is with the arrangements for communicating internally with adult members of the school community.

In common with most school staff handbooks, much of the literature concerned with school administration deals to a greater or lesser extent with the arrangements for communicating with pupils and parents, but the processes of staff communication tend to be neglected.

The approach adopted in this text is prompted by the belief that many of the problems encountered in the management of school staff might be avoided with the development and maintenance of effective staff communication systems. Moreover, in the absence of satisfactory arrangements for staff communication, the wider conduct of school affairs, including communicating with pupils, parents and other agencies involved, is likely to be adversely affected.

Since teachers are by their training and vocation professional communicators, emphasis is given to inquiry into current practices of staff communication in schools rather than a simple exposition of the principles of communication, though these are acknowledged. The discussion proceeds with a review of the purposes of staff communication. The main arrangements for staff communication which are common to most schools are then examined with the aid of a diagnostic framework and statements from school staffs which illustrate their perceptions of the effectiveness – or otherwise – of the various means of communication operating in their schools. A brief commentary on the various elements is included to highlight a number of salient issues. The aim is thereby to stimulate debate among headteachers and readers generally.

It is hoped that the participatory style of the text will encourage headteachers and other senior staff to examine the existing arrangements for communicating with staff in their schools and to seek to determine whether they are the most appropriate for the purposes that they are ostensibly designed to meet. This inevitably raises issues over and beyond communication *per se*, primarily because school organisation structures and leadership styles – which communication systems often reflect – cannot be ignored and these have wider implications for the management of staff in the school.

Staff communication: some preliminary considerations

Most headteachers would agree that 'good systems of communication' are a prerequisite for the effective management of a school community. They will also acknowledge that the rhetoric of communication theory sometimes obscures what happens in practice, and diverts attention from the need to review existing arrangements for communicating with staff.

The principles of good staff communication

Certain principles of good staff communication, self-evident though they may be, must be accepted at the outset. Only a few will be selected since most of the text will be concerned with the identification of ways of improving communication methods which are not working effectively.

The communication purposes must be understood by the sender and the receiver and should not be obscured by the language, medium, or context of the 'message'. The sender is usually clear about the purposes of his communication and does not intend to disguise these purposes from the receiver. Hidden or subliminal purposes are to be avoided. The sender should be able to anticipate the receiver's probable interpretation of the purpose and the receiver should be able to recognise these purposes as legitimate and inoffensive.

The formality of a communication must match the purpose. For example, an announcement of the date of the speech day differs both from a warning on late morning arrival and from a congratulation on the birth of a daughter, not only in the feeling and tone of the communication, but also in the medium employed and the degree of public exposure given to it.

Communication should not be used to smooth over bad management. Good communication cannot make a bad decision better, but bad communication can make a reasonable decision unacceptable. Communication should make use of prepared channels which are understood by both sender and receiver. Neither urgency nor rarity of an event are good grounds for employing forms of communication which are not generally understood by the receiver. The customs and practices of a school in communicating both up and down the staff hierarchy are difficult to change, and any change must be made explicit and familiar before being exposed to sensitive issues.

These few principles will suffice for the time being to begin an analysis of communication processes.

Communication by the headteacher

Many of the dimensions of communication considered here are self-evident, but are worthy of review so that a comprehensive profile can be assembled.

The ostensible purposes of communication by the headteacher may be seen to fall into the categories of:

- the transmission of information
- the transmission of decisions taken by the headteacher affecting the work or interests of the teacher
- instructions to the teacher
- requests to the teacher
- admonitions or approbation
- the combination of several of these.

It is not uncommon for one category of purpose to be disguised within another – for example decisions passed on in the form of information, or requests for views on various options as a means of seeking endorsement for a preferred decision.

Communication may be to an individual or to a sub-set of staff members or to the whole staff. The medium of communication may be:

- a personal encounter ranging from a chance meeting to an arranged interview
- an individually addressed note or letter
- a verbal statement in a public setting such as a school assembly or a staff meeting
- an indirect letter such as a circular addressed to a group of staff members
- a notice posted on a staff board.

Less evident is the variation that is possible in the language of communication, which may range from the impersonal to the intimate, from the empathic to the neutral, from the authoritative to the invitational, from the rational to the emotive, from the terse to the elaborated, or from the colloquial to the legalistic.

The effect of a communication on the receiver must always be considered, and while this is customarily assessed by anticipating how his or her interests will be affected, there are times when further action is necessary. Such occasions can be identified as follows:

- when the collective as well as the individual interests of the receiver are affected;
- when the interests of others who do not receive the communication are affected;
- whenever the communication is critical of the receiver or imposes on him or her additional work or a change in customary duties;
- whenever the communication may be understood to usurp the reciever's rights and privileges or to give to someone else authority over him or her to take authority away or to infringe 'title' to space or equipment.

In any of these circumstances it would be advisable to:

- *consider the full range of possible consequences and legitimacy of any grievance to which it might give rise;*
- *consider alternative courses of action before embarking on the one selected;*
- *consult a third person about the intention;*
- *consider whether a participatory mode of supporting the action can be undertaken and used to enhance the reasonableness of the communication, where such participation might take into account the views of others, including the feelings of the intended receiver.*

The receptive framework for communication

The receptive framework for communication is the most vital part of the communication network, and certain principles govern the effectiveness of that framework. The receiver will be more likely to accept a communication if:

- he or she recognises that the sender is acting within the proper and agreed field of activity and within the status and authority accorded by the staff;
- his or her representative has been consulted to the appropriate degree;

- it is authored (written, spoken, signed) by the sender in person rather than a delegated person, particularly one whose status is lower or no higher than the receiver's;
- the medium of communication is appropriate to the privacy of the message;
- the language of communication avoids offence and is fitting to the purpose of the message and to the functional relationship between sender and receiver.

The size of a staff affects the familiarity with its members that a headteacher can achieve, and also affects the diversity of collective interests of its members. The larger the staff, the greater the need for structured devolution of responsibility, including that for communication. Individual authority for areas of activity should be as clearly defined as possible. Committees should never be charged with responsibility for communication, most should be seen as advisory and the advice addressed to the person in authority who then becomes the sender of the communication.

Channels of communication throughout the management structure of the school should be explicitly formulated permitting two-way communication. No members of staff should be in doubt as to whom they should look to for information on a particular area of work, or who is authorised to give instructions. They should also know whom they should approach for help in professional matters, including those relating to the organisation of their work and the conditions of their employment. The purposes and procedures of meetings should be fully understood by staff in attendance and their role(s) should be clearly defined.

Crystal clarity will not prevent political activity taking place, since any community generates its own issues which will become causes to some and will bring about alignment of staff, which all too readily will be counterposed to the authority of a headteacher. The advantages of good communication practices lie in their being able to vent dissatisfactions before they reach the stage at which uncontrollable outbursts occur, in their reducing the risk that an unintended offence jeopardises the relationships between the headteacher and staff, and in their reducing the ambiguity and uncertainty of events outside the customary daily round of school tasks.

Exercises in communication

Readers will find it useful and occasionally amusing to attempt to amend the following communications in one of the ways indicated, i.e. the medium, the style, the audience, the context of delivery, the alternative courses of action. Occasionally a single message should be divided.

ITEM 1
A notice pinned to the staff noticeboard and sent individually to the heads of the science departments

Staff are asked to note that a recent inspection of the school premises by the Authority's security officer has revealed that the area around the upper school labs presents a fire hazard and that work will commence on Monday next, the 27th October, to install fire doors on the upper corridor. Additional work is required in the labs themselves which will put them out of use for the whole of the three-week period during which the operation will take place. Access to the upper corridor by the stairs in the west wing will be closed off during this period. Science staff are asked to ensure that all valuable and breakable material is removed from the benches in the labs to the store rooms and to instruct lab technicians accordingly. Since labs will be in use for the whole of Friday, and Friday night is the last night of the school play, which members of the staff are expected to attend, the clearing of the labs will be done on Saturday morning.

Science lessons will be conducted in form rooms, or in lower school labs when these are available, and members of staff who anticipate difficulties should contact the deputy head, Mr Braithwaite, who is co-ordinating arrangements. He will take the opportunity during morning assembly on Monday morning to warn the school about the risks that will be brought about through increased traffic on the stairs in the east wing.

ITEM 2
An interview with a probationary teacher on the first day of his first term

I asked you to come at 8.30 so that we could have this little chat. I do this with everyone on their first day, although I know that they have already had all the information about their teaching from the head of department and I gather that Miss Spinks has already spent some time with you. I read in the letter of recomendation from the college of education that you undertook some very exciting projects with the lower school during your last teaching practice. Well – you will probably find that we are a little more conservative here, and we can't forget that many of our pupils come from a lower class background and need to spend rather more time on their studies than perhaps they did in your school during teaching practice. In any case, now you are a proper teacher you must act more responsibly, so I would like to recommend that while you are finding your feet you should stick closely to the syllabuses that have been laid down and rely on the guidance of Miss Spinks who, for a woman, manages to maintain a firm hand in her teaching.

ITEM 3
A personal, hand-written note addressed to Mr Cowley, assistant teacher of history

While I was passing Upper V room this afternoon, my attention was drawn to your teaching by the noise emanating from the classroom. To my surprise I heard your own voice encouraging the students to argue more forcibly. It appears that you were conducting a simulation game and re-enacting a debate in the Houses of Parliament over the Corn Laws. Verisimilitude is an excellent means of motivating students and I appreciate that this was your intention. Nevertheless, the work of other classes must go on and a degree of decorum is necessary in the conduct of lessons. What concerns me most of all is the fact that you appeared to have become embroiled in the argument yourself and to have abandoned control of the class as such. I feel it important to record my displeasure immediately and to copy this note to your head of department who may be able to persuade you to adopt a less undisciplined approach to your teaching.

ITEM 4
A note handed to the school caretaker by the school secretary

Dear Brown,

Once again the girls' lavatories have been defaced with graffiti and I should like your advice on how best to clean off the offensive verses and drawings – short of requesting redecoration. Overtime for cleaning staff has already been running very high and I doubt that the office would be prepared to sanction further increases. Would you please try to reschedule the work of the cleaners so that all this can be accomplished by the end of next week. The senior mistress will speak to the girls about this so that, hopefully, it will not happen again, and will be asking for those responsible to be reported to her. Let me know how things are going from time to time. You know I always value your advice.

ITEM 5
An address to a full staff meeting

I realise that it's some time since we met, and yet when I came to consider what we should discuss at this meeting, items for the agenda looked very much the same as those that occurred at our last meeting, when you will remember that we decided to take no action on the matter of school uniforms and that all matters affecting the curriculum should be dealt with by our curriculum development committee. I have a number of matters to report, but perhaps the one which obscures all others is the message I have received from the Authority, that if our rolls continue to fall as they have done during the last three years, then the Director of Education will have no other recourse than to negotiate a merger of this school with Barnswood Comprehensive. That school, too, has been experiencing falling rolls, but since it is the larger of the two schools, is more recently built and could serve the catchment area of both schools, it would seem probable that this school would be run down and finally closed. I have discussed this matter with the governors and they agree with me that there is little we can do to increase our intake. There is no new building in the area and, therefore, no expectation that an influx of population will remedy our problems. I should be very interested to hear your views, but I have to tell you that I am not in a position to consider any specific proposals, nor do I have any knowledge of how redeployment or redundancies would be negotiated. Is there anyone who would like to speak?

ITEM 6
A note to the head of Stewart House

Dear Tom,

I know I can trust you to be discreet, and ordinarily I would be asking someone else to speak to young Blenkinsop, who joined us last year. You probably know that he has been spending rather a lot of time with one of the senior girls in your house, and comments have been made to me that the relationship is warmer than it should be. I don't have to remind you how seriously the governors view a breach of custodial trust between staff and pupils, however mature the latter may be. It may be that it would be a good thing to have a word with the girl herself. She is not due to leave until next July and if things continue as they have been then we can only anticipate trouble. Let me know how you get on with both of them, but try to avoid letting either of them know that I have been involved.

ITEM 7
A note to all form teachers

I have heard from the head of lower school that five cases of chicken pox have been reported in the last week and while this is not, in itself, a serious disease, it is one which quickly reaches epidemic proportions unless one is careful. The school medical officer believes that we should treat this as an infectious disease and that any pupil who betrays the symptoms, or who has siblings who have contracted it, should be asked to stay away from school for the necessary incubation period or until such time as the contagious period has passed. I am preparing a letter to parents but would like you to announce to your forms the precautions that I have indicated and also announce that anyone who stays away from school must supply a doctor's certificate covering the period of absence.

ITEM 8
An interview with two members of staff who have been in disagreement over the proposed timetable for Form 4 for next year

I have listened carefully to both points of view and cannot see why you are unable to agree with one another. Surely, it is obvious that one of you must have a double period on Thursday afternoon, although neither of you is willing to accept this. Since you can't agree, I shall just have to take the decision myself and you will have to accept the outcome. Anyway, let me know by Friday if you are able to resolve the matter, otherwise I shall let you know what I have decided.

ITEM 9
A meeting with the school secretary and the deputy head

Both Mr Corbet and I are sorry that you are contemplating resigning over such a trivial matter. We appreciate that the position of the school office, with its open counter, means that it is accessible to everyone and there is little privacy. There is nothing much we can do about that, and if staff did not come and do the photocopying themselves, you would find it difficult to manage all the work amongst the secretarial staff. It seems a pity that after fifteen years of service to us, things should suddenly have become intolerable, but I know that you will realise that we cannot allow the office to run the school, so you must do as you think best.

ITEM 10
A letter to the union representative on the staff

Charlie, I find it ridiculous to have to write a letter to you over a matter which ought to be sorted out by us in half an hour over a beer. Your insistence on taking an official stance on the matter of playground duties, when you and I know that it is only an excuse on the part of your association to press your other claim for additional pay for supervising public examinations when private candidates are involved, is typical of the head-in-the-sand attitude of many of your colleagues. I thought better of you. We both know that you can't win. Come over this evening and we'll walk down to the local together for a pint or two and I bet by the end of the evening things will seem much clearer.

Arrangements for communicating with staff

Many of the structures that make up the organisation of the school, including departments and committees, serve as vehicles for a multiplicity of functions usually as a consequence of tradition and convenience.

Staff communication is not immune from the forces of tradition and evolution. It is not uncommon to find staff continuing to use a particular forum for communicating with colleagues, without giving prior consideration as to whether it is an appropriate mechanism for what they are endeavouring to communicate. For example, if the purpose is to persuade colleagues about the merits of (say) a change in curriculum provision via a process of consultation, then which forum is most likely to facilitate the achievement of the objective – the curriculum committee, full staff meeting . . . ?

The emphasis that is placed on the various possible mechanisms and procedures for staff communications will inevitably vary according to the culture and traditions of the school, the objectives and leadership style of senior staff, and the nature of the decisions to be taken. Nevertheless, the key aspects of communication should be stressed:

- that it is essentially a two-way process, whatever its immediate purposes, because of the need to establish that staff understand what is required of them, have the resources necessary to carry out decisions, and are motivated to do so;
- that it is an essential means of ensuring the commitment of staff to the school as a whole, as well as to their role within it.

Barriers to communication

While commitment in principle to the notion of 'good communication' is widespread, in practice what is achieved often leaves a lot to be desired. Cynicism and disillusion among staff about the quality of communication between senior colleagures and themselves is not uncommon. This can be traced to a number of 'barriers' whose existence prejudices the effectiveness of communication processes and procedures.

For illustrative purposes, these may be placed in three categories: technical, semantic and attitudinal. As professional communicators, teachers are likely to be well aware of the first two, and to be able to overcome problems relatively easily once they are aware of them. Attitudinal barriers pose a more complex problem, since the parties to the communication process are often unwilling or unable to recognise their existence or, if they do, to find ways of overcoming them.

Technical problems relate to anything in the physical environment which interferes with the communication process, e.g. noise, lack of privacy, interruptions, poor telephone lines, badly reproduced documents, badly sited noticeboards, or even the defective sensory capacities of the communicators!

One of the other common causes of breakdown in ongoing communications is the 'language' or semantic barrier, i.e. the use of technical jargon which is not familiar to the recipient, or use of language which is imprecise, unclear, ambiguous or cliché-ridden. The end result is that the receiver fails to comprehend, or misinterprets what is being communicated. But attitudinal barriers often provide the key to understanding the long-term failures in communication which have an adverse effect on staff relations, because they derive from differing perceptions, expectations and interests of different individuals and groups. They reflect chronic emotions, beliefs and prejudices which affect the way in which messages are presented and interpreted. Many senior staff, for example, 'go through the motions' in communicating with junior colleagues, seeing the requirement to explain decisions they have made, or to consult before making them, as an affront to their own authority and an impediment to efficiency. Staff, for their part, may be unwilling to listen to a point of view if it conflicts with their prior assumptions. The reluctance to communicate often openly reflects a lack of trust between individuals and groups, which may be the main impediment to securing greater co-operation in organisations of all kinds.

The need to communicate is a social one, vital to the co-ordination of individual effort to achieve objectives in the school as in any organisation. But because no two individuals or groups see things the same way, inevitably there are problems. Where co-operation is needed, or if there is a need to discuss and solve problems of mutual concern, a genuine attempt has to be made by those involved to share their ideas. And they must be as precise as possible in the way they put those ideas across, selecting media and means with care and attention to their purposes.

Structures and processes of communication

Communication practices with staff vary between, and indeed within, schools, especially those applying to non-teaching staff.
With reference to teaching staff consider the check list below.

1 *Full staff meetings*
2 *'Cabinet' meetings*
3 *Heads of department meetings*
4 *Departmental staff meetings*
5 *Staff committees*
6 Ad hoc *working parties*
7 *Informal meetings*
8 *Staff associations*
9 *Liaison with staff union representatives*
10 *Open access to senior staff*
11 *Staff handbook*
12 *Staff noticeboard*

This is not an exhaustive list and it might have included, for example, staff pigeon holes and relayed verbal messages, but the structures and processes indicated will suffice for our purposes.

As it stands, the list identifies a fairly comprehensive set of 'vehicles' for internal communication, but this says nothing about their suitability for particular purposes nor about their effectiveness, which together form the underlying theme of this chapter.

Exercise

Consider how each of the following tasks would be handled in your school, selecting the 'vehicles' and writing its number alongside the task. Often, more than one 'vehicle' will be employed – if so, write their numbers in sequence alongside the task.

1   Announcement of a change to 35-minute periods

2   Consideration of a proposal to un-stream the first year

3   Deciding public examination arrangements for the following term

4   Assigning responsibility for teaching practice arrangements for graduate students

5   Making known rules for staff dress during school hours

6   Making arrangements at short notice to cover meal supervision during a withdrawal of labour by part of the staff

7   Taking action over verified complaints of inadequate cleaning of classrooms

8   Informing the whole school of detailed arrangements for sports day

9   Allocating budgets to departments for the next financial period

10   Deciding whether to allow a local college to conduct a research project involving questionnaires to examination forms

11   Considering what third-year optional subjects can be offered in the coming year

12   Dealing with an immediately reported theft of inflammable chemicals from the chemistry lab. during the lunch break

13   Arranging to remove posters supporting violent strike action of a union unrelated to school personnel but with which a teachers' organisation has expressed sympathy

14   Conveying the view of the governors that the staff request for participation in staff appointment procedures be denied

15   Negotiating a change to computerisation of pupil records

16   Processing a request by staff of the geography department for a photcopying machine to be located in the geography preparation room

17   Dealing with a complaint by a parent who bursts into your room saying that his son in Form 5 has been hit on the ear by a senior member of staff

18   Pursuing the validity of an accusation in an anonymous letter that the blatant homosexual relationship of two members of staff is undermining the moral fibre of the school

19   Inducting new teaching staff

20   Preparing items for the agenda of the next staff meeting

21   Arranging a leavers' party for fifth and sixth forms

22   Communicating through rules for staff a new directive from the Chief Education Officer concerning applications for leave of absence and absence through sickness

23 Ensuring that staff who have failed to attend instruction on safety precautions receive appropriate guidance

24 Recruiting a head caretaker

25 Suspending a teacher on probationary service

Discuss your answers with other respondents and try to identify in what respects your differences reflect variations in school organisation, in the system of communication, in the status relationships of those with whom you are communicating, in the choice of 'media', or in the underlying 'political' situation in your schools. This is a first step in the diagnosis of what may be your communication problems, a process which will be followed up in the next section.

A framework for the diagnosis of staff communication in the school

The first step in conducting a review of the internal communication system is the development of a frame of reference which facilitates the identification of strengths and weaknesses.

Given the complexity of the communication processes and structures, the task of devising a diagnostic framework, which allows for rigid distinctions to be made between the various elements, is fraught with conceptual and practical difficulties. Briefly, there will almost certainly be some overlap between the components of the framework, but this inherent problem can be countered by maintaining consistency in the analysis.

A diagnostic 'model' may take many forms and the following schema is simply an example, though it should be noted that it underpins the analysis and commentary which follows the presentation of this framework.

Do you have a staff communication problem in your school?

Before answering this question, readers may wish to consider the questions raised under the headings below, though it is stressed that they are not mutually exclusive.

Organisation

1 Do senior and middle ranking members of staff complain that they spend too much time at meetings and/or dealing with administration?

2 How is it ensured that members of staff get the information necessary to perform their tasks effectively?

3 Do specialist committees/work groups retain information which other staff could profit by if they had access?

4 Does essential information go through a number of channels or direct to the person(s) that it most concerns?

5 Do staff in the different units of the school organisation – faculties, departments, pastoral, academic, understand their respective problems and exchange relevant information?

6 Do any members of the senior and middle ranking staff spend so much time endeavouring to communicate that they have difficulty in carrrying out their other tasks?

System

1 Does each member of staff receive regular feedback on his/her perfor-mance – teaching, administration, extracurricular activities?
2 Is the performance of the units of school organisation systematically moni-tored, and are dysfunctions dealt with effectively?
3 Do members of staff know what the duties and responsibilities of their senior colleagues are?
4 How are relevant developments in the school's external environment monitored?
5 Does information get 'censored' or filtered out between management levels and between departments?

Status relationships

1 Do senior and middle ranking staff talk to junior colleagues other than to issue instructions?
2 Are individual members of senior and middle ranking staff aware that their personal attitudes and modes of behaviour can inhibit/facilitate effective com-munication with colleagues?
3 Do junior members of staff talk to 'management' other than to ask questions?
4 Do senior and middle ranking members of staff meet with their junior col-leagues as a group or singly?
5 Irrespective of their positions in the school hierarchy, do staff listen to each other?
6 Do 'managers' pass on as much or as little information as possible?

'Media'

1 How do staff find out about the school plans and achievements, and about changes that might affect or interest them?
2 How do new members of staff, including probationers, find out about how the school operates and who is responsible for what?
3 Does the school have a staff handbook, bulletin, newsletter? What do staff think of these?
4 Are there separate staff noticeboards for notices about school administrative routines, and announcements concerned with social/extracurricular activities? Are the noticeboards cleared of redundant papers and how often?

'Political'

1 Which departments and/or staff cliques are powerful and what is the source(s) of their power?
2 Are staff resisting change because they do not understand the purpose, or because they think it is against their individual/collective interests?
3 Is there a lack of trust between senior members of staff and their more junior colleagues and/or union representatives? Is this because of poor communi-cation or other factors, e.g. incompatible personalities?

4 Do many staff feel indifferent or hostile to the school because they are not kept informed about what is going on or claim they are not told anything?
5 How and when are staff told about changes in the *modus operandi* of school affairs? What opportunities do they have to influence the changes?
6 Do staff wish to be informed about 'management' intentions, or to be consulted, or to share in decision making and at what level?*

The questions raised under these headings are illustrative of the sorts of issues that might require attention, and readers may wish to add or delete questions according to their particular circumstances and preferences.

Having devised a diagnostic instrument the next task is to carry out a review of the effectiveness of the communication practices in the school.

Conducting a review of staff communication

An assessment of the effectiveness of staff communication has to start with an investigation of what staff actually think about the different structures and processes used to communicate. This may be accomplished by interviewing colleagues, but the size of the staff body and the time required can make this an impractical proposition. However, the burden of interviewing members of staff may be considerably reduced by conducting a survey of staff opinions with the aid of questionnaires. The investigation may be undertaken in two stages.

A preliminary survey using a questionnaire can be conducted with staff to identify the main problem areas which require further investigation (see Example 1 below).

Having identified the main weaknesses and strengths in the communication network, attention can then be addressed to establishing what the particular problems are in any given case. These may be ascertained by using a follow-up questionnaire (see Example 2 below), and if circumstances allow interviewing the staff concerned.

When using questionnaires, care should be taken to ensure that individual respondents cannot be identified. This may present a problem where (say) seventy per cent of staff indicate dissatisfaction with departmental staff meetings, since there is no way of telling which department(s) they are referring to.

This potential difficulty can be avoided by using colour codes or numbers. For example, the maths department is coded red or alternatively is given a number, so that all the members of staff in that department receive a questionnaire with the appropriate colour or number. Each department should be distinguished in this way.

Before conducting such surveys staff should be informed of the purpose of the exercise and it should also be made clear that action will be taken to improve any weaknesses in the communication system highlighted in the review.

---

* Adapted from British Institute of Management Checklist No. 76, 'Effective Communications'.

Example 1. *Finding out what staff think about the value of the structures and processes of communication in the school: a preliminary survey*

Please indicate, by circling a number, the degree of effectiveness you attribute to the means of communication used in this school which are presented in the left-hand column.

	Very effective	effective	ineffective	very ineffective
Full staff meetings	4	3	2	1
'Cabinet' meetings	4	3	2	1
Heads of department meetings	4	3	2	1
Departmental staff meetings	4	3	2	1
Staff committees	4	3	2	1
Ad Hoc working parties	4	3	2	1
Informal meetings	4	3	2	1
Staff associations	4	3	2	1
Liaison with union representatives	4	3	2	1
Open access to senior staff	4	3	2	1
Staff handbook	4	3	2	1
Staff noticeboard	4	3	2	1

Example 2. *Departmental staff meetings*

Please indicate by circling a number your degree of satisfaction/dissatisfaction with the aspects presented in the left-hand column.

	very satisfactory	satisfactory	unsatisfactory	very unsatisfactory
Notice of meetings	4	3	2	1
Time of meetings	4	3	2	1
Length of meetings	4	3	2	1
Location of meetings	4	3	2	1
Formulation of agenda	4	3	2	1
Circulation of agenda	4	3	2	1
Accuracy of the minutes of the meetings	4	3	2	1
Circulation of the minutes	4	3	2	1
Chairman's conduct of the meetings	4	3	2	1
Other (Please specify and use the scale)				

Analysing the questionnaire responses

The task of analysing the completed questionnaires can be simplified by using or adapting the matrix on pages 107–8.

A demonstration of how this frame of reference may be used in the school is provided in the next section.

Diagnostic matrix

Communication Arrangements	Staff perceptions	Organisation problem	Systems problem	Status relationship problem	'Media' problem	'Political' problem	Apparently satisfactory
Staff meetings	1 2 3						
Cabinet meetings	1 2 3						
Heads of department meetings	1 2 3						
Departmental staff meetings	1 2 3						
Staff committees	1 2 3						
Ad hoc working parties	1 2 3						

continued

continued

Communication Arrangements	Staff perceptions	Organisation problem	Systems problem	Status relationship problem	'Media' problem	'Political' problem	Apparently satisfactory
Informal meetings	1 2 3						
Staff Association	1 2 3						
Liaison with staff union representatives	1 2 3						
Open access	1 2 3						
Staff handbook	1 2 3						
Staff noticeboard	1 2 3						

Applying the diagnostic framework

In the preceding section it was indicated that a review of staff communications has to begin with an investigation of staff preceptions of the communication system. Thus, to illustrate differences in perception, the communication arrangements listed on page 101 are set alongside a range of views expressed by headteachers, heads of department and staff. For ease of reference, these are presented in a series of tables.

They represent a summation of data collected from over fifty schools and any similarity in perceptions spanning more than one table is purely coincidental. Almost without exception, the headteachers felt reasonably confident about the effectiveness of staff communication in their schools, although many could point to particular weaknesses.

After each series of statements applying to specific communication arrangements, a number of issues are presented for consideration. It is, however, stressed that they are not mutually exclusive and are included to stimulate discussion among readers about the underlying problems and implications.

The *authors' diagnosis* of the statements presented in the tables is indicated in the matrix at the end of this section.

Staff meetings

	Headteacher perceptions	Head of department perceptions	Staff perceptions
(1)	Staff meetings were becoming increasingly acrimonious so I now have an upper and lower school meeting. This way staff are given more opportunity to participate and the stirrers can only perform to half the staff.	Staff meetings in this school are very formal affairs in which the headteacher (to be fair) tells us about his plans for the school, but the main purpose seems to be the issuing of instructions.	We have staff meetings but they are largely a waste of time because the Head does not circulate an agenda beforehand and whenever we have submitted items to be included he says they are inappropriate.
(2)	I hold two staff meetings a term and because I have an open style of management they tend to be very productive, though of course some of the staff suggestions are silly and I sometimes think I spend an inordinate amount of time explaining why they are not on.	Our staff meetings are invariably lively and informative even if it is not always clear what is to occur as a result of the discussions.	Staff meetings tend to go off in all sorts of directions but at least staff are encouraged to have their say. Sometimes I think the Head should be a little more directive but if he was I suppose it would discourage staff participation.
(3)	Staff like the ceremonial of the staff meeting even though it achieves nothing. So I hold one a year to make announcements.	I have never fathomed why the Head doesn't simply send a memo to staff since we don't discuss anything at the staff meeting.	The Head uses the occasion of the staff meeting to welcome staff especially new members, but the rest of the meeting is given over to a sermon of do's and don't's as if we were pupils.

Diagnosis of the range of views about staff meetings – review of some issues

It is evident from the statements of the participants that there are differences about:

- what the purposes of full staff meetings are;
- how they should be conducted.

In your view what should be the purpose of full staff meetings? Is it to:

- issue instructions;
- provide information
- make general announcements
- provide an opportunity for staff to exchange views and information with the headteacher and senior colleagues;
- develop staff camaraderie;
- some or all of these reasons;
- other?

Do the staff in your school know the purpose of the full staff meetings? How do you know they know? Do the majority of staff agree with the reasons given?

On matters of procedure and the general conduct of full staff meetings, could communication be improved by:

- preparing a formal agenda and circulating it in good time before the meeting;
- keeping formal minutes of the meetings, and where appropriate, identifying those members of staff who have been given specific responsibilities?

How do the staff in your school feel about procedures and the general conduct of full staff meetings?

While there may be many different responses to the matters raised above, it is perhaps reasonable to assume that most headteachers would agree that in general terms the aim of a full staff meeting is to communicate. The central question then becomes: If there is little communication taking place, is there any point in continuing to hold full staff meetings? One answer to this question (among others) is that it depends on staff expectations and the extent to which the headteacher feels able to accommodate them.

Cabinet meetings

	Headteacher perceptions	Head of department perceptions	Staff perceptions
(1)	Every Friday the senior management team meets to review matters arising and to plan for the coming week. I do not circulate an agenda. . . there are only 3 of us and it is more flexible this way. Heads of department are rarely	I know that the head-teacher meets with the deputies ever Friday and I presume they discuss any problems which have arisen but I don't really know.	We know the senior management meet every week because at the time they are unavailable but beyond that we have to rely on the grapevine for any snippets of information. It is difficult in our position to know what the head does. . .

continued

Headteacher perceptions	Head of department perceptions	Staff perceptions
involved – it would not be fair to add to their burdens and in any case the school's performance is my responsibility not theirs.		
(2) I have weekly meetings with my 3 deputies and department heads and senior teachers attend as and when they are needed. In the main we discuss things like cover for absent staff, pupil discipline etc. but we also exchange ideas and make plans for the future. We don't have a formal agenda but I have a list of items and ask colleagues if they have anything to add. Any decisions taken are subsequently fed through the system but formal minutes are not kept.	Heads of department in this school are asked to attend the senior management meeting when matters of direct concern to their department are on the agenda.	The head of department sometimes tells us that he has to attend a senior management meeting but he never seems very clear why. . . . With one or two exceptions the heads of department in this school do not carry much 'weight' so it is no surprise that they can't tell us much. We accept that we are not in a position to see the total picture and make important decisions but why should we be kept almost completely in the dark especially where our future is concerned?
(3) I have weekly briefing meetings with the deputies and senior teachers but we also have monthly meetings where we discuss ways of improving the school's performance, especially the ways departments are coping and any initiatives they are considering. As part of this process heads of department are required to submit monthly reports to the senior management team. Formal minutes are kept and I give feedback to the heads of departments.	Heads of department have to submit monthly reports on the operation of their departments and these are reviewed by the 'inner cabinet'. Sometimes we are called to clarify issues but usually the feedback is via a memo from the Head.	We are not told of the details of what is discussed at 'cabinet' meetings but we know that the school's performance is a standing item on the agenda. The Head monitors the work of the departments very closely and they have to submit a monthly report. This keeps us on our toes because while the Head will give praise where it is due he will also quickly notify the head of department of any deficiencies he sees in the way the department is running.

Diagnosis of the range of views about cabinet meetings – review of some issues

The headteachers' statements indicate a variety of school management styles and these almost certainly stem from their personal preferences which may also be influenced by a host of variables including:

- the calibre of senior staff and head of department
- the calibre of junior staff
- the expectations of staff
- staff relationships
- the organisation of the school
- the particular circumstances of the school, e.g. growing, declining, amalgamating, the degree of autonomy granted by the LEA.

The air of mystery surrounding the cabinet meetings – not matters of detail but general lack of awareness among staff, and indeed some heads of departments, about an important aspect of senior management's function can greatly assist the circulation of rumours, with all that implies for staff relations. There is also a very real risk that the status and authority of heads of departments and other staff who have management responsibilities will be undermined when it is apparent to their junior colleagues that they wield little influence in the 'corridors of power'.

If the calibre of the heads of departments is a cause of concern to the head-teacher, this raises questions about the policies and procedures relating to recruitment and selection, promotion and staff development.

Do you know what the staff in your school feel about senior management meetings? Do you take the view that senior management meetings are of no interest to staff? Do staff in your school know what the headteacher does, apart from x hours teaching? Could communications in your school be improved by (say) circulating a typical schedule of the headteacher's working day to staff? Could communications be improved in your school by ensuring that staff are informed of the nature of senior management meetings?

You may find these questions provocative, but in view of the statements presented in the table concerned with cabinet meetings they may need to be addressed.

Heads of department meetings

	Headteacher perceptions	Heads of department perceptions	Staff perceptions
(1)	Heads of department regard the meetings as the forum for marking out territorial rights. Although they do occa-sionally discuss what we do and what we should do they invariably run out of steam. Some heads of department would feel that I talk too much but there has to be some direction especially when there is a lack of sensible ideas coming forward.	On paper the heads of department meetings in this school look good. . . the agenda and papers are circulated in advance, but in practice the head-teacher dominates the meetings and if we raise any queries you get smashed down. I have never raised anything and won't.	As far as we can gather heads of department meetings are rather bad tempered affairs where very little is decided, at least that's our impression.

continued

Headteacher perceptions	Head of department perceptions	Staff perceptions
They see their role as one of resistance to me rather than acting as my middle management.		
(2) The difficulty is that heads of department have vested interests and built in prejudices which tend to be of a personal rather than academic nature. When you ask them to discuss their aims and objectives it is clear that administrative convenience overrides academic considerations. They need training.	The Head refuses to acknowledge our concerns or if she does it is to the effect that they are unimportant. We have tedious discussions about where we see our respective departments in the future but we can only speculate because we have insufficient information to assist us to make sensible plans. These meetings are very frustrating. . .	Nothing much seems to emerge from the heads of department meetings and if there is we are not party to it. . .
(3) The heads of department and head of year meetings are the main axis of the management of the school. They have meetings every two weeks and if that is what is required to make them feel part of the policy making of the school I am willing to go along with it. I have adopted a lot of their suggestions.	We are expected to provide items for the agenda as well as the Head and minutes of the meeting are kept. The topics we discuss are very wide ranging (not just curriculum matters) and we express our views in the knowledge that whilst action may not necessarily follow the general wishes, our preferences will be noted.	It is the practice in this school for the heads of department to keep their staff informed of the topics under discussion at their meetings. Proposals for change are not always enthusiastically received but staff generally prefer to know earlier rather than later so that they can make their views known.

Diagnosis of a range of views about heads of department meetings – review of some issues

A common feature of the views presented about heads of department meetings is the subject of change and the processes adopted to that end. The headteacher's apparent attempt to stimulate dialogue via heads of department meetings seems to be largely ineffective in two instances and fairly successful in one case.

In these circumstances a number of issues need to be addressed. The immediate question which presents itself is: Are the heads of department resisting change *per se*? If this is the case, what might be the causes of such resistance? Could it be because:

- they are not involved in the decisions they are asked to implement;
- the reasons for change have not been adequately explained;
- they have not been persuaded by the explanation;

- change threatens their existing powers of jurisdiction over their department boundaries;
- they are totally pre-occupied with the 'here and now' because of existing pressures and workloads;
- they are unclear about their roles and responsibilities;
- they are not equipped intellectually and emotionally to cope with change?

Alternatively, are the heads of department resisting change because they resent the headteacher's intervention and general management style?

Were that to be so, might it be because:

- the headteacher's behaviour inhibits or precludes a meaningful dialogue among and between the participants;
- it is known that the headteacher is filtering the flow of information;
- the headteacher does not have sufficient information upon which to base future plans or changes in existing practice;
- it is known that the headteacher (for whatever reason) cannot deliver the necessary support for implementing change;
- the personalities of all those concerned are such that the meetings are a catalyst for emotional responses rather than reasoned debate?

The issues raised under both sets of questions are not mutually exclusive but it would be surprising if at least one of them did not emerge in a review of the effectiveness of heads of department meetings.

What do heads of department meetings achieve in your school? How do you know what occurs? Do you have a monitoring system to evaluate the merits or dysfunctions as the case may be?

Departmental staff meetings

	Headteacher perceptions	Head of department perceptions	Staff perceptions
(1)	The purpose of the departmental meetings is to review the work of the department in the context of the overall aims and philosophy of the school. Before any departmental meeting takes place I expect to receive a copy of the agenda and subsequently the minutes.	The headteacher insists that we have regular departmental meetings to ensure we have the commitment of our staff and to keep issues and grievances within bounds. But this is difficult when he vets the agenda and removes any item that doesn't meet with his approval. . .	A typical agenda of our departmental meetings includes such items as open evening, pupils' homework and pupil discipline. . . of course we need to discuss these aspects of our work but we would also like to raise things like staff promotion policies in the school but such matters seem to be taboo subjects at our meetings. . .
(2)	Some departments regard coffee and a chat as adequate but as I keep telling them, that's not a substitute for a business meeting. I suppose that's a comment about my	We have a departmental meeting at the end of each term. . .they are social occasions really. . .staff tend to 'let their hair down' after a hard term's work. I	We do not have what you would call formal departmental meetings. Our meetings (once a term) take place after school hours which we regard as our own time. . .the

continued

Headteacher perceptions	Head of department perceptions	Staff perceptions
heads of department, who really aren't up to the job. . .	regard this as extremely important for harmonious relationships. Problems arise almost daily and they have to be resolved then and there. . .in most cases they do not call for a department view.	headteacher never seeks our views about the way the school is run so there is little point in raising issues in a formal sense though, of course, some of us have a good moan, it helps to relieve our frustrations.
(3) Departmental meetings are an essential part of the communication process. A typical agenda would be matters that have arisen from senior management meetings. There are two main purposes: feeding information and instructions down to departments; and to provide an opportunity for staff to feed back their views to senior management.	We have a formal agenda and minutes are kept of our departmental meetings. The agenda invariably contains items of concern to senior management but staff also contribute items for the meetings. Staff sometimes get a bit emotional about what seems to them to be criticism of their work but on the whole the meetings are orderly affairs. . .staff know that the headteacher receives their views via the minutes of the meetings.	The head of department is very meticulous about procedures and encourages staff to submit items for the agenda. He also keeps accurate minutes so we know what was said. We would like to see more of our suggestions taken up but at least the headteacher and deputies cannot pretend they are unaware of our aspirations and concerns.

Diagnosis of the range of views about departmental staff meetings – review of some issues

Here the differences between the contributors as to what should be the proper concerns of departmental staff meetings and the way they should be conducted are highlighted. Such differences serve to bring into focus some of the difficulties associated with the exercise of management functions in the professional setting of the school. This potential dichotomy is perhaps exemplified in the following list of class teachers' comments about heads of department.

He has to share the culture of the department.

She has to be a peer among peers rather than one of the top brass.

He cannot be a dictator – he cannot say 'you will do that' – it has to be done on a discussion basis.

If necessary, she must be capable of saying unpleasant truths when it comes to it.

He should not necessarily be formal. He should adopt the role suitable to the occasion.

She needs to regularise meetings, make the best use of staff, get all possible work done beforehand so that no time is wasted, e.g. two staff take a task and report on it.

It should not be inferred from the above that the exercise of management functions cannot co-exist within a general collegiate ethos: indeed this is commonly found in schools. However, those who press for a collegiate mode of operation tend to overlook the possibility that this too can create tensions among staff. This is most likely to occur where individuals and/or groups of staff pursue hidden or personal agendas without reference to the needs of the pupils, department and the school generally.

The inherent dangers of adopting a wholly managerial stance, or at the other end of the spectrum, exercising zeal for collegiality, may be avoided by initiating effective systems of communication.

What purposes do departmental staff meetings serve in your school? Are they to:

- provide a forum for staff to air their grievances;
- facilitate consultation between staff and senior management;
- develop staff cohesion – team building;
- review current practices and plan for the future;
- encourage staff to innovate and take initiatives;
- provide a convenient mechanism for issuing instructions to staff;
- other?

Do the staff concerned know the purposes?

This list has been compiled from a much larger number of responses from headteachers, but for our purposes the significant feature is that, with a couple of notable exceptions, the stated purposes convey a desire to involve staff in the decison making processes. However, the statements in the table about departmental staff meetings perhaps exemplify why the reality does not always accord with the stated purposes.

Staff committees

	Headteacher perceptions	Head of department perceptions	Staff perceptions
(1)	Staff in this school expect me to provide purposeful leadership and look to me to get things going. To assist me I have a number of committees who look at various aspects of the work of the school, the main one being the Curriculum Committee. They need guidance so its my practice to advise them of the sorts of issues they ought to consider and where possible provide them with appropriate documents.	From my position the staff committees are part of both the communications network and INSET, and I believe the head sees them in that way too. This is not to undervalue the work the committees actually do which for the most part provides the main impetus for all that we do here. . .	Practically every activity undertaken in this school has a specialist committee. The headteacher manipulates the system by giving each committee their terms of reference and insisting they report direct to him.
(2)	I am a member of a number of staff committees	I know one or two members of staff are not	I resist serving on committees bcause I think the

continued

Headteacher perceptions	Head of department perceptions	Staff perceptions
including the theatre committee which means a lot of hard work. There are five members of staff who don't want to participate in committee work and they know I know. . . If everyone adopted that attitude the school, and especially the pupils, would be much the poorer in every sense.	keen on committees because they never volunteer their services, but I share the Head's enthusiasm for involving people and the committees give junior members of staff, especially, the chance to contribute to the work of the school outside the classroom.	heads of department and senior staff abdicate their responsibilities by passing tasks to the teachers who serve on them.
(3) This school is spread over three sites and staff committees are an essential part of the management of the school. They: help to develop staff camaraderie; act as a focal point for the development and implementation of ideas; and through the involvement of staff at all levels from across the school, enhance communication. Younger teachers who have a lot to contribute are very much encouraged to participate. . .	In principle I have no objection to staff committees but experience is that in practice the people who serve on them are not always the best equipped to deal with the concerns of the committee(s) they serve on. There is also a danger that staff committees can undermine the management structure in the school. This might be avoided if we had a clearer reporting back system.	While committee work can be very time consuming, I am sure a lot of things would never get done if the committees ceased to exist. It's nice to work with people you would normally have little contact with and I am sure that my service on a number of committees has helped to broaden my experience which must be useful for my future career.

Diagnosis of the range of views about staff committees - review of some issues

The practice of establishing standing staff committees (e.g. curriculum committee) varies considerably between schools. Some have a plethora of committees, many have one or two, while others have none at all. There are also variations in the profiles of committee membership, locations of the committees in the school organisation structure, and the rationale for their existence.

The uneven pattern of the arrangements for standing staff committees reflects headteachers' personal preferences and the particular circumstances of the school. These observations are made in the light of some headteachers' responses to the question: Why do you have standing staff committees?

Headteachers' responses were:

- vehicle for INSET
- means to overcome inertia of senior staff and heads of department
- motivate staff
- identify staff potential
- staff consultation and involvement

- team building
- develop staff camaraderie
- academic innovation.

Do you have standing staff committees in your school and, if so, would you include any of the reasons presented in the above list as an explanation for their existence?

In your school:

- Who chairs the committee(s)?
- What is their membership profile?
- Is their brief tightly prescribed?
- What actually occurs as a result of their activities?
- Are non-members aware of the work of the committee(s)?
- To whom do they report?
- How do they obtain access to information necessary for their work?
- Is the work of the committee(s) systematically monitored?
- What are the expectations of staff in relation to committees?

Such questions are prompted by the views expressed by some of the contributors to the preceding table which suggests that in some schools at least there is perhaps a need to review the committee system.

Ad hoc working parties

	Headteacher perceptions	Head of department perceptions	Staff perceptions
(1)	*Ad hoc* working parties can be a useful means of getting staff involved especially in innovative projects, but in my experience they must be given a brief setting out what it is they are supposed to be doing and why. . .	I am not keen on *ad hoc* working parties . . . because they are a recipe for achieving very little and they give unworthy promotion seekers the opportunity to gain visibility without actually doing very much.	*Ad hoc* working parties are to be avoided if at all possible although this is not always easy because we are conscious that the headteacher takes a keen interest. . . and nowadays particularly you need a very good reference to have any chance for promotion. It is not so much that we are not interested but our teaching burden is so heavy that we just don't have the time. . .
(2)	I do not maintain 'standing staff committees' because they quickly suffer from atrophy, so when there is a need I set up a working party with a clear remit and specified time when I expect the task to be completed. This way	Because I am a head of department it doesn't necessarily follow that I will be invited to join one of the Head's working parties. She does not appear to value our contributions and she said to me on one occasion that as an ex grammar school	. . .I must confess that as a member the work can be very frustrating. I am not sure why but I think it might be because the head lays down the terms of reference so tightly that it is almost impossible to consider things we think are important

continued

Headteacher perceptions	Head of department perceptions	Staff perceptions
younger staff can get involved and the professional committee people are not given the opportunity to establish a power base in the school.	head of department I had not fully grasped the comprehensive ideal, whatever that's supposed to mean. . . a lot of ideas dreamed up by the working parties are laughable and not worthy of consideration. . .	and relevant to the task of the working party. I get the feeling sometimes that I am just a cipher. . .
(3) I don't discourage working parties being set up to (say) organise a school outing, I don't see any merit in leaving strictly academic matters to the tender mercies of *ad hoc* work groups. It is the senior management's responsibility to develop and implement academic policies and you cannot delegate this function to junior members of staff who obviously haven't got the necessary administrative and pedagogic experience.	In an unguarded moment the Head told me he regarded himself as a benign autocrat and that is one thing we totally agree on. On academic matters it would be pointless to suggest setting up working parties to consider issues though I must say that we do have them now and again to review social activities etc.	I am fairly new to this school and compared with my last one staff have very little say in the way things are run. Most of them accept the situation and indeed expect the Head and deputies to take all the decisions. They tend to be very apathetic so I don't see a future for working parties though I am convinced that if run properly they can be beneficial to the school.

Diagnosis of the range of views about *Ad Hoc* **working parties** – **review** of some issues

Ad hoc working parties or committees are a fairly common feature of school management, and they can provide a useful forum for staff involvement in the decision-making processes, especially (though not exclusively) in the sphere of curriculum review and development.

It is perhaps axiomatic to note that curriculum reviews carry implications for the school timetable, but in practice these are often conducted as quite separate activities rather than in tandem.

However, the effectiveness of working parties drawn from the general body of staff and charged with the task of curriculum development must remain in doubt where they are excluded from examining the implications of their work for the organisation of the school and the timetable.

Many of the issues reviewed earlier with regard to staff committees apply to *ad hoc* working parties and they will not be rehearsed here. But it may be anticipated that staff will wish to know what any proposals for changing the curriculum imply for their timetables and the future of their department or unit of operation. Specifically they will be concerned about:

- the areas of the curriculum that are to be expanded/dropped;
- the changes that are envisaged in the contraction of the timetable.

The head of department who suddenly discovers midway through the summer term that half the department's work has disappeared as a consequence of curriculum development, or the member of staff who discovers that the subject(s) he/she is currently teaching do not appear in next year's timetable, are unlikely to feel kindly disposed to the changes.

Some, if not all, of these sorts of problems might be avoided if the divisions between the activities of the working party concerned with curriculum development and the processes of timetabling are not so tightly drawn.

What is the practice in your school? Is curriculum development mainly the province of:

- senior management
- standing staff committee
- *ad hoc* working parties?

Would an *ad hoc* working party normally have access to the master timetables? How is the master timetable presented, e.g. booklet, on an office wall, in classes, to individual members of staff? Are heads of department involved in the construction of their own department's timetable? When would a head of department first see the department timetable – is it in force when the points allocation is known? When would a Scale 1 teacher receive his/her timetable? Is it normal practice for working parties to consult with other members of staff?

The assumption underlying these sorts of questions is that the rationale for setting up an *ad hoc* curriculum working party is to provide a vehicle for wider staff involvement and to improve communication. In the light of the statements presented in the table you may feel that such assumptions are erroneous.

Informal meetings

	Headteacher perceptions	Head of department perceptions	Staff perceptions
(1)	I keep in touch with the body politic as I go through the corridors and leisure areas. I know all the staff by name and during my tours of the school, I have informal chats with individual and small groups of staff.	The head is a very warm person but he is also very shrewd and knows practically everything that's going on because he doesn't rely on the deputies for information. . . he is always talking to staff in corridors and wherever. . .	The headteacher has a very 'laid back' style and has never been known to ignore a member of staff however lowly. . . He has a clever way of introducing apparently unrelated topics into the conversation and we all know that he is sounding us out about things so we are usually frank with him. . .
(2)	There is a lot to be said for talking to people systematically in rotation. It's easy to fall into the habit of talking to two-thirds of the staff and you think you are talking to	The Head never comes to the staffroom but she is highly visible around the school and will pass the time of day with members of staff though she refuses to be drawn into	You always get the feeling that the Head finds it difficult to converse informally with staff and somtimes it's a strain trying to keep a conversation going. . . informal

continued

Headteacher perceptions	Head of department perceptions	Staff perceptions
everyone. It's important to talk to all even if you have to manufacture reasons to do so.	discussions about operational matters. . .	meetings are not very productive as far as we are concerned.
(3) To maintain authority and respect I believe you have to remain rather aloof and not get involved in idle chatter with staff. . .	The headteacher is a strong believer in the filter system and avoids informal meetings like the plague. You have to go through the proper channels, i.e. senior teachers – deputies. To the staff he is a very remote figure and I am not even sure he would recognise me although I have been at this school for nearly five years.	I think informal metings with the Head and senior staff can help to forge good social relationships, but in this school the staff hierarchy is so formal that junior members of staff just do not engage in banter with senior staff and certainly not with the headteacher who scarcely acknowledges you.

Diagnosis of the range of views about informal meetings – review of some issues

The distinction between formal and informal meetings is usually taken to be that the former are properly convened and minuted whereas these procedures do not feature in the latter case. In the context of the school this distinction is not very helpful because the protocol of meetings varies considerably between schools.

In this review 'informal meetings' refers to the informal network of communications, that is to say conversations and discussions among staff which occur in corridors, common rooms and so forth.

In many schools this continues to be the dominant approach to dealing with matters that arise. This *modus operandi* contrasts sharply with the tightly structured regime necessary for coping with the movement of large numbers of pupils and the activities they undertake.

Assessing the effectiveness of informal meetings is obviously extremely difficult, and headteachers (among others) tend to point to the apparent absence of tensions among staff and the general atmosphere in the school as evidence that all is well.

While staff contentment is obviously desirable, the old adage that people see what they want to see should be continually borne in mind. Auden, in his poem 'The Unknown Citizen' wrote:

Was he free? Was he happy?
The question is absurd:
Had anything been wrong,
We should certainly have heard.

Most headteachers will recognise the import of Auden's observations but human frailties often inhibit an accurate construction of social reality.

For many headteachers and senior school staff, informal meetings serve a number of purposes:

- to develop staff camaraderie;
- to deal quickly with matters arising in the school;
- to gather information.

These seem very laudable reasons: why then do some headteachers discourage the practice? Is it simply because of their personalities, or could it be because they believe such informality may:

- undermine the formal management structure in the school;
- create a bad impression with pupils and visitors;
- expose them and senior colleagues to 'special pleading' by members of staff;
- encourage rumour-mongering;
- not accord with staff expectations about how the school should be run?

In casual conversations with members of staff, how do you know that they are not telling you what they think you want to hear rather than what they actually believe?

An awareness of what might occur as a consequence of adopting a more informal style does not necessarily mean that the dangers can be avoided. Much will depend on the particular circumstances of the school.

Staff Association

	Headteacher perceptions	Head of department perceptions	Staff perceptions
(1)	The Staff Association is run by elected members and deals with such matters as election of staff governors, social events and retirement arrangements. I have to admit that the Association is not very successful and they come up with a lot of silly ideas. It's really a problem of leadership.	To my knowledge most heads of department do not take an active part in the Staff Association. I am not sure whether it is because we see it as essentially a forum for junior members of staff to have their say, or because it doesn't carry much weight with the Head. In any event the Association does not do very much.	The Staff Association is moribund in the school and as far as I can see the only useful function it performs is to arrange farewells to staff either retiring or leaving the school for another post. . .
(2)	The principal mechanism for communication is the Staff Association which meets 2 or 3 times a term. Although I am just an ordinary member many things are referred to me. . . These meetings enable me to keep my fingers on the pulse as it were and they give me a	There is an expectation that heads of department will atend Staff Association meetings and functions but we tend to keep a low profile. . . probably because the head dominates the proceedings.	The headteacher attends the Staff Association meetings supposedly as an ordinary member, so most people play it safe and either defer to him or say nothing.

continued

Headteacher perceptions	Head of department perceptions	Staff perceptions
good ear as to what staff are thinking. . .		
(3) There is a Staff Association and the officers are elected. They meet every week and are concerned with a large range of topics such as social events and school discipline (pupils or staff). The Association acts as a safety value for the staff and is a valuable source of information to me.	As a general rule heads of department do not put themselves forward for election to the Staff Association committee but we do take a very keen interest and get involved in all sorts of ventures organised by the Association. I think most of us feel that we ought to set an example to younger colleagues and, more importantly, help to maintain good social relations.	The Staff Association is very active and the meetings are well attended. Staff generally believe the Association gets things done. . .not only social events but the committee also conveys to the headteacher staff grievances and suggestions for improving the way the school is run.

Diagnosis of a range of views about school staff associations – review of some issues

A utopian vision of school staff associations is that they are a major vehicle for communication and teacher involvement. Alas, there are few headteachers who would be prepared to take an oath that this observation applied to the staff association in their school, and the reckless minority may be unpleasantly surprised if they sought the views of their staff.

It is axiomatic that the vitality of the staff association is dependent on staff enthusiasm and commitment. Where staff support is obviously lacking it might be profitable to seek explanations. Might any one or more of the following reasons signal some possible causes of staff apathy towards the school staff association:

- the burden of staff timetables inhibits their active membership;
- the election processes are such that younger and junior members of staff are excluded from holding office;
- the constitution of the association does not include a provision for joint consultation;
- the constitution allows for joint consultation but staff are positively discouraged from raising matters of substance;
- the meetings are poorly conducted;
- senior staff do not participate in the affairs of the association;
- staff reaction to the way the school is run?

These questions are not mutually exclusive and indeed most of those listed point to many other issues worthy of consideration. What is the purpose of the staff association in your school? Is it a forum for:

- joint consultation;.
- social events;
- discussion of educational matters?

These are just some of the reasons cited by headteachers in seeking to explain the role of staff associations in their schools. There may also be reasons which are never articulated but which the staff might suspect.

- Is it felt that the staff association will serve to counter union influence?
- Is it believed that the staff association may avert the emergence and growth of powerful cliques?

Do you actually know what the teachers in your school think about the staff association?

Liaison with staff union representatives

Headteacher perceptions	Heads of department perceptions	Staff perceptions
(1) One of my staff union representatives is the local president of her association and she is frequently better informed than me so I do compare notes with the union representative quite often but not in any formal sense. That could undermine the bond of trust I share with senior and middle ranking staff in the school.	The staff union representatives are much better informed than us . . . not only about issues outside the school but also about plans the Head has in mind. I find this very irksome and wish the Head would confide in the heads of department and at least let us know of any proposals before alerting the union representatives. In the present circumstances, what little standing we have is being whittled away.	Staff tend to rely quite a lot on their union representatives. . .not just when they have a grievance, but they are a mine of information, especially about what is going on in the LEA which perhaps explains why they have regular access to the Head.
(2) I make my decisions and the union representatives consult with me if they feel their members are getting a raw deal. I take an old fashioned view (that) I represent the staff and union people represent the views of their association and I see no reason therefore to give them any information that the rest of the staff would not receive.	I think the unions have an important role to play outside the school, e.g. protecting our conditions of employment, but I don't believe they should intervene in internal school matters.	The Head is very paternalistic and staff tend to go to him if they have problems rather than their union representatives – in any case they are generally very apathetic when it comes to union affairs although most are members.
(3) I speak to staff union representatives on an individual basis at times of crisis to ascertain their standpoints on particular issues – but otherwise I see no need to meet with them – and in any case I	The Head has let it be known that he expects us to approach him before pursuing any matter with the union representatives and this suits us because we get easy access to the Head's room. The union	It seems that the only time the head acknowledges the existence of our union representatives is when he wants some information. Staff are getting fed up with his attitude. I think it is

continued

Headteacher perceptions	Head of department perceptions	Staff perceptions
am not in the business of elevating the status of union representatives in this school, that would be a recipe for chaos.	representatives are very much kept at arms length by the senior management team.	because they do not seek his patronage and certainly many believe that the union is better equipped to look after their interests than the Head. . .

Diagnosis of a range of views about liaising with staff representatives – review of some issues

A characteristic feature of voluntary organisations is the relatively low membership participation in the daily conduct of their affairs. Teachers' professional associations share this characteristic as they are highly dependent on the work of a fraction of their members for their general vitality and the services they provide.

While the overwhelming majority of teachers are members of one of the professional associations covering the education service, the pattern of membership in schools varies enormously. Teachers' motives for joining a particular association are obviously born out of individual aspirations and concerns. But few would deny that the associations' traditional involvement in education provision, including curriculum matters, is legitimate, though the nature of such intervention is a matter of continuing debate among teachers. At one end of the spectrum of opinion is the belief that the teachers' associations should restrict their activities to national forums, which stands in sharp contrast to the view that they should adopt a more interventionist stance at the level of the LEA and school.

The degree to which union activity impinges on the life of the school is obviously a consequence of inumerable factors but it may be predicted that staff will become more union conscious as a result of:

- threats to their security
- attacks on their professionalism
- unilateral decisions which have implications for existing ways of working
- decline in their living standards
- undue delay in dealing with their complaints
- a call for support by their associations.

Teachers have demonstrated that they will embark on campaigns of non co-operation and have also resorted to striking where they believe the situation merits such actions. In such circumstances the headteacher's relationship with the staff representatives can determine to a very great extent the level of disruption in the school.

While the role of staff representatives varies in accordance with the respective policies of the associations and the perceptions of the individuals concerned, there are a number of functions which are more or less common to all staff representatives. The most notable are:

- recruitment of members
- union correspondence
- alerting members about union policies
- assisting members including helping them to process their complaints
- negotiating and consulting with representatives of the LEA usually via the local branch of the association.

The headteacher can, of course, make it difficult for staff representatives to exercise such functions, but the list serves to underline their position in the communication network.

Are your relationships with the staff representatives based on mutual accommodation and trust? Are you confident that you have an effective communications network with the staff representatives and the local union branch? Do you take an antagonistic stance towards the staff representatives and, if so, is it because:

- their activities undermine the management of the school;
- they do not have the support of the staff;
- they create tensions in the staffroom;
- of personal doubts about their calibre;
- of previous undesirable experiences;
- other?

Open access

	Headteacher perceptions	Head of department perceptions	Staff perceptions
(1)	Teachers have open access to me, it is the only way I could gain credibility.	This headteacher's door is almost always open to members of staff and I think that to some extent that's as it should be. However, junior members of staff (it seems to me) abuse the system and automatically bypass the heads of department and that makes a mockery of our position.	I know from personal experience that the head is very accessible to any member of staff who wishes to see her. If she is tied up she will come looking for you as soon as she is free.
(2)	I see staff quite a bit. I go into classrooms and they come in here (sometimes) a bit too much. They also have free access to the deputies.	The Head is strict on protocol and before you can see him you have to go though the proper channels, i.e the deputies, and also state the purpose of the visit.	The Head and deputies say that individual members of staff can go and see them at any time, but in practice we have to make an appointment and it becomes all very formal.
(3)	I operate an open door policy and I am aware that it's a weakness in my system but it is an essen-	From the number of individual members of staff who seek advice from me about both their	The headteacher is very approachable but it is difficult to obtain an answer from her so that when

continued

Headteacher perceptions	Head of department perceptions	Staff perceptions
tial part of the communication process. . .the problem is that things are brought to me that should be dealt with elsewhere, e.g. by deputies or heads of department.	academic and domestic problems, I doubt whether the headteacher is bombarded with requests for an audience, but I could be wrong.	you leave her room you are never quite sure where you stand.

Diagnosis of the range of views about open access – review of some issues

Most headteachers will identify with the statement that 'my door is always open to any member of staff who wishes to see me'. The phrase is, of course, open to a number of interpretations which are reflected in different practices. Thus, to some headteachers the statement is a literal truth; for others it will apply at a given time during the day/week; and perhaps in a minority of instances the belief may be sincere but for a variety of reasons staff visits to the headteacher are a rare occurrence.

Staff access to the headteacher and indeed other senior colleagues is a crucial aspect of communication and human relationships within the school. But like so many facets of school management, it is prudent to examine the opportunity costs of immediately responding to the whim of members of staff (almost regardless of the circumstances) and limiting their freedom of access to senior management. This is particularly necessary where there are (say) in excess of fifty members of staff and in circumstances of tight staffing ratios.

For headteachers who maintain an open door policy the following questions need to be addressed:

- How many staff visits in a normal day/week?
- Does it tend to be the same individuals?
- What is the average time per visit?
- What reasons did members of staff give for visiting?
- What advice was given during such visits?
- What decisions were taken as a consequence of staff visits?
- What impact did the visits have on your work schedule?
- Could most of the matters raised by staff have been dealt with by senior colleagues?
- Could any of the issues raised have been dealt with informally outside the timetabled day?

The process of monitoring staff interventions during the course of a week will almost certainly be a salutory experience for headteachers who encourage staff to 'drop in'. It is, of course, too simplistic to judge the effectiveness of such practice according to the degree of disruption imposed on the headteacher's pattern of activities. By virtue of staff visits the headteacher gets to know individuals – their strengths and weaknesses – and is constantly updated about what is going on around the school.

However, apart from the fact that it is unlikely that the majority of staff will pay *ad hoc* visits to the headteacher, good social relationships and knowledge of what is happening in the school are not conditional on the headteacher inviting 'free access'. Many headteachers maintain good relationships with staff and are sensitive to the mood of the school, without granting unlimited access to anyone who wishes to see them.

While practice varies it is not uncommon to find that:

- the headteacher schedules a particular time during the day/week for meeting individual members of staff;
- staff are normally required to make an appointment giving the reasons for the meeting;
- staff are normally expected to state why it is necessary to see the headteacher rather than a senior colleague;
- in exceptional circumstances it is made clear to staff that the above conditions do not apply, e.g. where a pupil has been involved in an accident.

Teachers who have been used to 'open access' may find it difficult to adjust to a rather more formal system but they might be asked to consider this question: Would you rather the headteacher devoted time to (say) discussing the vagaries of the vending machine or planning the future of the school? Where staff have a full appreciation of the sheer breadth of the role of the headteacher such questions would be unnecessary, but this is the exception rather than the rule.

Staff handbook

	Headteacher perceptions	Head of department perceptions	Staff perceptions
(1)	There is no point in producing a staff handbook because the changes are so rapid it is impossible to keep it up to date.	I am not sure what you would put in a staff handbook. . .most of the staff have been here for a long time and are very familiar with school routines.	I think a staff handbook could be useful especially if staff responsibilities were included. I only found out that the head of chemistry was in charge of visual aids when he came to repair an overhead projector. I am new to the school. . .
(2)	I regard the staff handbook as an important part of the communication system. It provides information and guidelines for staff which are easily amended because we use a loose-leaf binder.	I am sure I must have a copy of the staff handbook somewhere but I must confess I can't remember the last time I referred to it. . . Perhaps I have been here too long. . .	Staff call the staff handbook the yellow peril because of the colour of its pages and because it is like an instruction manual full of 'do's' and 'don'ts'.
(3)	A staff handbook can be a useful part of the communications process but you need to think very hard about its purpose	The staff handbook is very informative and useful especially for new members of staff and probationers. It is an extra	The sort of information in the handbook is not only helpful in coping with administration, but it can be a useful source

continued

Headteacher perceptions	Head of department perceptions	Staff perceptions
and having decided that, you need to ensure the presentation appeals to staff otherwise they will not look at it. You will note that ours is not solely concerned with administrative routines but contains information about the school's achievements and so on.	burden on us because the Head expects us to comment on any changes that are being proposed and to offer contributions and sometimes this can be a rather delicate exercise.	of reference when parents and other visitors ask questions about the school which we ought to know but often don't.

Diagnosis of the range of views about staff handbooks – review of some issues

The compilation of a staff handbook, which will capture and retain the interest of staff, calls for imagination about content and flair for presentation, but these features are rarely exhibited in such publications. Many handbooks may be characterised by the paucity of information (beyond administrative instructions) and drab presentation. It is perhaps not surprising, therefore, that they hardly register on staff consciousness and as a consequence are placed in a file and quickly forgotten.

Most headteachers will acknowledge the force of this observation but some seem resigned to continue to produce and update a staff handbook which they know will receive scant attention from staff. Some headteachers have responded in kind and the staff handbook has ceased to exist other than as an historical document. A small minority of headteachers have recognised that a staff handbook can be a very effective medium for communicating with staff and others, including visitors to the school. Accordingly, they have devoted considerable time and effort to raise the status of the handbook in the eyes of the recipients.

An investigation as to why staff often display little enthusiasm for the staff handbook can be a painful yet profitable experience, and you may find the responses summarised below revealing, notwithstanding that they may not apply to your own school's staff handbook. Indeed they may be worthy of consideration when engaged in the task of revamping the current edition of the handbook.

A summary of some staff responses to the school staff handbook

The aims and philosophy of the school are unclear.

Conveys the impression that staff are like pupils.

Contains nothing about the relationship between the school and the LEA.

It seems to be designed to stifle staff initiative.

The sheer size of it is off-putting.

There is no index and the organisation of the sections seems arbitrary.

It does not mention the local community and school catchment area.

It is produced on very poor quality paper and is full of typing errors.

Ancillary staff are barely mentioned.

Ours is stapled. A loose-leaf binder would be more convenient for new insertions.

The school motif could be used to brighten up the front cover which doesn't even tell you what the document is.

Ours could be greatly improved if the headteacher would seek the help of some members of staff, e.g. Art and Design.

Policies applying to staff are not specified though some can be deduced from the content devoted to instructions and rules.

Potentially useful information, e.g. list of school governors, should be included.

Space does not permit detailed comment on the staff responses about the staff handbook. Suffice to note that they do serve to promote a number of questions as follows:

- Is the purpose of the handbook clear to staff?
- Has consideration been given to the need to achieve a reasonable balance between administrative routines and other useful information, bearing in mind the issue of size?
- Can its size be made more manageable by dispensing with information that is now redundant?
- Does the style of writing reflect the professionalism of staff?
- Can the presentation be improved, especially the layout and organisation of content?

While acknowledging that the school staff handbook should reflect the particular circumstances of the school, the contents list below (which was extracted from a school staff handbook) might stimulate discussion in your school.

Staff handbook index

A THE SCHOOL
   School calendar
   School terms and holidays
   Governing body – list of members
   1 Aims and philosophy
   2 Catchment area
   3 Academic structure
   4 Pastoral structure

B PUPILS
   1 Uniform
   2 School council and prefect system
   3 Rewards and sanctions
   4 Pupil records
   5 Admissions
   6 Casualty action

C STAFF
   1 Form teacher list
   2 Ancillary staff and hours of work

  3 Staff roles
  4 The supportive services
  5 Consultative procedure/communication
  6 The Staff Association
  7 The induction year
  8 The staffrooms, staff lunches, salaries, personal absence, school timetables, clubs and societies, publicity

D DAILY ROUTINE
  1 The school day – times
  2 Registration
  3 Assemblies
  4 The use of form periods
  5 Notes on the supervision of children
  6 The school supervision system
  7 Emergency clearing of buildings procedure
  8 Educational visits
  9 Lost property, accidents and medical rooms
  10 School rules

E PATTERN OF STUDIES
  1 Curriculum – pattern of studies
  2 The remedial department and special education services
  3 Fourth and fifth year options procedure
  4 Sixth form – choice of study procedure
  5 Guidelines for class organisation and control
  6 Reports and consultative evenings
  7 Homework
  8 Examinations

F BUILDINGS AND RESOURCES
  Care of buildings
  1 The school building and environment
  Resources
  2 Maintenance
  3 Subject areas and 'a room of one's own'
  4 Audiovisual equipment
  5 Reprographic facilities
  6 The school fund

G PARENTS
  1 Parent Teacher Association
  2 Communication with parents:
    (a) letters home – duplicated
                      – individual letters
    (b) appointments
    (c) the school bugle
    (d) middle school prospectus
    (e) upper school prospectus
    (f) parents' prospectus

Staff noticeboard

	Headteacher perceptions	Head of department perceptions	Staff perceptions
(1)	In my experience people do not read the written word and I say that with some feeling because they never read notices.	The Head frequently complains that staff don't bother to look at the noticeboard, but if he did not flood our pigeon holes with paper perhaps staff would refer to the noticeboard more often.	. . .notices placed on the staff noticeboard are usually about trivia so you won't find staff looking there much. . .
(2)	The staff noticeboard can be likened to a chart in the central operations room. In addition to daily operational matters I insist that the minutes of meetings (if appropriate) are placed on the notice-board. I believe in keeping staff informed and I have found that this procedure avoids a lot of misunderstandings and undermines the rumour-mongers.	The staff noticeboard is the chief source of infor-mation in this school. If ever I have to see the Head about something I check the board first. . .	Staff tend to flock around the noticeboard first thing in the morning to get the 'orders of the day'. . . you need a pen and pad because it's impossible to remember everything and the instructions are not always clear either. . .
(3)	The staff (I think) do read the noticeboard. I try to encourage this by only placing notices that apply to all the teachers on the noticeboard or to alert them to matters of general interest. I make good use of the head of department network, and staff pigeon holes. . .	The staff noticeboard tends to get a bit cluttered but nobody seems to mind too much. . .perhaps it is because we know that our attention will be drawn to things that directly con-cern us via memoranda or the deputies.	Compared with my last school the staff notice-board is not a subject of great interest to staff though I should say that I am one of those people who looks and never sees anything so I am pro-bably, biased.

Diagnosis of the range of views about staff noticeboards – review of some issues

Staff noticeboards are potentially a very important means of communication, but there seems to be a great deal of ambivalence in many schools about their effectiveness. This suggests that the purpose of the noticeboard is very unclear to all concerned and as a consequence its potential remains unexploited.

In some schools anything which is considered to be even of the remotest interest to staff is displayed on the board along with memoranda of a directive nature. Any member of staff is free to use the board and nobody appears to have direct responsibility for its upkeep. Important notices are submerged by trivia especially where board clearance is an *ad hoc* activity. Such problems may be compounded in schools on split sites where each location has its staff noticeboard.

In these circumstances important messages are frequently missed by those they are intended for and a typical response is to replicate notices via the staff pigeon holes. Apart from the resource implications, staff easily get out of the habit of referring to the noticeboard and as a result its use as a vehicle for communication is seriously undermined.

Schools which have adopted the practice whereby the use of the noticeboard is reserved for specific purposes, and a member of staff is charged with the responsibility for its upkeep, avoid many of the sorts of problems alluded to above. Staff are expected to read the notices displayed and acknowledge their responsibility for so doing by taking action where appropriate.

Consider the practice in your school. Is it your experience that:

- senior colleagues frequently complain that staff do not read the noticeboard;
- the board is normally cluttered with out-of-date notices and trivia;
- notices are misdirected to boards on other sites;
- notices are not clearly dated;
- it is not clear to whom the notices refer;
- there is an absence of headings on the board to assist the appropriate display of notices;
- notices are invariably replicated and sent direct to members of staff?

If these are features of the practice in your school the effectiveness of the staff noticeboard as a means of communication must be in some doubt.

The completed matrix on pages 134–5 provides an instant overview of the perceived strengths and weaknesses of the communication structures presented in the tables. Additional information would be required to confirm the outcome of the analysis, but the main purpose here has been to direct readers' attention to a range of questions and issues that need to be addressed when reviewing the effectiveness of staff communications.

Reference to support staff has been delayed in order to sustain a coherent approach to the topic under review. However, the guidelines for reviewing existing communication arrangements apply equally to non-teaching staff, though the questions raised would need to reflect the culture and patterns of communication associated with support staff.

Communication and non-teaching staff

Most headteachers would agree that non-teaching staff do not always get the recognition they deserve in helping to ensure the school runs smoothly. They will also acknowledge that from time to time they have witnessed the withdrawal of co-operation and goodwill by support staff and this is frequently caused by a breakdown of communications within the school.

Notwithstanding that most schools would find themselves in severe difficulties without the support provided by non-teaching staff, the latter tend to be on the periphery of the school community rather than an integral part of the whole.

One headteacher when asked if non-teaching staff attended the 'full' staff meetings declared 'that he nearly got lynched when he made such a suggestion to the teachers'.

Analysing the questionnaire responses

The task of analysing the completed questionnaires can be simplified by using or adapting the matrix below.

Diagnostic matrix

Communication Arrangements	Staff perceptions	Organisation problem	Systems problem	Status relationship problem	'Media' problem	'Political' problem	Apparently satisfactory
Staff meetings	1	✓	✓	✓	✓	✓	
	2	✓	✓	✓	✓		
	3		✓				
Cabinet meetings	1	✓	✓	✓	✓		
	2	✓	✓	✓			
	3							✓
Heads of department meetings	1	✓	✓	✓	✓	✓	
	2	✓	✓	✓	✓		✓
	3							
Departmental staff meetings	1	✓					
	2	✓	✓			✓	✓
	3						
Staff committees	1	✓					✓
	2	✓	✓	✓		✓	
	3	✓					
Ad hoc working parties	1	✓	✓	✓		✓	
	2	✓		✓		✓	
	3			✓			

continued

Communication Arrangements	Staff perceptions	Organisation problem	Systems problem	Status relationship problem	'Media' problem	'Political' problem	Apparently satisfactory
Informal meetings	1						✓
	2	✓	✓	✓		✓	
	3			✓			
Staff Association	1	✓		✓			
	2	✓		✓			
	3						✓
Liaison with staff union representatives	1			✓			
	2					✓	
	3					✓	
Open access	1	✓					
	2	✓					
	3	✓					
Staff handbook	1	✓	✓				
	2				✓		
	3				✓		
Staff noticeboard	1	✓					
	2	✓			✓		
	3	✓			✓		✓

This anecdote is a sharp reminder of the traditional division between professionals and other staff. However, in an age when authority is increasingly under challenge and wider societal pressures are forcing schools to become more open to the communities they serve, artificial barriers between teachers and support staff will be difficult to sustain. This is not to suggest that the caretaker *et al.* should be directly involved in strictly pedagogic matters, but that it may be prudent to involve them rather more in the affairs of the school than is generally the case.

Many teachers (among others) will doubtless get on quite well with the support staff in their school and they may be entirely justified in their belief. But it is difficult for a school to claim that it is a community of people with shared aspirations for its well-being, whilst a minority of its citizens are not integrated into the mainstream of school life.

Publication of support staff names and roles

Communication problems between teaching and support staff often occur in schools because the former do not fully appreciate the role and duties of the latter. Many staff handbooks include the status, names and duties of teaching staff but few give similar details for support staff. Their inclusion may help to avoid silly misunderstandings and to this end readers might find the example presented below a useful model which they may wish to adapt for their particular needs.

Ancillary staff

School office staff

Middle school based:		*Hours of duty*
Administrative officer & head-teacher's secretary	Mrs G Knowles	8.45 a.m. – 12.30 p.m.
Clerical assistants:		
Financial matters (capitation, school fund)	Miss M Clark	8.30 a.m. – 3.30 p.m.
Typing, telephone & general duties	Mrs J Cooper	9.00 a.m. – 2.00 p.m.
	Miss J Lee	1.30 p.m. – 4.30 p.m.
Lower school based:		
i/c Lower school office	Mrs L Rolfe	8.45 a.m. – 12.30 p.m. 1.00 p.m. – 4.15 p.m.
i/c Reprographics room	Miss P Howard	9.00 a.m. – 1.00 p.m.

Caretaking staff

Middle school based:

School caretaker	Mr M Sutton	6.00 a.m. – 8.00 a.m.
		9.00 a.m. – 11.00 a.m.
		2.00 p.m. – 6.00 p.m.
Assistant caretaker	Mr G Cooper	6.30 a.m. – 9.30 a.m.
		1.00 p.m. – 6.00 p.m.
Male cleaner	Mr E Alexander	6.30 a.m. – 9.30 a.m.
		12.45 p.m. – 5.45 p.m.

Lower school based:

Senior assistant caretaker	Mr L Rowe	Alternate weekly shifts
Assistant caretaker	Mr N Neill	6.00 a.m. – 3.00 p.m.
		2.00 p.m. – 10.00 p.m.

School laboratories

Senior laboratory technician, biology laboratories, lower & middle schools	Mrs C Williams	8.30 a.m. – 4.30 p.m.
Technician – chemistry laboratories	Miss M Slater (part-time during school closures)	8.30 a.m. – 4.30 p.m.
Technician – physics laboratories	Mrs D Berne (part-time during school closures)	8.30 a.m. – 4.30 p.m.
Technician, lower school	Mrs T Bone (part-time during school closures)	9.00 a.m. – 3.30 p.m.

Mid-day assistants

Middle school based:

Mrs P Queen	11.40 a.m. – 1.10 p.m.
Mrs B Barclay	11.40 a.m. – 1.10 p.m.
Mrs F Churche	11.40 a.m. – 1.10 p.m.

Lower school based:

Mrs V Wallis	11.40 a.m. – 1.10 p.m.
Mrs R Nixon	11.40 a.m. – 1.10 p.m.

Technical studies workshop

Workshop Technician   Mr P Durant (part-time)

Language laboratory assistant

Mrs K O'Reilly   (part-time, 3 hours daily)

Rural studies stockman

Mr W Greenham

Mettings with support staff

A common practice in schools is for the headteacher to see the caretaker first thing in the morning to sort out any problems and to discuss tasks that should receive attention during the day. The headteacher will also usually see the catering supervisor fairly regularly and, of course, works very closely with the principal school secretary who organises the work of other clerical staff.

Apart from these people it is unusual for a headteacher to meet formally with other members of the support staff though pleasantries may be exchanged. This style of leadership is very much in line with conventional management practice of operating through a chain of command. Here the assumption is that the supervisors are competent and will reflect the concerns of their colleagues in discussions with those higher up – in this case the headteacher or deputy.

Unfortunately, as many headteachers will vouch, not all supervisors operate at the level of competence required, and individual personalities are sometimes unsuited to the assigned role. In the case of supervisors of school support staff, the consequences are numerous. Most significant, perhaps, is the likelihood that the concerns of other support staff may never be communicated to the headteacher or senior colleagues, though the latter may receive complaints from teaching staff about the behaviour of certain members of the non-teaching staff.

Regular scheduled meetings with support staff can help to overcome these kinds of communication problems. But where these are introduced it is important to avoid undermining the position of the supervisors, especially in the eyes of the people for whom they are responsible. Ideally, such meetings should be chaired by the headteacher or deputy so that there is no doubt about their status among the school adult community. A typical agenda might look like this:

Caretaking and cleaning staff meeting
Monday, 20 February, 1984 at 10.30 a.m.

AGENDA
(1) Changing accommodation
(2) Cleaning materials and equipment
(3) Condition of classrooms, particularly furniture in classrooms
(4) Waste bins
(5) Chewing gum
(6) Evening use of school

(7) Toilets
(8) Library
(9) Date and time of next meeting

Signed:

Minutes should be kept of these meeings to reduce the possibility of misunderstandings about what was discussed and also to remind those concerned what action was agreed.

Wider involvement of support staff

Meetings with support staff are, of course, only one step towards their closer involvement in school life. There is a very real danger that devising exclusive arrangements for communicating with particular sections of staff may strengthen and perpetuate existing divisions between them. Consideration needs to be given, therefore, to exploring other means for developing camaraderie and communication among school staff generally, regardless of the particular roles individuals normally perform.

- Does the school staff association have to be the exclusive domain for teaching staff?
- Is it possible that members of the support staff may have some useful contributions to make at parents evenings apart from arranging chairs etc?
- Are there any (say) scout leaders among the support staff and could their knowledge and skills be utilised by teachers engaged in extracurricular activities?

These questions are simply included to stimulate discussion about some possible ways of bringing staff closer together, and any proposal must be carefully examined in the light of the particular circumstances of the school.

Aspirations of support staff

The main concern of this section has been to promote discussion in schools about how existing communication arrangements applying to support staff might be improved, especially by providing them with more opportunities to get more closely involved in school affairs.

It should be borne in mind that many people besides teachers have been attracted to working in schools because they have a strong empathy with young people, and are dedicated to playing a part in providing a service which enables pupils to flourish and realise their full potential.

If such committed members of school support staff are discouraged from becoming more involved in the wider activities of the school, it may be anticipated that difficulties in recruiting people of high calibre will be exacerbated. Equally, frustrations born out of failure to communicate with each other are likely to reinforce latent tensions among the various occupational groups with all that implies for the effective running of the school.

It is axiomatic that solutions to communication problems must, if they are to be effective, take cognizance of the particular circumstances of the school. Accordingly, no attempt has been made in this chapter to provide general answers but rather to indicate some possible guidelines for action.

This chapter represents a preliminary excursion into what are essentially the nuts and bolts of staff management. The temptation to rehearse the other major themes explored elsewhere in the book has generally been resisted, but it should be stressed that the discussion here does not stand in isolation from the other elements of staff management treated in the following chapters.

Many of the grievances and disciplinary issues which are examined in the following chapters have their origins in ineffective staff planning and communication practices. The incident which follows is included as an example of the sorts of issues explored in the complementary set of training materials.

Incident: The caretaker's memo

Headmaster

I request that the following memo is distributed to all staff, both teaching and non-teaching.

If adhered to, it will do much to improve the cleanliness and security of the premises.

Mr Smith
Caretaker

MEMORANDUM

1 The swimming pool is not to be used after 5.00 p.m. without *prior* consultation with the duty caretaker.

2 Staff are to be off the premises by 6.00 p.m., unless there is an officially organised function *scheduled* to finish later.

3 Staff are not to enter the school after 6.00 p.m. without the knowledge of the night caretaker.

4 Staff and pupils leaving the sports complex after 6.00 p.m. are to leave via the outside gate and not to go through the school.

5 Staff are not to enter the school at any time over the weekend without the *prior* approval of the caretaker.

6 During closure periods (all holidays) staff visiting the school are to enter and leave by the main entrance, signing in and out in the register provided.

Trainer's guidelines: issues for consideration
It would seem that a breakdown in relationships and communication between the caretaker and other staff has occurred. So often it seems that boundary disputes and arguments as to whose job it is to do what, and when, arise as a consequence of resentment engendered by feelings of isolation and problems of status.

What would you advise the headteacher to do to resolve the apparent problem? In the short term, should he:

- consult with senior colleagues;
- discuss the matter with the caretaker and endeavour to establish what is the root of the problem;
- inform the caretaker that he has given full consideration to the request to circulate the memo and explain to him that it would serve no useful purpose and might create further dissension among staff;
- assure the caretaker that if the points raised in the memo are as a consequence of a lack of staff co-operation, he will personally draw their attention to the difficulties arising from their apparent disregard for the security and cleanliness of the school premises?

In the longer term the headteacher will wish to promote more harmonious relationships between the caretaking staff, other members of the adult community and pupils. To this end, would you advise the headteacher to:

- review the existing processes of communication;
- hold regular meetings with the caretaking staff to discuss matters arising;
- where appropriate, invite caretaking staff and other members of the support staff to participate in the wider affairs of the school;
- other?

Further reading

Deverell, C S, *Successful Communication*, G Bell & Sons Ltd, London, 1973.

Evans, D W, *People and Communication*, Pitman, 1978.

Eyre, E C, *Effective Communication Made Simple*, W H Allen 1979.

Hart, J, *The Secondary School Secretary – Some Hidden and some Developmental Aspects of the Secretary's Role*. Paper presented to the Annual General Conference of the British Educational Management & Administration Society (BEMAS), Cambridge, 1984.

Lyons, G, *Heads' Tasks – a Handbook of Secondary School Administration*, NFER Publishing Co., 1976.

Mahoney, P, 'The business of communicating and the communicating business', *Journal of the Institute of Personnel Management*, December 1983.

Coping with individual and collective grievances

Introduction

The term 'individual grievance' refers to complaints raised by individual members of staff, and 'collective grievances' is used to designate all forms of concerted action by some or all of the staff of a school. The origins of the problems giving rise to complaints or collective grievances may lie inside or outside the school, may relate to conflicts of views with the employer, the headteacher, other members of staff, the central government and may or may not involve action disrupting the normal working of the school. Naturally, as fellow professionals, headteachers may have sympathy with the views of their colleagues, but find themselves, as managers, obliged to act in a non-partisan manner. It is this conflict, with the traditional role of headteachers as senior colleagues exercising their influence by virtue of their wider experience and the authority of the post they hold, which makes the more recent trend towards industrial action by school staff so uncomfortable.

Action which begins with an incident in some other school or as a result of a union decision is usually well signposted in the media and has the benefit of prior discussion. The premonition is no guarantee that adverse consequences can be avoided since all of us are prone to the misconception that our own colleagues are too sensible, too loyal, too responsible to disrupt the harmony of normal working. Alas we may find that the reality is harsher than our expectations and we run the danger of allowing disillusionment to alter the relationships on which the former stability was founded. We are forced to face preparation for radically disruptive events, in which case, despite the increased and seemingly unfair burden falling upon us as managers, we must maintain the means of recovering the calm that has been temporarily suspended.

Preparation is a matter of both organisational readiness and a shock-protected frame of mind. We must be able to disguise our incredulity at the triviality of some of the points at issue, our annoyance at the truculence, officiousness and militancy of our friends, and our bitterness at the dereliction of duties which seems to threaten the ideals commonly pursued until now.

Both forms of preparation are necessary to cope with action which pops up unexpectedly in our schools, although it is more patently a domestic problem in which our personal involvement, either through our own acts or through our general responsibility, rarely leaves us room for dispassionate response. To consider the kinds of preparation open to us, we ought first to survey the issues which have in recent years led to collective disputes. The list below reminds us of the topics, even though some may represent surface features of more fundamental grievances.

Sources of collective grievances

- pupil–teacher ratios
- supply cover for absent staff
- lunchtime supervision
- redundancy
- redeployment
- changes in contracts of employment
- curriculum provision
- school closures/mergers
- headteachers' management style
- salaries and wages
- reorganisation of school catering

The pervasiveness of the issue in its effect on school life is not necessarily commensurate with the extremity of the action. An issue which divides the staff along union or terms of service lines may well disrupt the normal life of the school more, through the acrimony it creates, than a withdrawal of some services on which staff are either agreed or at least not at variance. Nevertheless, since collective action has become more common and since its purpose is to draw public concern to the grievance, the nature of the common instruments of protest listed below cannot be ignored. Individual staff grievances defy neat categorisation, but the list identifies the main forms for collective action taken by school staff in recent years.

Types of collective action

- refusal to cover for absent or striking staff
- strike
- 'work to contract'
- demarcation
- picketing
- public demonstration
- pressure group activity via local press
- withdrawal from extracurricular duties
- refusal to attend meetings outside school time

The isolation of the headteacher, in the face of collective action which exposes the school to unwelcome publicity, to avid sensation-seeking of the press, to parental anxieties and to mischievous exploitation by some pupils, can turn one grey overnight. The isolation may of itself provoke unwise response or inaction and must be avoided by building links with others which are not forged merely by crisis. The formal links with boards of governors, LEA officers and committees, professional associations, other headteachers, PTAs etc. must be maintained in good standing; so too must the internal staff and pupil consultative groups, since these will provide the supporting infrastructure for the headteacher's response to the dispute. If they are to be capable of support, they must be involved functionally on a continuing basis in matters which affect the school. They cannot be taken out of the cupboard and dusted off for totally unfamiliar service.

While acknowledging that articles of school government are sometimes 'subject to the direction of the governors and the education committee' it is customary for the headteacher to be charged with the responsibility for the internal organisation and structure of the school, and the supervision of staff. Among other duties then it may be inferred that the headteacher is obliged to:

- strive to create and maintain harmonious staff relationships;
- endeavour to resolve individual and collective staff grievances arising from within the school;
- cope with the consequences of individual and collective staff grievances which emanate from beyond the confines of the school;
- act in accordance with the demands of employment law and the legislation covering negligence and pupil safety.

Given access to advice and support, the headteacher is free to turn attention to the unaccustomed and somewhat unpalatable grievance processes and procedures which impose formality upon the conduct of negotiations and discussions. It is not unlike book-keeping in the meticulousness of the recording operations and the rules by which they work.

Therefore the main purpose of this chapter is to explore some of the effective measures adopted by headteachers who have had to contend with the consequences of staff grievances and associated collective action, which have been engendered by factors outside the school and sometimes beyond the ambit of the LEA. However, in the light of employment legislation, the initial concern is with the processes involved in handling staff grievances generated within the school.

While attention is addressed to both teaching and support staff, the main emphasis is given to the teachers since the manifestations of their discontent are usually more disruptive to the life of the school than other groups of the school adult community.

Grievance procedure and the law

Under the Employment Protection (Consolidation) Act 1978, the LEA as the employer (governing body for voluntary aided schools) is responsible for informing each member of staff as to how they may pursue grievances.

The legal provision applies only to individuals and there is no statutory obligation for the employer to make arrangements for the resolution of collective grievances. However, because an individual grievance may lead to a collective grievance, the convention is to link the arrangements for dealing with each kind under one procedural agreement.

Most LEAs have adopted the model grievance procedure agreed at national level by the agencies representing the employers and those unions that act on behalf of teachers and support staff respectively. Copies of the model procedures are provided in the appendices for reference.

Grievance procedures and the role of the headteacher

Most staff grievances within schools are best dealt with informally and this practice continues to be the most appropriate in the majority of cases. However, in the light of the law, and the rise in the number of both individual and collective grievances, formal procedures are a necessary adjunct to the traditional common sense approach favoured by headteachers.

As the agent of the employer, the headteacher is obliged to:

- administer a grievance procedure within the school;
- check that staff are aware of, and understand, the grievance procedure;
- ensure that the procedure is applied in a way which is consistent with the external arrangements for resolving grievances at the LEA level.

Therefore, the headteacher is primarily concerned with deputing the appropriate senior staff to deal with grievances which arise in the school. There is, of course, the additional task of counselling and advising staff as to how they should proceed with a grievance which arises from factors outside the school.

Dealing with grievances

Both individual and collective grievances may be somewhat arbitrarily divided into those concerned with the application of the contract of employment and the associated collective agreement between the employers and union, and those grievances which arise because of interpersonal differences among staff, or problems an individual is experiencing.

While most grievances about contractual matters originate from outside the school, there are occasions when a grievance which has contractual implications arises within the school. Thus it is important for the headteacher and senior colleagues to identify, at an early stage, the precise nature of the grievance so as to avoid an unnecessary escalation of the issue, and to ensure the grievance is processed through the appropriate procedural channels.

The following incidents serve to illuminate the above points.

> The caretaker complained to the headteacher that staff from the drama department were not finishing rehearsals on time and as a result he was having to close the school in his own unpaid time.

> A junior member of staff complained to her head of department that the deputy headteacher always selects her to cover a colleague's class when there are others in the staffroom who are never asked to cover.

> The staff union representatives advised the headteacher that staff were complaining about their increased workload as a consequence of the LEA decision to cut back on supply cover for absent teachers.

> A senior teacher complained to the headteacher about the general attitude of the school secretary towards members of the teaching staff.

Apart from the third incident cited, the grievances appear to have originated within the school. But note the differences in the nature and substance of the grievances.

As presented, the first case raises an issue of a contractual nature in addition to questions about organisational arrangements; the second case points to an unfair discrimination; the third case may be distinguished from the others as it is a collective grievance which carries implications for contracts of employment and collective agreements; the fourth case is ostensibly about interpersonal relationships.

As a general principle, the headteacher will wish to resolve such grievances within the school, though inevitably there will be occasions when they will be referred for resolution to the external grievance procedure. Cases are often referred because of the inexperience of those staff to whom the headteacher has entrusted the responsibility for handling grievances. The check list below alerts the headteacher to some common failings.

A check list

- *No grievance should be considered too trivial for attention.*
- *Ensure that the information about the grievance is as complete and as accurate as possible.*
- *Clarify with senior staff the limits of their authority in dealing with grievances and ensure that they receive the necessary training for handling these grievances.*
- *Keep those concerned fully informed of the progress of the grievance.*
- *Demonstrate personal concern by following through promptly on any action required and in the event that action is inappropriate, inform the individual concerned of the reasons for not pursuing the complaint.*
- *Keep adequate written records to ensure consistency and effectiveness.*
- *Insist that staff follow the appropriate channels to ensure the integrity of the internal grievance procedure is maintained.*
- *Beware of setting precedents which may lead to future problems.*
- *Where appropriate, check the individual contract of employment and/or the relevant collective agreement.*
- *Beware of encouraging the habitual complainant.*
- *Monitor and evaluate the operation of the grievance procedure.*

Most of the items listed require no elaboration, but headteachers may wish to consider their practice for handling individual grievances. There is a tendency among headteachers to spend a disproportionate amount of time in dealing with complaints from members of the adult community in the school. This is not to suggest that they should not be involved, but simply to state the obvious, which is that many complaints could properly be dealt with by heads of department and other senior staff. This does, of course, mean that attention will need to be addressed to developing the counselling skills of senior colleagues and delegating the appropriate authority to them to enable them to carry out their responsibilities effectively.

A grievance procedure signifies the presence of orderly arrangements for handling differences between the parties concerned and the purpose is to achieve a mutually acceptable resolution to the issue in question. However, there is no legal requirement that this must occur; conciliation and/or mediation may fail, and the end result may be some form of collective action including the ultimate sanction – a strike of school staff.

A detailed commentary on the various sorts of collective action which have been taken by teachers and support staff is provided in the appendices for reference.

It was indicated in the introduction to this section that irrespective of the underlying issues giving rise to collective action by school staff, the headteacher is expected to cope with the consequences. Next, attention is addressed to coping with collective grievances.

Coping with the consequences of collective action

Regardless of who is involved or the circumstances of the school when collective action is impending, the headteacher will first wish to ascertain:

- *the issue(s) which is in dispute;*
- *whether the issue(s) is internally or externally generated;*
- *who will be taking part;*
- *whether there is to be a strike or 'work to contract';*
- *what proportion of the group will be undertaking the action;*
- *details of the action;*
- *whether the action is to occur on specified/unspecified day(s) of the week or continuously;*
- *whether the participants are acting on their own initiative or following union instructions;*
- *the normal duties of the staff involved.*

Here the sources of information would include:

- *the LEA*
- *senior members of staff*
- *union representatives*
- *local, national and educational Press*
- *individual contracts of employment*
- *job description*
- *staff timetable/work schedules.*

Having assembled this information, the headteacher can begin to make an assessment of the likely impact the collective action will have on the school. This will vary according to a host of structural and attitudinal factors, the most significant of which are listed below.

Impact of collective action: factors for consideration

- *response of headteachers and senior colleagues*
- *status and duties of the participants*
- *organisational arrangements made by the LEA*
- *instructions issued by the CEO/education committee*
- *proportion of staff involved*
- *reaction of staff working normally*
- *nature of the support given by the union(s) concerned*
- *policies of unions not directly involved*
- *response of the school union representatives*
- *parents' reaction*
- *pupils' reaction*

- *school catchment area*
- *internal organisation and siting of the school*
- *reaction of the wider community*
- *time of the year*

All forms of collective action taken by school staff are likely to have a disruptive impact on the life of the school, but the two kinds of dissent which present the headteacher with the greatest difficulty are the 'work to contract' and the strike. The next concern is to explore some of the main features of 'work to contract' by teaching staff and the way(s) in which the headteacher copes with the consequences.

But first it must be stressed that before taking action to resolve a dispute, the headteacher will be strongly advised to ascertain whether the proposals have the support of the LEA. In the event that the LEA does not sanction the headteacher's action, he or she may be totally exposed to the wrath of both the LEA and staff, especially where assurances have been given to the latter. In these circumstances the headteacher's precipitate action may serve only to prolong and deepen the rift between the parties concerned.

'Work to contract': some implications for the school

In many ways the tactic of 'working to contract' is a more attractive proposition than a strike for union members seeking to bring pressure to bear on their employers. For the participants the chief advantages are as follows:

- It normally entails no significant loss of earnings.
- The demands on the union's financial resources are relatively small.
- It may be implemented in a large number of schools and thereby increase the pressure on employers to make concessions.
- It can be sustained for relatively long periods of time.
- It enables the participants to maintain a relatively low public profile with all that that implies for their standing in the local community.
- It can be an effective challenge to employers' policies with little apparent risk to the individuals involved.

'Working to contract' is most often associated with the issue of the 'teachers' day'. However, such collective action is undertaken in response to all sorts of issues. Teachers have resorted to 'working to contract' in response to LEA policies of reducing supply cover to schools, and have declined to carry out administrative tasks traditionally reserved for more senior colleagues.

From these two examples, it will be apparent (certainly to headteachers) that this form of action can have a very disruptive effect on the school, particularly as it can last for a relatively long time, and from the standpoint of the LEA and headteacher, is often difficult to counter.

While introducing more detailed and specific teachers' contracts of employment may assist in resolving differences about their duties, the national collective agreements still offer considerable scope for different interpretations of teachers' conditions of employment. These, too, may be reduced through negotiation, but 'working to contract' (like other forms of collective action) is essentially a symptom of deep-rooted concern, such as a decrease in teachers' career opportunities and/or lack of job security.

As long as the circumstances prevail which induce fears and frustrations among teachers, the employers will continue to be faced with a central dilemma. Thus, by making it more difficult for people to register dissent by (say) 'working to contract', there is a possibility that they will take alternative forms of collective action which can be potentially more disruptive to the school, including strikes.

Notwithstanding this observation, many LEAs have gradually moved towards issuing relatively detailed employment contracts in the light of legislation and problems arising over differing interpretations of the provisions. Here the practice of the headteacher is crucial. While it is acknowledged that national and, in some cases, local collective agreements remain outside the headteachers' influence and control, this does not apply to staff contracts of employment, job descriptions and so on. The headteacher interviews and selects staff (usually with others) and a great many schools issue job descriptions and staff rules. Therefore, in this sense, the headteacher is in a position to determine many, but by no means all, of the contractual duties and obligations of staff.

The headteacher who is confronted with the possibility of staff 'working to contract' will wish to check on the following documentation:

- *the individual contracts of employment*
- *the individual job description*
- *the relevant national and local collective agreements*
- *the school rules applying to staff*
- *the LEA rules and regulations applying to the category of staff in question.*

While superior knowledge based upon experience and familiarity with contracts and procedures can be an advantage to the headteacher endeavouring to cope with the consequences of staff 'working to contract', the ability to maintain good interpersonal relations is probably more important.

Consider these statements:

My staff refuse to cover for colleagues who are absent for more than three days.

When I came to this school I was astonished to learn that the majority of the teachers would not attend staff meetings outside of school hours.

We have had a number of occasions when the laboratory assistants have refused to clear up the mess left by teachers, because they say it is not their responsibility.

Without detailed knowledge of the circumstances of these incidents, any advice may be challenged. However, the headteacher will invariably have a number of options, any one or more of which may be worth exploring in such situations.

What options would you suggest to a newly promoted headteacher faced with the incidents above? Would you advise the headteacher to:

- appeal to their professionalism and sense of responsibility;
- seek the assistance of the LEA;
- check on the contracts of employment of those involved and confront them with their duties and obligations;

- obtain the advice of his/her association;
- endeavour to negotiate with the relevant union representatives;
- take disciplinary action;
- ask the chairman of the school governors to mediate;
- accept the situation and get on with the business of running the school insofar as circumstances allow;
- actively seek the co-operation of staff not directly involved;
- delegate the responsibility for sorting things out to a deputy headteacher?

These approaches are not mutually exclusive but different headteachers have used such tactics to cope with the sorts of incidents provided above, with varying degrees of success as measured by the level of disruption inflicted on the school.

As a general rule the headteacher should:

- *avoid taking action which could exacerbate the situation*;
- *refrain from acting in a way which is contrary to LEA practice*.

The key to coping more or less effectively with staff management issues is the headteacher's ability to identify the most appropriate action to take in any given circumstances.

Finally in this context, it should be borne in mind that if 'work to contract' continues for any length of time, the mode of operation can become customary and accepted practice, at least by the participants. Thus, for example, where teachers have ceased to attend parents' evenings because of working to contract, it may be extremely difficult to get them to resume this activity when the issue which has led to the action has been resolved.

The school: teachers' strike action

In some ways a strike by the entire teaching staff of the school simplifies the task of the headteacher since he/she will have little choice but to close the school. In the circumstances the headteacher will bear the chief responsibility for informing parents which will place considerable pressure on the administration. Furthermore, arrangements will need to be made to cope with inquiries from parents and the press. The position of the support staff also has to be considered and they will need to be notified as to any changes in their work routine. For example, the services of the school meals staff may not be required on the day or weeks the strike is occurring.

However, it is only on rare occasions that teaching staff will exhibit such unison because many teachers refuse to strike on grounds of conscience and the fact that the teachers' unions rarely agree to take concerted strike action. Thus, the headteacher is more likely to have to cope with a situation in which only a proportion of the teaching staff will be taking strike action. Such circumstances present a considerable challenge to the school and the stance adopted by the headteacher and senior colleagues is of crucial importance. Indeed, deputy heads and other senior staff may be directly involved in the action, in which case the headteacher is likely to feel extremely isolated and under siege especially if he/she has not prepared for such an eventuality.

Impending strike

Perceptions of the headteacher

When faced with an impending strike or, indeed, any other kind of collective action, the conflicting pressures and personal dilemmas which are a feature of headship become much more sharply focused.

Consider these statements:

I am a long standing member of the teachers' association which is supporting the strike, and while I refuse to participate I will not do anything to undermine the action.

While I have every sympathy with the aims of my staff who will be taking strike action, I simply cannot condone that sort of behaviour especially where teachers are concerned.

Teachers have a professional obligation to teach the children in our care, and it is utter nonsense to suggest that by striking they are acting in the best interests of the children.

Such opinions serve to confirm the view that a strike is characterised by strong moral convictions which co-exist with considerable moral confusion and complexity. It is important that headteachers do not view collective action prompted by external factors as a personal affront, or an attack on their school, because such perceptions act as a powerful constraint to making effective judgements and decisions.

Headteachers who appear to cope most effectively with the consequences of strike action are those who abide by the dictum that 'it is not who is right but what is right in the circumstances'. This also applies to the LEA as the employer. Indeed, while the school may be the focal point of the strike, it is the LEA which retains overall responsibility for administrative support and the provision of education within the Authority.

The LEA stance

In the absence of sound advice and general support from the LEA, the head-teacher's ability to cope effectively with the consequences of a strike will almost certainly be undermined. Consider this statement from a headteacher:

Immediately following the announcement that a strike was pending, I received instructions from the LEA, via the elected members, that I was to keep all the children in school. This decision appeared to stem from the belief that we could teach 500 pupils in the school hall.

The LEA cannot, of course, insist that the school be kept open if the head-teacher believes that to obey such an instruction would be to put the pupils at risk. However, taken at a superficial level, this incident serves to raise a number of fundamental questions, namely:

- On what information was the decision based?
- Were they aware of how many teachers in this school would be participating in the strike?
- Had they prior information about the implications for curriculum provision?

- Were they aware of the examination schedules in this school?
- Did they know in advance the degree of co-operation that would be forth-coming from the teachers who would not be taking strike action?
- To what extent were the 'political' exigencies overriding the plans of the LEA officers?
- Had prior attention been addressed to potential health and safety hazards?

The central point that emerges is that the LEA officers can only formulate plans in the light of the probable impact of the strike on the school. This requires an intimacy with the school's affairs which the headteacher will have acquired from the day-to-day running of the school.

Having obtained the relevant information from the headteacher, the LEA officers will have a clearer picture of the difficulties likely to be encountered during the course of the strike and, indeed, immediately after the action has ceased. In short, a strike demands a degree of co-ordination between the LEA and headteacher over and beyond normal practice.

Thus it is incumbent on the LEA to:

- *have a sound knowledge of the organisation of the school and its ethos;*
- *collect the necessary information from the headteacher before the strike actually begins;*
- *provide expert and timely advice for the headteacher concerning legal matters;*
- *provide guidelines which leave the headteacher in no doubt as to who is responsible for what;*
- *monitor developments and act with alacrity when the situation requires an immediate response;*
- *keep the headteacher informed of developments within the LEA;*
- *clarify with the elected members, especially the chairman of the education committee, the policy stance in relation to the strike, and plan accordingly.*

Where this action is taken by the LEA, the headteacher tends to suffer much less ambivalence and therefore operates more effectively. Moreover, the delineation of responsibility does inhibit the temptation to avoid making difficult decisions by referring the matter in question elsewhere.

Of course, the above assumes a degree of rationality which is rarely present in circumstances of overt conflict. For example, LEA officers frequently give advice supplied by the Authority's legal department, but this offers no guarantee that the unions involved will share the LEA's perception of the legal position and act accordingly. Thus the headteacher cannot presume in advance that those participating in collective action will feel bound by legal prescriptions emanating from the LEA.

Headteachers' action
The check list which follows is designed to provide a reference to those tasks the headteacher can usefully undertake after receiving notification that a strike involving school staff is due to take place.

It should be stressed that the table is a summation of over fifty headteachers' responses to different kinds of collective action by teachers and support staff. Those who have experienced a strike by teachers articulated with some precision their concerns and coping strategies, while the response of their more fortunate colleagues tended to be more limited in scope. This is reflected in the table, and it is not suggested that the concerns listed, and the coping strategies adopted, carry equal weight regardless of the type of collective action and status of the participants.

The various components of the check list are briefly explored in the text following.

Collective action: headteacher's check list

Individuals and agencies to be contacted	Internal actions required	Headteacher concerns
Teaching staff	*List of staff intending to participate in the action*	*Staffing resources, curriculum provision, response of the teachers working normally*
LEA	*Action on guidelines, liaison procedures*	*Quality of advice, legal liabilities*
Chairman of governors	*Meetings schedule*	*Ill-conceived advice, public announcements*
Parents	*Office procedure, telephone, staff workload*	*Parent co-operation, ancillary support*
Pupils	*Timetables*	*Teaching and supervision, pupil response*
Union representatives	*Consultation processes, names of people to contact at local union headquarters*	*Picketing of the school: parent and children involvement, delivery of supplies, future relationships*
Building and maintenance	*Security of site(s) and buildings, access for delivery*	*Building debris, excavations, pupil safety*
Public services:		
Police	*Liaison procedures*	*Building/site security, pupil road safety, vandalism*
Fire	*Audit of fire procedures, laboratories, domestic appliances*	*Inadequate pupil supervision*
Health	*Audit of safety procedures*	*Inadequate pupil supervision, toxic substances*
Transport	*Pupil travelling arrangements*	*Catchment area, pupil safety and behaviour*
Support staff	*Audit of stocks, supply schedule*	*Fuel, stationery, meals, level of co-operation*
The Press	*Arrangements for handling enquiries from the Press*	*Public standing of the school, misquoting of statements, editing of prepared Press release*

continued

Individuals and agencies to be contacted	Internal actions required	Headteacher concerns
Headteacher associations	*Identify appropriate contact, correspondence*	*General and especially legal advice about the position of the headteacher*
Headteacher colleagues	*Arrangements for meetings*	*Feeling of isolation, effect of LEA policies and procedures*

Some explanatory notes on the check list

The comments below follow the format of the check list which should be read from left to right. For convenience the agencies and the individuals noted in the left-hand column are used as sub-headings.

Teaching staff   The headteacher, and indeed the LEA, will wish, at an early stage, to ascertain the number and names of staff who will be participating in the impending strike. Arrangements will have to be made to stop payment of salaries to those concerned and, to avoid misunderstandings, the headteacher ought, in consultation with the staff representatives, to obtain the signatures of the individuals involved.

Prior knowledge of the proportion of staff intending to undertake strike action will not in itself allow for a meaningful evaluation to be made of the likely impact on the school. This process also requires information about the duties and responsibilities of the individuals concerned. It may be that the striking members of staff form the main core of (say) 'English' teachers in the school. On the other hand, they may be spread across subjects. In the former case the impact on the teaching of English could be such that the subject may have to be abandoned for the duration of the strike. This is unlikely to be necessary where the teachers are normally involved in teaching several areas of the school curriculum. Their administrative and extracurricular responsibilities also need to be determined.

The headteacher must further consult with the remaining staff and their union representatives to establish the degree of co-operation that may be expected while their colleagues are absent from the school. For example, will they be prepared to teach much larger classes and/or cover the duties normally undertaken by their striking colleagues? Much will depend on the policies of those unions not directly involved in the dispute, and this will have to be clarified.

These preliminary tasks will enable the headteacher and senior school staff to assess what impact the impending strike is likely to have on the school. An evaluation of the possible consequences will raise many imponderables, but the central questions to which the headteacher should give priority are:

- *Will it be possible to keep the school open?*
- *If so, what activities will have to be suspended?*

The LEA then has to be advised in detail of the implications for the school arising from the effects of the teachers' collective action.

The LEA In consulting with the LEA, the headteacher will be acutely concerned about the nature of the advice and support that he/she will receive, and the possibility of personal liability in the case of (say) a pupil being injured.

In discussion with officers of the LEA, the headteacher will be well advised to seek guidance and assurance over the sorts of issues listed below:

- *how the Press should be handled*;
- *what information should be sent to parents*;
- *the position of school meals staff where there will be a substantial fall in the demand for school meals*;
- *arrangements for supplying the school with heating oil and other supplies, especially where it is likely the school will be picketed*;
- *the level of administrative support that may be expected from the LEA*;
- *if appropriate, the arrangements for pupils to take public examinations*;
- *availability of additional financial resources for such things as school educational visits which may be arranged as a consequence of the strike*;
- *employment of additional support staff, e.g. mid-day assistants*.

This list is by no means exhaustive and is provided merely to indicate some common concerns of headteachers when confronted with a strike by school staff.

In the potentially fraught circumstances of collective action, the law applying to 'negligence' and 'duty of care' is of particular concern to headteachers, primarily because of the issue of pupil supervision.

Under the law, the LEA as the employer (governing body in the case of voluntary aided schools) is vicariously liable for the civil wrongs that staff commit while engaged on legitimate activities during the course of their employment.

The duty placed on the headteacher flows from his/her responsibility for the organisation and discipline in the school. In essence this amounts to taking all *reasonable* steps to prevent any of the pupils from suffering an injury. The test of what is reasonable seems to rest on foresight. Thus, the headteacher should consider this question: Is it possible (not 'certain' or even highly 'probable') that injury could occur to a pupil as a consequence of a decision by the headteacher or by inaction on his/her part?

In addition to the common law duty, alluded to above, the headteacher should consider the implications arising from the Health and Safety at Work Act.

Readers who seek further clarification about the headteacher's responsibilities in relation to 'negligence' and 'care' should refer to the bibliography provided at the end of this section.

Chairman of governors A characteristic feature of a school facing a crisis is the rise in the number of meetings that require the presence of the headteacher. Some of this burden may be shared with the chairman of the school governing body, who is in a position to intercede with the LEA on behalf of the headteacher, and is also ideally placed to act as an intermediary between school and parents.

Much will depend upon the personal standing of the chairman within the LEA and wider community, but in any event the headteacher will obviously wish to work as closely as circumstances permit with the school governors. Liaison of this kind is more likely to be effective where the headteacher has previously established a good working relationship with the chairman of the governors.

Parents Parents will probably have already heard something about the impending collective action from their children or the Press, but such sources are notoriously unreliable. Therefore the headteacher will wish to clarify with parents as soon as possible the position faced by the school. In particular, it is important to inform parents about such things as timetable changes and whether, for example, the children will be kept in school or sent home at specified times of the school day.

If the latter is to occur, it may present working parents with considerable difficulties in making satisfactory alternative arrangements for the well-being of their children. The headteacher also has to consider the possibility of a rise in the incidence of vandalism committed by pupils outside school with all that that implies for the standing of the school in the local community.

Thus, it is important for the headteacher to enlist the support and co-operation of the parents and this necessarily means keeping them regularly informed of developments. While most school secretaries are well versed in the processes of corresponding with parents, the sheer volume of letters, and the uncertainty that a strike inevitably engenders, can give rise to a breakdown of communication between school and parents. A parents' association may be able to assist the processes of communication.

An early review of normal school office practice is to be recommended to see how the predicted increase in administrative matters can best be handled.

Pupils A disruption in the normal pattern of their school day will provide an interesting challenge for some children, but others will find it causes difficulty especially, for example, if they are studying for examinations. Yet others will be suspicious of the teachers' motives in engaging in strike action and will feel let down. Such feelings can undermine relationships between pupils and staff which, in the case of older children, have been nurtured over four or five years. Once the mutual bond of trust has been broken, it may be predicted that staff will be hard pressed to re-establish the degree of rapport with the children which they may have previously enjoyed. This has obvious implications for pupils' motivation and the maintenance of discipline in the classroom. For these reasons (among others) the headteacher will wish to take special care when informing the children of the impending strike and what that means in terms of their timetables and extracurricular activities.

Pupils will be left in no doubt as to the expectations of their behaviour and the need to maintain school discipline. Attention will also be addressed to safety hazards both inside and outside the school, but these are mundane matters which are part of the routine of school life.

The dilemma for the headteacher is to maintain the integrity of the staff involved in the forthcoming strike without appearing to justify the teachers' action. Should the children be told of the circumstances underlying the decision to strike? Apart from the inherent danger of being accused of biased reporting (from whichever party to the dispute), the headteacher also has to consider the ability of pupils to comprehend the intricacies and complexities of a strike.

There are no simple answers to such questions and much will depend on the particular circumstances of the school. However, what is clear is that the pupils must be reassured that they are not pawns in an adults' game and that everything possible is being done to ensure the disruption of their education is being kept to the minimum.

Union representatives A key source of information for the headteacher is the staff union representatives, especially those directly concerned in the dispute.

It is the usual practice for the union(s) involved to set up a local strike HQ to direct and co-ordinate the collective action in the schools. The headteacher who liaises effectively with the union representatives has the advantage of obtaining information about changes in union (or indeed LEA) strategies, frequently before some of the officers of the Authority have received confirmation of developments. This presumes, of course, that relationships prior to the action are cordial and underpinned by mutual trust.

Moreover, by maintaining a communications link with the union representatives, the headteacher can more easily engage in some special pleading on behalf of the school. In the early days of a strike, there tends to be a great deal of confusion and a lack of 'ground rules'. For example, it is not unknown for some parents and one or two pupils to join a picket line at the school gates. These sorts of issues can be quickly dealt with where the headteacher has instant access to the local strike committee.

The headteacher will be well advised to consider the appropriate channels of communication and consultation which may be established with the union representatives at an early stage in the dispute, and certainly before the strike takes effect.

Building and maintenance contractors Where building works are in progress or general maintenance is being undertaken on the school premises, it is normal practice for school staff to be especially vigilant as part of their duty of care. One of the consequences of a strike by some members of the school staff is that the normal level of pupil supervision cannot be sustained.

The headteacher should therefore give advanced warning to those concerned with school building and maintenance of the impending strike, and the problems this may present in terms of site security and safety. If the school is to be picketed there may also be problems of delivering building supplies and this possibility should also be considered and reported to the LEA (governors for the voluntary aided school).

Public services It is with more than a faint touch of irony that some headteachers have suggested that a strike by school staff serves to remind people of the complexity and scope of activities undertaken in the modern school. Chemicals and a wide range of potentially hazardous and expensive equipment are used extensively in the process of delivering the curriculum. While all schools will be visited from time to time by representatives of the appropriate branches of the public services, their expertise and support can be particularly helpful to the headteacher endeavouring to cope with the consequences of a strike.

The police can advise on road safety matters, and provide additional security protection to deter would-be thieves and vandals. They can also advise the headteacher about some of the legal implications arising from staff picketing the school, and the role they normally adopt in such circumstances. Here, it may be prudent for the headteacher to seek advice from the LEA before approaching the police.

In the light of a possible reduction in the number of staff available for pupil supervision, the fire service can assess the adequacy of the existing fire procedure and the storage of inflammable substances.

The transport authorities may be able to assist with the problem of sending children home outside the normal pupil travelling times. This is especially important when the children come from a wide geographical catchment area. In such circumstances the headteacher may be able to arrange special dispensation arrangements with the strike committee to ameliorate the most hazardous effects of strike action.

While the LEA will necessarily be involved in liaising with the public services, the headteacher should not hesitate to take the initiative and establish close liaison with the various representatives.

Support staff   Contingency planning includes taking stock of existing supplies of heating oil and a host of other items without which it would be difficult if not impossible to keep the school open.

While some teaching staff will usually be involved in this process, support staff, particularly the school caretaker, are responsible for taking deliveries and monitoring fuel gauges etc. Depleted stocks may be replenished before the strike begins but the headteacher also needs to ascertain the degree of co-operation which might be forthcoming from support staff during the course of the strike. For example, with pickets in attendance, will the caretaker refuse to accept an oil delivery?

The Press   Most, if not all, headteachers will be familiar with the horror stories about the 'goings on' in such and such a school which appear in the local and national Press with almost monotonous regularity. The accuracy of such reports is usually dubious to say the least, but subsequent denials by the headteacher and LEA concerned rarely erase community suspicions engendered by the initial Press report. Unfortunately, editorial licence tends to be particularly rampant in reports about collective disputes.

Even if it were desirable, it is virtually impossible to impose a news blackout about a strike and its attendant ramifications in a school, but arrangements can be made which, at the very least, may help to limit the worst excesses of the Press. While many Local Authorities have standard procedures for dealing with the Press, a strike situation demands a rigorous review of existing arrangements because (among other reasons) many headteachers are unaware of normal practice. Thus, as soon as it is confirmed that strike action is to go ahead in the school, the headteacher should consult with the LEA to work out a plan of action for handling the news media. The co-operation of the union(s) concerned should also be sought because they will probably share many of the concerns of the other parties involved.

The 'ground rules' for dealing with the media should be clear and unambiguous, and made known to school staff via the headteacher. Early contact should be made with the local newspaper editor(s) to seek agreement on the most appropriate arrangements for dealing with matters arising. Here it would be the responsibility of the LEA to take the initiative.

As a general rule, the headteacher should resist the temptation to be interviewed by TV and radio reporters, and particular care needs to be taken when responding to telephone inquiries from seemingly well-meaning citizens, but who may in fact be emissaries of the media. The bona fides of those telephoning the school can usually be checked, simply by asking the caller for their number so that a return call can be made when it is more convenient. The headteacher should also impress upon members of staff the dangers of responding in an *ad hoc* way to questions from representatives of the media. Pupils, too, should be advised of the importance of refusing to comply with suggestions by a minority of unprincipled reporters to do something foolish such as staging a riot, or some other form of disturbance. This will obviously require judicious handling if only to avoid alerting pupils to actions they had not previously considered.

Headteacher associations A headteacher caught up in a collective dispute will normally contact his/her professional association for two main reasons. Firstly, to ascertain the policy of the association in relation to the dispute in question, and to seek advice about the appropriate response which may be made to the LEA; secondly, to obtain guidance about specific issues, frequently of a legal nature, which are of considerable personal concern.

The professional advice and reassurance given by the Association to the hard-pressed headteacher can be invaluable in restoring the confidence necessary to cope effectively with the consequences of a strike. Equally, the mutual support of headteacher colleagues in the Authority is seen by many to be extremely valuable, especially in dealings with the LEA.

Running a school during a strike

When I was promoted to headship I never imagined in my wildest dream that one day I would find myself remonstrating with teachers on a picket line for playing football in the road.

The processes and procedures undertaken in advance of collective action by members of school staff represent only the first part of a coping strategy. The headteacher will also wish to consider the most appropriate action to take during the course of the collective action.

During a strike, some aspects of school administration, for example the rescheduling of timetables and corresponding with parents, are likely to take up more of the headteacher's time than they might in normal circumstances, and it may be anticipated that there will be occasional difficulties. For example, it only takes one or two teachers to be absent through sickness (when the school is already understaffed) to upset the emergency timetabling arrangements. But the greatest challenge to the headteacher and senior colleagues is the occurrence of events which are beyond their own experience, and which place strains on interpersonal and group relationships.

Therefore, the primary intention here is to explore briefly a range of coping styles adopted by headteachers in the light of relatively common features of any strike action. While procedural matters merit attention the main concern is with interpersonal relationships. This dimension is treated in much greater depth in the training materials complementing this handbook, and the immediate concern is to alert the headteacher to some implications arising from the coping styles reviewed.

The table on pp. 162–5 has been devised to facilitate a brief examination of a range of stances adopted by headteachers in the light of the particular circumstances and background to a number of issues and their personal preferences. While in each case the responses of the headteachers have been limited to three, the number could have been significantly increased, only at the risk of repetition.

It cannot be stressed too strongly that in the absence of intimate knowledge of the circumstances and the people involved, it would be extremely foolhardy to suggest that one particular approach is better than another.

Despite the fact that any categorisation of human behaviour is to some extent arbitrary (if only because some responses do not precisely 'fit' the label attached to them), the classification used in the tables does indicate that the headteachers' two preferred modes of coping were Accommodating and Avoiding, followed by Collaborating, whilst Confronting was a virtual rarity.

As indicated, any one of these approaches might have been appropriate depending on the circumstances underlying the issues confronting the headteachers. However, it seems that the headteachers who cope most effectively with the sorts of issues identified in the table, are those who retain a flexible stance and choose the appropriate strategy(s) in the light of all the known and anticipated circumstances including, of course, any LEA policies. Some implications arising from the different coping styles identified in the table are briefly discussed below.

Coping style: Confronting   This approach is inherently competitive and combative. It is inspired by a determination to win and the success or otherwise of this style rests in a large part on the mutual recognition of the headteacher's power. Expressed bluntly, a confronting stance is little short of survival of the fittest, in which one party wins and the other loses. This has implications for future staff relationships which the effective headteacher will invariably consider before adopting such a style.

Coping style: Collaborating   This approach stems from the belief that the individuals and/or groups concerned share a problem that can best be resolved jointly. Collaborative tactics require significantly greater skills than the other categories of responses identified in the table below. A prior condition for success is the existence of a high degree of mutual trust, and the headteacher needs to be fully aware of the possibility of being seen to offer some sense of legitimacy to the actions of those involved in the dispute, especially where his/her stance is clearly at variance with the LEA position.

Coping style: Accommodating   This form of behaviour is characterised by a reference for resolving problems through the processes of compromise. It is prompted by a sense of powerlessness and an inability to influence significantly the course of events by independent action.

Compromise solutions to problems are at the heart of negotiations and success rests on a mutual desire by the parties involved to be seen to be reasonable and willing to make concessions acceptable to the other side.

Coping style: Avoiding   This stance is usually prompted by a desire to avoid involvement. It is often a calculated decision to withdraw because intervention or involvement is perceived to be inappropriate in the circumstances. For example, where the interaction might exacerbate the situation with the associated risk to the authority of the headteacher.

Finally here, attitudes tend to harden and mutual trust deteriorates, in proportion to the length of time the strike action lasts. The headteacher, therefore, needs to be particularly sensitive to such phenomena and endeavour to weigh the pros and cons of decisions prior to their implementation.

After the dispute

Some general observations

Overt conflict of the kind discussed above is one symptom of a decline in mutual trust and understanding, and the headteacher will wish to restore confidence and a spirit of co-operation among school staff immediately following the settlement of a dispute. It may be predicted that where people have been on strike there will be 're-entry' problems that require the headteacher's early attention. While this applies to all categories of school staff, the headteacher will be primarily concerned to restore, as quickly as possible, the level and quality of education provision in the school.

The issues presented below are examples of the sorts of factors that can impede a swift return to normal working and which, therefore, merit contingency planning before the strike action is officially concluded.

The pupils claimed the staff were working them too hard in order to catch up on time lost during the dispute.

Some junior members of staff were finding it extremely difficult to maintain order in the classroom after the dispute.

The parents were primed to complain about the predicted poor examination results.

The deputy headteacher, who had experienced considerable personal abuse from some of the more militant members of staff when they were on strike, refuses to speak directly with the teachers concerned.

The school meals staff are very resentful over the teachers' strike, largely because a few of their colleagues lost their jobs as a consequence.

It is very noticeable that since the dispute the staff demand to be considered about even rather trivial matters, whereas before they did not seem to be particularly interested in school administration beyond their immediate domain.

When the dispute was over staff seemed more prone to air their personal grievances than before.

A senior mistress who refused to go on strike was sent to 'Coventry' by some of her colleagues after the dispute was settled.   (*continued p. 166*)

Categorisation of the headteacher's coping styles

Issues	Confronting	Collaborating	Accommodating	Avoiding
Picketing the school		I talked regularly to staff on the picket line and readily agreed to their request to use the school toilets and to come in for a cup of tea.	I was somewhat taken aback to discover staff were picketing the school, but I usually spent twenty minutes chatting with them when I arrived in the morning.	I arrived at the school to find that members of staff had formed a picket line at the school gate. I totally ignored them and continued to do so for the duration of the strike.
Relationships with staff union representatives		The staff union representative is a very responsible person and I often sought his help in overcoming certain problems which arose from time to time.	I tried to meet with the union representatives of the staff on strike on a daily basis to trade information.	I made no attempt to contact staff union representatives during the strike or for that matter any other time.
Pupil timetables		In the periods when the staff were unavailable to teach the children, we made extensive use of TV education programmes and brought in extra films. We also advised parents about suitable TV programmes and places the children could profitably visit.	I was under considerable pressure from parents and elected members to keep the children in school. We compromised by adopting a system of block timetabling which meant the children did not have to keep going in and out of the school.	I did not succumb to parental pressure and simply blocked out the periods on the timetable normally taken by staff on strike and sent the pupils home.

continued

Issues	Confronting	Collaborating	Accommodating	Avoiding
Parents' meeting		Parents were invited to attend a meeting called at the initiative of the local strike committee to explain why the teachers were on strike. I agreed that the meeting could take place on the school premises and also accepted the invitation to chair the meeting.	The local strike committee asked me if I would co-operate to arrange a meeting with parents on the school premises in order to put the case of the teachers on strike. I agreed but declined the offer to chair the meeting.	I was asked by the local strike HQ to call a meeting of parents so that the union representatives could present the union's case. I refused because staff working normally were specifically excluded from the invitation.
School deliveries	The postman refused to cross the picket line to deliver the mail, so I collected it myself and told the staff outside the school gates that I would be responding to requests for job references in the usual way.		The postman refused to deliver the mail to the school so I arranged for it to be left at the caretaker's house (which is outside the school boundaries) and the caretaker and I shared the task of bringing the mail into the school.	After a few days the postman declared he was no longer prepared to deliver the mail whilst the strike lasted. I contacted the postmaster and told him the Post Office was legally obliged to ensure the mail was delivered to the school. Normal mail deliveries were maintained.
Relations between staff	A number of staff working normally were extremely distressed by the verbal abuse they were subjected to by their colleagues on the picket line. I was incensed by such behaviour and told		Staff relations in this school were good before the dispute and whilst there was a little tension between a few members of staff during the strike, I managed to persuade those	At first relations between the staff on the picket line and teachers attending school were friendly but deteriorated because a head of department persisted in making jokes at the expense

continued

Issues	Confronting	Collaborating	Accommodating	Avoiding
	those responsible that I would not tolerate conduct of that kind and if necessary would call the police.		concerned that it would not be in anyone's interest to let emotions gain the upper hand.	of those on strike. The staff union representative asked me to intercede and to stop the HoD deliberately riling the staff at the school gates, but I refused to become involved.
Resumption of normal working		During the strike I was acutely conscious of the deepening rift between sections of the teaching staff. I therefore planned a series of staff briefing meetings and 'coffee mornings'. These took place on the first day back to school after the dispute and for some time thereafter.	On the first morning back after the strike I held a staff meeting and advised staff to put the recent unhappy period behind them and to work together for the good of the school.	When all the staff returned to the school I held a staff meeting but refrained from mentioning the dispute and business was conducted in the normal way.
Relations between teachers and support staff			The support staff in this school had little sympathy for the staff on strike. I told them that whilst I recognised their difficulties I was relying on them to co-operate with the teachers on their return to the school.	I was aware of the ill-feeling that some sections of the support staff (especially school meals people) had towards those teachers on strike. However, there was little I could do and in any case it was important that I

continued

Issues	Confronting	Collaborating	Accommodating	Avoiding
				maintained a position of neutrality.
				During the strike one of my deputies told me that one or two members of the support staff were threatening to refuse to co-operate, when the dispute was over, with the teachers who had been absent from school. I passed this information on to their supervisor at the LEA and suggested she deal with the people concerned.

Relatively minor issues are now elevated to an importance they hardly deserve.

A common feature of these statements is that relationships and traditional ways of working are undergoing a process of change. Conflict is undoubtedly a powerful catalyst for change, but perceptions as to whether change arising from a dispute is desirable will, perhaps inevitably, vary enormously among the staff. The lists below seek to clarify potentially desirable and undesirable outcomes to a dispute though it should be stressed that they are by no means exhaustive.

Dispute – potentially desirable outcomes:

- pupils more self-reliant/motivated;
- personal development of senior staff as a consequence of managing a school in a crisis;
- expansion of the horizons of junior staff as a result of engaging in curriculum activities outside their normal roles;
- headteacher's awareness heightened especially with regard to employment relations procedures and agreements;
- a critical review of the staff job descriptions and contracts of employment;
- improvement in the processes of communication/consultation within the school and between the school and the LEA;
- a greater willingness of staff to undertake a critical review of the school organisation, structure and curriculum;
- parents more actively involved in the life of the school.

Dispute – potentially undesirable outcomes:

- continuing tension between members of the school adult community;
- authority of headteacher and senior staff undermined;
- heightened sense of distrust between school staff and the LEA including elected members;
- parents lose faith in the standard of education provision;
- increased union intervention in the life of the school;
- pupils' respect for staff diminished, leading to more cases of indiscipline;
- pupils' future career prospects reduced because of the interruption in their studies;
- staff status in the local community undermined.

While it is acknowledged that many of the elements identified in the above lists could be reversed according to the perceptions of the individuals concerned, what is irrefutable is that the headteacher will need to be alert to the possible outcomes of a dispute and reflect upon the opportunities as well as the constraints.

The process involved in coping with the consequences of strike action by teaching staff has been dealt with at some length. This is because a strike is a symptom of some deep-rooted conflict and dissent between the parties involved and it, therefore, represents a great challenge to the headteacher's leadership of the school community.

For those withdrawing their services, the prospect of a strike can raise anxieties about the potential harm to the pupils' education, their personal standing in the community and, of course, the loss of income. As far as the employer and unions are concerned, a strike is a testimony of their inability to resolve their differences amicably. Questions are raised in the public forum about the general conduct of employment relations in the education service, which in turn undermines public confidence in those charged with the responsibility for secondary education.

These factors (among others) serve to put pressure on the employers and unions to continue negotiations in the search for a satisfactory settlement of their differences. The call for strike action usually follows a breakdown in negotiations, and if this seems likely to occur a strike may still be avoided with the help of third party intervention, in the form of mediation, conciliation or arbitration. In any event, a strike remains the ultimate sanction at a union's disposal and while other options exist, strikes will continue to be very much an exceptional event in the school's calendar. Among the alternative forms of collective action open to unions, perhaps the most significant as far as the school is concerned is the 'work to contract', increasingly manifest in the withdrawal of goodwill.

Collective action by school support staff

Coping with the consequences
Whilst there will be some variation, school support staff consists of the following occupational groups:

- librarians
- secretarial/clerical
- technicians
- caretakers/cleaners
- caterers
- welfare assistants
- groundsmen.

No useful purpose will be served by rehearsing the preliminary steps that a headteacher may take pending collective action by support staff, and reference should be made to pages 147–8. While some of the considerations and suggestions presented earlier will not be applicable to support staff, others are relevant and may be of interest. The main concern here is to explore some features of collective action by support staff which have not yet been discussed.

The LEA and support staff
Traditionally, support staff have been the responsibility of the headteacher, but there has been a trend in recent years for LEAs to appoint a supervisor who is centrally located in the LEA offices. This applies chiefly to caretaking, groundsmen and catering staffs and while the normal process of reporting to the headteacher remains common practice, major difficulties can arise as a consequence of dual systems of supervision, especially in a situation of collective action. The incident below exemplifies this observation.

> The school caretaker was on strike and I insisted he handed me a duplicate set of keys. The caretaker refused and said that he was personally responsible to his LEA supervisor for the safekeeping of the sets of keys.

This incident illustrates how support staff engaged in collective action may exploit a dual system of reporting to serve their immediate aims. In such circumstances the headteacher will have to liaise closely with the relevant LEA supervisor.

Largely because of insurance purposes, many LEAs prescribe who should hold keys, including the master keys, for the premises. In such cases it is unlikely that the situation illustrated above would arise.

Support staff unions

Unions representing support staff, such as the Transport and General Workers Union, will usually be far removed from the normal day-to-day concerns of the headteacher. This is in sharp contrast to the status of teachers' unions since the headteacher will usually have, if not a close working relationship, an awareness of union policies and the key figures in the local union hierarchy.

The absence of any kind of relationship with local officials of support staff unions can be a disadvantage to the headteacher for a number of reasons. Coping effectively with the consequence of collective action depends largely on the existence of channels of communication and access to accurate information. It is extremely difficult to negotiate or engage in special pleading on behalf of the school, without at least some knowledge of the predilections of those local union officials who are directing the collective action. The headteacher is, therefore, solely reliant on the LEA for information and/or the staff union representative in the school who may or may not be particularly well informed.

Finally, attention should also be addressed to the possibility that some members of the teaching staff will refuse to cross the picket lines manned by support staff and the degree of disruption this is likely to have on the life of the school.

It has been clearly illustrated in this chapter that collective action invariably undermines the staff code of conduct. The maintenance of staff discipline and professional standards is a crucial aspect of the headteacher's role and this is the subject of the next and last chapter.

The incidents which follow are included as an example of the sorts of issues explored in the complementary set of training materials.

Incident: Deputy head v head of department

The head of the history department in this school sent me a memo in which he complained about the deputy head's absence from departmental meetings held during the previous two terms.

I asked the deputy if the allegations were true. She informed me that the head of department had refused to comply with her request for the meetings to be timetabled at the beginning of the year, and as a consequence she had already committed herself by the time she received notification of the departmental meetings.

The deputy was extremely upset by the head of department's action in writing to me, and said that she would be giving serious consideration to invoking the formal grievance procedure against the head of department.

Trainer's guidelines: issues for consideration

Is it appropriate for a senior member of staff to instigate a formal grievance against a more junior colleague?

Is the deputy at fault for not ensuring that the head of department timetabled the departmental meetings at the beginning of the year?

Is there a requirement for departmental meetings to be scheduled at the beginning of the year, and how is this conveyed to the heads of departments?

What does the headteacher do now? Should he:

- let the matter rest;
- ask the head of department to explain why he had not complied with the deputy's instruction to schedule the departmental meetings well in advance;
- ask the head of department why he had not raised the matter with the deputy;
- tell the deputy that she was remiss in not informing him of the head of department's lack of co-operation in this matter?

Incident: Collective action and the media

The national Press interviewed the teachers picketing the school, and we found ourselves at the centre of much attention. Facts were invented, confidential papers and reports were leaked and used as ammunition.

Trainer's guidelines: issues for consideration

This kind of incident raises many implications for the school, including the following:

- standing of the school in the local community
- impact on pupils and parents
- exacerbation of tension already existing between those affected
- future relationships with other schools
- teachers' standing in the local community
- time and energy expended to put the record straight
- future relationships among teachers and non-teaching staff.

What advice would you give to a headteacher when a collective dispute is pending, to reduce the possibility of this sort of incident arising? Should the headteacher endeavour to reach prior agreement with the school-based trade union representatives on:

- how to respond to enquiries from the Press and other media;
- the code of conduct of those on picket duty;
- arrangements to avoid misunderstandings arising between the parties concerned?

Appendix I: The nature of disputes

Disputes are broadly of two kinds:

- disputes of right, which relate to the application or interpretation of current collective agreements between employers and unions, or contracts of employment;
- disputes of interest, which arise from claims by staff or proposals by 'management' concerning revised terms and conditions of employment.

This analytical distinction serves to highlight the problems which can arise where collective agreements and/or contracts of employment are badly drafted. The 'School Meals Agreement' (1968) illustrates the sorts of difficulties which can arise as a consequence of a lack of clarity in collective agreements and the individual contract of employment. Reference to all the intricacies of that agreement need not detain us; suffice to say that it allowed for significant differences in interpretation and as a consequence has served to exacerbate problems, especially in relation to lunchtime supervision.

Disputes procedures

The main objects of institutional machinery for reconciling differences between the Authority and the unions are to devise, apply and interpret collective agreements and to facilitate the settlement of grievances. Essentially, disputes procedures are treaties of 'peace' and devices for avoiding 'war'. The existence of such machinery means that the parties concerned accept the limitations that the arrangements impose on either side, especially the provisions that the procedures be exhausted before either party takes unilateral action against the other.

The problem for handling disputes varies between LEAs, ranging from the *ad hoc* response to relatively sophisticated formal procedures. It is difficult to assess the relative effectiveness of the different approaches to reconciling differences, but there are a number of factors that seem to be significant, including the following:

- the degree of trust in the general sphere of employment relations in the LEA
- the degree of organisational and technical change occurring
- the degree of consistency in administration and 'political' decisions
- the availability of financial and other resources.

With the possible exception of resources, none of these aspects can be measured with any precision. Nevertheless, where there is an apparent lack of trust, rapid organisational and technical change, inconsistency in decisions and a low level of resource, it may be predicted that numerous differences will arise between the LEA and school staff. In such circumstances it is doubtful whether the *ad hoc* approach to resolving disputes is appropriate.

Providing they are strictly adhered to, formal disputes procedures have the advantage of imposing orderly arrangements upon the parties concerned. However, they offer no guarantee that the differences between the parties will be reconciled and much will depend on the provision for arbitration, conciliation and mediation. These different activities are outlined below.

Arbitration   This is a process whereby the arbitrator(s) determine the outcome of the dispute by making a decision or 'award' which the disputing parties agree to abide by at the outset.

Conciliation   Here a neutral third party meets the opposing parties and endeavours to help them reduce their differences and so reach a settlement. It must be emphasised that when conciliation is successful, agreement is reached by the parties themselves. The conciliator has no mandate to impose a settlement upon the parties; he/she acts as a catalyst to enable them to reach agreement.

Mediation   This refers to a method of settling disputes whereby an independent person makes recommendations as to a possible solution. The mediator goes further than the conciliator by putting forward positive proposals aimed at resolving the dispute.

Arbitration, conciliation and mediation   Provision is made in the 'burgundy book' (*Conditions of Service for School Teachers in England and Wales*) for the parties in dispute to seek the assistance of the 'National Conciliation Service'. Similar provision is made for non-teaching staff in the 'silver book' (*NJC for Local Authorities' Services – Manual Workers*) and the 'purple book' (*NJC for Local Authorities' Administration, Professional, Technical and Clerical Services*). If these existing arrangements are unacceptable to either the LEA or unions concerned, then an approach may be made to the Advisory, Conciliation and Arbitration Service (ACAS) which can provide local assistance.

Collective action: strike   Strike action by teaching or support staffs can take many forms. The one common feature is that the individual participants are in breach of their employment contract since they have not presented themselves for work and are, therefore, not fulfilling their contractual obligations. Under the law, strikers may be dismissed because of this contractual breach; but if the Authority subsequently retracts the dismissal notices it cannot act discriminately; all the dismissal notices must be withdrawn. This is to ensure that the Authority does not use the strike as an opportunity to get rid of staff representatives because of their role in the strike, for example.

Strikes can be 'official', 'unofficial', and/or 'unconstitutional'.

'Official' strike   Almost invariably the power to make a strike 'official' rests solely with the executive council (or its equivalent) of the union(s) concerned. There is usually provision in the union rules for strike pay; and where a strike is declared 'official' a payment may be made to those on strike.

'Unofficial' strike   This refers to the circumstances where the executive body has not given its support to the strike action. In this case the strikers will not normally receive any payment from union funds.

'Unconstitutional' strike   This occurs where action is taken in breach of the disputes procedure, i.e. when all the stages have not been fully exhausted. On occasion the executive body of the union may grant approval for a strike and thereby make it official in the eyes of the union, although procedurally the action remains unconstitutional. This usually happens when the union believes management is using delaying tactics by dwelling on the technical aspects of the disputes procedure, or in displaying a reluctance to negotiate in 'good faith'. Many unofficial strikes are also unconstitutional.

'Work to contract'   In essence 'work to contract' means working according to specific rules (it is sometimes referred to as 'working to rule'), and in this case any task or activity which is not covered by the rules may be refused to be undertaken by those engaged in this type of action. In the absence of a highly detailed employment contract and rules, this form of action may be very difficult to cope with. It should also be noted that this sanction may be applied with or without union backing.

Picketing   This refers to a situation in which strikers gather outside (say) the school to persuade other groups of workers to support their strike action, such as delivery drivers, to persuade staff continuing to work normally to join the strike, or simply to gain publicity for their cause. Under the law, picketing may be carried out only in 'contemplation or furtherance of a trade dispute; and only at or adjacent to the place of work'. Such action remains very controversial, largely because it raises the thorny problem of individual versus collective rights. However, to remain within the law pickets must act in a peaceful manner. If violence or other forms of intimidation occurs, the perpetrators are liable to prosecution under criminal law, and under civil law pickets may find themselves open to a wide variety of charges including obstruction of the highway. In such matters the police have considerable powers of discretion and can severely restrict the impact of picketing if the circumstances appear to warrant their intervention.

Appendix II

Appendix II   Model Grievance Procedure:
Collective Disputes Procedure

Section 1: Individual Grievances

Section 2: Collective Disputes

SECTION 1
A MODEL GRIEVANCE PROCEDURE
for Teachers in Primary and Secondary Schools
to meet the requirements of the
Contracts of Employment Act 1972

Association of Education Committees
Association of Municipal Corporations
County Councils Association
Welsh Joint Education Committee
Joint Committee of the Four Secondary Associations
National Association of Head Teachers
National Association of Schoolmasters
National Union of Teachers

Following discussions between the Associations of local education authorities and of education committees and the Inner London Education Authority and the Teachers' Organisations on the requirements of the Contracts of Employment Act 1972 relating to Grievance Procedures, the model procedure set out below is commended to all employing local education authorities, managing and governing bodies, and individual members of the teaching profession employed in county, voluntary controlled and special agreement schools. It is emphasised that the procedure indicated in this document is designed to deal with *individual* grievances or disputes. It is not intended that it should be applied to collective disputes.

A MODEL GRIEVANCE PROCEDURE
(Contracts of Employment Act 1972)

Teachers' grievances can arise from a variety of sources. They can arise among members of the teaching staff or with the headteacher. They can be of a relatively simple nature or of fundamental importance. They can involve the managers or governors of the school or the administration of the school and the local authority. To meet this situation it seems desirable to set out:
first, a procedure which may enable a grievance to be resolved informally and without recourse to any subsequence stage;
secondly, a completely formal procedure where the first kind of procedure is inappropriate or has failed.
Advice on a similar procedure for headteachers in their relations with their managers or governors or the local authority follows a section dealing with members of the teaching staff.

A. Members of the Teaching Staff
A.1 (i) Where a member of the teaching staff has a grievance with the local authority or with the managers or governors which does not involve any other member of the staff, a

---

Source: *Conditions of Service for School Teachers in England and Wales* ('burgundy book'), Council for
Local Education Authorities (C L E A).

direct approach should be made to the chief education officer or the managers or governors, as may be appropriate.

A.1 (ii) Where a teacher has a grievance which involves other members of the staff he should first of all endeavour to resolve the matter by direct approach to the member of staff involved or in discussion with the head of department, or other appropriate senior member of staff or, if necessary, in discussion with the headteacher.

A.1 (iii) Where a member of staff requests a personal interview with head of department or other appropriate senior member of staff or headteacher it should be granted within five working days of the request being made.

A.1 (iv) The head of department or other appropriate senior member of staff or other headteacher (as in (iii) above) should seek to resolve the problem personally or, by mutual agreement, in consultation with other member(s) of the staff. The headteacher may also, by mutual agreement, seek consultation with the chairman of the managers or governors, officers of the LEA, or with representatives of the teachers' organisation(s) as may be thought appropriate.

A.2 (i) Where the matter has not been resolved under any of the procedures referred to above, the member of staff concerned should submit a formal written notice of the grievance to the headteacher, and to the person concerned, if other than the headteacher. The headteacher should then forthwith make a formal written report to the managers or governors and send a copy to the chief education officer.

A.2 (ii) The managers or governors, in consultation, where appropriate, with the chief education officer or his representative, should seek to settle the problem. All relevant documents should be submitted to them and they should allow the parties concerned, if they so wish, to make their submissions, each of them being accompanied, if they so wish, by a friend or an official representative of their union or association.

The meeting for this purpose should be arranged within ten days.

A.2 (iii) There should be a right of appeal on the part of any person or body involved in the issue to such standing or *ad hoc* body as may be agreed locally in consultation between the authority and the organisations of teachers in the area.

A.2 (iv) All relevant documents should be submitted to the body so constituted, which should meet within ten days or as soon as practicable thereafter and should allow the parties concerned, if they so wish, to make their submissions, each of them being accompanied by a friend or an official representative of their union or association.

B. Headteachers

B.1 (i) Where a headteacher has a grievance he should first of all endeavour to resolve the matter by direct approach to the person concerned. If not resolved he should then discuss the matter personally with the appropriate officer of the local education authority, who may be a member of the advisory staff of the authority or a member of the administrative staff.

B.1 (ii) Where the matter remains unresolved the headteacher should discuss it with the chief education officer or his representative, who may, also by mutual agreement, seek consultation with the Chairman of the managers or governors, or with representatives of the teachers' organisation(s) concerned, as may be thought appropriate.

B.2 (i) Where the matter is not resolved under B.1 above the headteacher should submit a formal written notice of the grievance to the chief education officer and/or to the managers or governors of the school, as the nature of the grievance makes appropriate.

B.2 (ii) Where the grievance lies with the managers or governors a meeting should be arranged by them within ten days, or as soon as it is practicable thereafter. The head and any other teacher who may be involved should be entitled to be accompanied by a friend or by a representative of the teachers' organisation(s) concerned.

B.2 (iii) Where the grievance lies with the local education authority, whether or not the support of the managers or governors of the school has been sought by the headteacher, the chief education officer should refer the grievance to the appropriate committee or subcommittee of the local education authority with all the relevant documents and, where this is relevant, with the observations of the managers or governors of the school. Such a meeting should be arranged within ten days or as soon as is practicable thereafter. The parties should be entitled to be accompanied by a friend or an official representative of their union or association.

B.2 (iv) Where the grievance has been with the managers or governors and the appropriate procedure under B.2 (ii) above has been applied, reference will be to the appropriate committee or sub-committee of the local education authority. Again all relevant documents should be placed before the committee concerned and a meeting should be arranged within ten days or as soon as is practicable thereafter to resolve the issue. The parties should be entitled to be accompanied by a friend or an official representative of their union or association.

B.2 (v) Where the procedures outlined in B.2 (ii), (iii) and (iv) above have been followed, and the problem is still unresolved, there shall remain a right of appeal as under A.2 (iii) and (iv) above.

_____

Note on the application of this procedure to Voluntary Aided Schools

In subsequent discussions with representatives of the Church of England and the Catholic Education Council the modifications set out below were agreed in order to take account of the dual relationship of teachers in aided schools on the one hand to the managers/governors as their employers, and on the other to the L E As in respect of many of their conditions of employment. It is hoped that L E As will find the amended model useful when consulting the managers/governors of non-C of E and non-R C aided schools. It is a matter of consideration whether the amended model should be applied to controlled or special agreement schools in the light of the rules of management or articles of government and of the provision of the Education Acts relating to religious education.

Preamble: procedures must not conflict with rules of management or articles of government.

A.2 (iii) line 3 After 'authority' add 'the appropriate voluntary school authorities'.

B.1 (i) line 3 After 'personally' insert 'with the Chairman of the managers or governors or, is the nature of the grievance makes it appropriate for him to do so.'

B.1 (ii) Amend to read—'where the matter remains unresolved the headteacher, after consultation with the Chairman of the managers or governors, where appropriate, should discuss it with the chief education officer or his representative or with representatives of the teachers organisation(s) concerned, as the nature of the grievance makes appropriate.'

B.2 (i) Amend to read—'Where the matter is not resolved under B.1 above, the headteacher should submit a formal written notice to the managers or governors of the school, or to the chief education officer, as the nature of the grievance makes appropriate, and if the latter, the headteacher should inform the Chairman of the managers or governors of his action.'

B.2 (iii) Amend to read—'Where the grievance lies with the local education authority, the headteacher should report the matter to the chief education officer and inform the Chairman of the managers or governors accordingly'

line 3 Start a new sentence—'The chief education officer should refer . . . etc.'

B.2 (iv) Delete.

B.2 (v) Delete reference to B.2 (iv).

September, 1972
Revised September, 1973

SECTION 2

RELATIONS BETWEEN TEACHERS AND L E As
COLLECTIVE DISPUTES PROCEDURES

Introductory

1.1 Representatives of the teachers' organisations and of the local education authorities' associations have examined the possibility of formulating, for consideration by their parent bodies, recommendations designed to achieve certain objectives. The first objective is to reduce the possibility of disputes arising between teachers and their employing authority. The second is to establish procedures at local level which should facilitate the resolving of disputes if they should arise. The third is to establish at national level a conciliation body to which reference could be made for resolving disputes which for any reason were not resolved at local level.

1.2 The recommended procedures should be regarded as complementary to the 'grievance procedures' on which agreed recommendations have already been approved by the national bodies representing teachers and authorities. They should relate to conditions of service and matters affecting the general relations between teachers' associations and local education authorities. The procedures would not be applicable in the case of disputes which properly fall to be dealt with under specific legislative provision, e.g. the arbitration provisions of the Remuneration of Teachers Act or the Teachers' Superannuation Acts. Nor would the acceptance of the procedures affect the normal arrangements for discussions at national level of matters of common interest between representatives of teachers' organisations and of the local education authorities' associations.

Consultative Procedures at Local Level
2. With a view to achieving the first of the objectives set out in paragraph 1.1 it is recommended that in the area of every local education authority there should be established agreed procedures for consultation and negotiation between representatives of the teachers' associations and representatives of the employing authority, including members of the authority. (This might be by means of a standing joint committee, or otherwise, as might be agreed locally.) This recommendation should enable the teachers' associations or the authority to refer any matter through agreed procedures for discussion and report to the authority before policy decisions are taken relating therein. It is not, therefore, a part of the disputes procedure, but rather a means likely to avoid disputes arising.

Conciliation Procedures at Local Level
3.1 The subsequent recommendations in this memorandum are directed towards the second and third objectives set out in paragraph 1.1. They should be considered in the light of these general propositions:
   (a) The recommended procedures constitute a major development in relations between teachers and local education authorities, singly and collectively. It may well be that experience will reveal defects or inadequacies in the procedures; arrangements should be made, therefore, for their working to be kept under regular review at the national level so that, if desirable, revised recommendations could be made without delay.
   (b) The recommendations presuppose the acceptance by all concerned of the basic principle that authorities and teachers will do their utmost to settle potential or actual disputes at the local level. Such acceptance implies, firstly, that reference to the proposed national body of any dispute essentially local in origin or nature would be made only as a last resort and, secondly, that a local education authority or an association of teachers involved in a dispute would take no action to implement decisions relating to the dispute until the conciliation procedures set out below had been fully utilised.
3.2 Any organisation of teachers signatory to this document would retain the right, through its appropriate associations, to meet and negotiate with the employing authority on any question affecting its members. If the subject matter of the point at issue involves departure from a locally negotiated agreement to which other teachers' organisations are parties, before approaches are made by the organisation concerned to the employing authority there should be discussion with the other teachers' associations who are party to the agreement in question.
3.3 When a difficulty which has arisen between an association, or associations, of teachers and an authority is not resolved through consultation and negotiation with the authority, the question should be referred to conciliation with a view to recommendations for the resolution of the dispute between the parties. The conciliation should be at local level unless it is agreed that having regard to the origin and nature of the dispute it would be appropriate for the matter to be referred directly to the national body described in subsequent paragraphs of this document.

The conciliation machinery at local level might for example, be either through an ad hoc body, each party to the dispute nominating a member or assessor, with a chairman acceptable to both parties, or through the establishment of a panel from which, for a particular case, appropriate representation to consider the matter and to advise is agreed between the parties.

3.4 Where local arrangements are made, the conciliation body should meet within 14 days of its establishment in the case of an ad hoc body, or of the reference to it in the case of a standing body; in either case the body should report within a stated period or as expeditiously as possible. In the event of the recommendation of the local body not being acceptable to any of the parties the matter should be dealt with under the national procedures described immediately below.

Conciliation Procedures at National Level

4.1 The local education authority associations and the teachers' organisations who are signatories to this document should establish a national conciliation body. The composition of the body, and the duration of appointments to it, would be determined from time to time by agreement between the bodies signatory to this document. Initially it might comprise 12 persons acceptable to all those bodies, of whom 4 would serve for three years, 4 for two years and 4 for one year, subsequent appointments or re-appointments being for three years. In addition there should be a chairman and deputy chairman as agreed by the signatory bodies. The Chairman (or the Deputy Chairman when necessary) after considering the nature of a particular dispute referred to the national body and after such consultations as he deemed appropriate should determine how many and which members would be invited to deal with the dispute in question.

4.2 In accordance with the objectives and general principles set out in the introductory paragraphs of this memorandum it should be accepted by all concerned that a dispute would not be referred to the national body unless (*a*) it were claimed by either party that it involved an issue which was essentially national in nature or origin or (*b*) it could be shown that all reasonable efforts had been made to settle the matter at the local level. In case of doubt the ruling of the Chairman (or Deputy Chairman) as to whether the conditions specified under (*a*) or (*b*) above had been complied with would prevail.

4.3 The national conciliation body should determine its own procedures for dealing with matters referred to it, but should follow the normal procedures for committees of enquiry into disputes of this kind. It should initiate proceedings within two weeks of a dispute being referred to it. Its findings or advice to the disputing parties should be made public.

4.4 In the event of the findings or advice of the national conciliation body not being acceptable to one or other of the parties, no action, either to implement the decision of the authority on the one hand or to initiate industrial action by the teachers' organisations concerned on the other, should be taken without their giving at least two weeks' notice of their intention.

4.5 The bodies signatory to this memorandum are agreed that the initial arrangements for the servicing and financing of the national body should be based on the presupposition that every effort will be made by all concerned to settle disputes at the local level as emphasised in paragraph 3.1*b*) of the memorandum. They are also agreed, as stated in paragraph 3.1*a*) that all the procedures recommended in the memorandum should be kept under constant review during their early years. With those two points of agreement in mind they recommend as follows:

(*a*)   that the responsibility for the basic servicing and financing of the national body (i.e. correspondence leading up to meetings of the body, provision of accommodation, recording of proceedings, and so on) should rest with the associations represented on the management panel of the Burnham Primary and Secondary Committee;

(*b*)   That the parties to a dispute referred to the national body should be responsible for meeting the specific costs of that reference other than those covered under (*a*) immediately above: Such of those costs as are common to both sides in a dispute, should be shared in equal parts between the authority (or authorities) on the one hand and the teachers' organisation (or organisations) on the other;

(*c*)   That any disagreement as to the apportionment of costs should be referred to the

Chairman (or when necessary to the Deputy Chairman) of the national body for determination by him;

(d) that the arrangements set out in (a), (b) and (c) above reviewed jointly by the signatory bodies after they have been in operation for 12 months.

Council of Local Education Authorities (Association of County Councils and Association of Metropolitan Authorities)
Assistant Masters Association
Association of Assistant Mistresses
Association of Head Mistress
Head Masters Association
National Association of Head Teachers
National Association of School Masters
National Union of Teachers   *1974*

Manual Workers
SECTION 6 APPENDIX B
GRIEVANCES AND DISCIPLINARY PROCEDURES

1. PROCEDURE FOR SETTLING GRIEVANCES

(a) Each employee should be informed that a grievance on relevant subjects should be discussed with his foreman supervisor.

(b) The foreman supervisor should reply orally as soon as possible (and in any case within . . . . days*).

(c) If the complainant is dissatisfied with the reply he should be allowed to see his shop steward trade union representative, who may then take up the matter with the foreman supervisor.

(d) It is recommended that both initial steps should be kept at the foreman supervisor level. Should this be impracticable another officer should be specified in the agreement by name or by reference to his post.

(e) If the employee continues to be aggrieved he or his representative should submit the grievance to the foreman supervisor for transmission to the head of the department (or other senior nominated officer). The grievance may be put in writing on a form to be provided and available for the purpose. The employee or his representative should keep at least one copy.

(f) The head of department (or other senior nominated officer) should, as soon a possible*, arrange a meeting with the interested parties and, if desired, with the full-time union official. It is recommended that this meeting be arranged after consultation with the personnel administrator establishment officer.

(g) As soon as possible after this meeting, the officer should confirm the decision in writing. The designated officer (or an officer responsible at a further stage in the procedure) may refer the matter back with appropriate comments or reject the grievance.

(h) If the employee continues to be aggrieved in respect of his original complaint, his grievance may thereafter* be taken to an appropriate committee of the council, or a joint committee representative of management and the employees, or any other similar arrangement suitable for the purpose. The factors influencing an authority's decision in this regard will make allowance for local conditions and the likelihood of settlement. It may be possible to substitute a Joint Works/Staff Committee for one of the above, if the issue falls within the sphere of that Committee.

(i) Thereafter further procedure where appropriate should lie with the existing conciliation machinery.

* *It may be considered desirable to incorporate appropriate time limits for the sake of dealing with grievances expeditiously. The time limits should be capable of notification according to the circumstances.*

Source: *National Joint Council for Local Authorities' Administrative, Professional, Technical and Clerical Services Scheme of Conditions of Service*, Eighth edition, 1975.

Note:
(a)   *It may be considered desirable to identify items to be excluded from consideration under the procedure.*
(b)   *The procedure should not exclude the following possibilities:*
    (i)   *that a man and his representative approach the foreman in the first instance;*
    (ii)   *that a man be represented or be without representation;*
    (iii)   *that a group of employees be represented by a trade union official or by a committee; or that the procedure should be available to a group of employees sharing a grievance.*

2.   LOCAL DISCIPLINARY PROCEDURE

(a)   Where an employee's work, conduct or omission are such as to warrant disciplinary action, the appropriate supervisor or officer should give a warning to the employee.

(b)   This may be done orally or in writing depending on the circumstances. A written warning will give the nature of the complaint and any implication therefrom, and the fact that the employee has been notified of the warning.

(c)   The further commission of a similar act, or of a subsequent but different offence, may result in a further warning, which may be a final warning according to the circumstances. The employee's attention must be drawn to the issue of a final warning, and he must be informed that he may ask his trade union official to be formerly notified. Any final warning must be confirmed in writing as soon as possible.

(d)   Certain types of gross misconduct may lead to instant dismissal.

(e)   Should any disciplinary action be reconsidered and effectively withdrawn, any written reference should be expunged from the employee's file and the employee notified accordingly.

(f)   A head of department (or other senior nominated officer) where authorised may dismiss an employee in cases where previous warnings have been ineffective, or for gross misconduct. Where the possibility of serious disciplinary action arises (including dismissal), the employee should be interviewed by the officer concerned and told why his services are considered unsatisfactory. The employee should be given adequate opportunity to explain or defend himself. In particular he will have the right to be accompanied during the interview by his trade union or other representative. It is recommended that this interview be arranged after consultation with the personnel administrator establishment officer.

(g)   Dismissal or other serious disciplinary action should be confirmed by letter (using recorded delivery when otherwise unavoidable) under the signature of the Chief Executive to the authority (or other nominated chief officer). This letter should state the grounds for the action taken and confirm that the employee may appeal in the appropriate way to a committee where he may appear in person and/or with a representative.

(h)   The contract of employment may be suspended either to enable investigations to be made where the possibility of dismissal may arise or where there are grounds for doubt as to the suitability of the employee to continue at work pending criminal investigations or procedure or as an alternative to dismissal. The procedure recommended in the event of dismissal should also apply to an employee thus suspended. During a period of suspension the employee shall be paid an allowance of not less than half pay. Except where suspension has been used as an alternative to dismissal,
    (*i*)   in the event of it being adjudged that the employee was not blameworthy, the suspension shall be terminated and employee shall receive all monies to which he would have been entitled but for the suspension;
    (*ii*)   if the employee is adjudged blameworthy, but is allowed to continue in employment, the local authority shall have discretion whether to make up the suspension allowance to equal the whole or part of wages withheld during the period of suspension;
    (*iii*)   if the employee is dismissed, he shall not be entitled to wages other than the sum (if any) due up to the date of suspension, but shall be allowed to retain any sum already paid to him as suspension allowance during the period of suspension.

(i)   If at any time in this procedure the employee wishes to exercise his right of appeal

against any form of disciplinary action taken against him, he must do so within . . . .
working days* of receipt of the warning or notification of termination of employment
on disciplinary grounds, or written advice of other disciplinary action.

* *The appropriate period will be for local determination. It should not be longer than the equivalent of four weeks.*

(j)   Normally no disciplinary action should be taken against a shop steward until the
circumstances of the case have been discussed with a full-time official of the union
concerned.

(k)   This procedure does not apply to notice given,
(*i*)   on termination of employment for which an employee has been specifically
engaged;
(*ii*)   in the event of redundancy; (a grievance on account of redundancy should be dealt
with under the local redundancy agreement);
(*iii*)   where less than six months' probationary service has been completed and dismissal arises from unsuitability for confirmation of appointment

(l)   A model procedure for hearing of appeals to the authority against dismissal or other
serious disciplinary action, is set out in Paragraph 3, below.

Ancillary APT & C staff

81. Grievances

(*a*)   Employing authorities shall ensure that officers are fully aware of the steps available to
them as individuals under the 'grievance procedure' drawn up by the authority in accordance with their particular circumstances. However, matters arising which would be appropriately dealt with under paragraph 80 (Appeal) of this Scheme shall continue to be dealt
with in the manner required by that paragraph.

(*b*)   Employing authorities are recommended to adopt a grievance procedure in accordance
with the model below:

Model Grievance Procedure
Note. *The following procedure does not apply to matters appropriately dealt with under paragraph 80 (Appeal) of this Scheme.*

(i)   Where an officer is aggrieved on any matters (other than the grading of his post) he
should discuss the matter initially with his immediate superior.

(ii)   The immediate superior should reply orally to the grievance as soon as possible
and in any case within seven days.

(iii)   If the complainant is dissatisfied with the reply he should report his grievance to
his staff (or trade union) representative who may then raise the matter with the
head of the department (or other senior nominated officer). Where an officer is not
in membership of a trade union or staff organisation he should be allowed personally to make representation to his head of department (or other senior nominated
officer).

(iv)   The head of department (or other senior nominated officer) should reply to the
complaint as soon as possible and in any case within seven days.

(v)   If the complaint is not satisfactorily resolved at this stage, the local authority is
recommended to try and settle the matter, wherever practicable, through the
machinery of the local joint committee or in its absence directly with the trade
union(s) involved.

(vi)   The matter to end at employing authority level except where it is agreed between
the parties that an important issue of principle arises which could be considered
through the conciliation machinery.

82–89. (Reserved)

75. Disciplinary Rules and Procedures

(*a*)   The National Council believes it is important for local authorities to have rules and procedures which assist in setting standards of conduct, to stimulate order and fairness in the

treatment of individuals. These rules and procedures should be readily available to and understood by both management and staff at all levels.

(*b*) The National Council has not issued detailed guidance on the formulation of disciplinary rules and procedures, but recommends local authorities to determine, by operation of the procedures normally adopted by the local parties, arrangements appropriate to local circumstances which have full regard to the principles and standards set out in the A C A S Code of Practice on Disciplinary Rules and Procedures.

3. **MODEL PROCEDURE TO BE FOLLOWED AT LOCAL HEARING OF APPEALS AGAINST DISMISSALS OR OTHER SERIOUS DISCIPLINARY ACTION**

Employing authorities are recommended to institute the following procedure at local hearing of appeals against dismissals:

(a)   The local authority shall appoint an Appeals Committee which shall be constituted from among members who are not members of the employing committee which decided the issue in the first place. It is desirable that in normal circumstances and for the sake of dealing with the appeal expeditiously the Committee should be given power to act.

(b)   The employee shall be given notice in writing at least seven days in advance of the time and place of the hearing, and shall be allowed to be represented by his trade union representative or some other person of his choice and shall be enabled to call witnesses and produce documents relevant to his defence at the hearing.

(c)   The local authority's representative(s) shall put the case in the present of the appellant and his representative and may call witnesses.

(d)   The appellant (or his representative) to have the opportunity to ask questons of the local authority's representative on the evidence given by him and any witnesses whom he may call.

(e)   The Committee may ask questions of the local authority's representative and witnesses.

(f)   The appellant (or his representative) to put his case in the presence of the local authority's representative and to call such witnesses as he wishes.

(g)   The local authority's representative to have opportunity to ask questions of the appellant and his witnesses.

(h)   The Committee may ask questions of the appellant and his witnesses.

(i)   The local authority's representative and the appellant (or his representative) to have an opportunity to sum up their case if they so wish.

(j)   The local authority's representative and the appellant and his representative and witnesses to withdraw.

(k)   The Committee, with the officer appointed as Secretary to the Committee, to deliberate in private only recalling the local authority's representative and the appellant to clear points of uncertainty on evidence already given. If recall is necessary both parties are to return notwithstanding only one is concerned with the point giving rise to doubt.

(l)   The Committee to announce the decision to the parties personally or in writing as may be determined, unless for special reasons the Committee has only the power of recommendation to the authority in which case a report will be submitted to the authority and the parties so advised.

Further reading

Adams, N, *Law and Teachers Today*, Hutchinson, 1983.

Barrell, G R, *Teachers and the Law*, Methuen, 1978.

Croner, S, *Heads' Legal Guide*, Croner Publications Ltd, 1985.

Harrison, G, and Bloy, D, *Essential Law for Teachers*, Oyez, 1980.

Taylor, G, and Saunders, J B, *The Law of Education*, 8th edition, and *Supplement* to the 8th edition, Butterworth, 1976, 1981.

Maintenance of the code of staff conduct

Introduction

Some headteachers will doubtless be loath to admit that incidences of staff indiscipline ever occur in their school, while others will concede that there are occasions where a minority of individuals do not always observe the staff code of conduct, but such aberrations are best sorted out informally within the school.

These stances are entirely consistent with the spirit of professionalism which traditionally underpinned relationships among school staff. Fortunately, the vast majority of teachers continue to be imbued by the attendant moral strictures and their contracts of employment. Nevertheless, as with other professional groups, there are those individuals who either flout the rules or for various reasons are unable to meet the exacting standards demanded by the profession. These observations also apply to school support staff.

For the headteacher, the small minority of individuals who breach the rules can, and frequently do, take up an inordinate amount of time and energy, especially where the action taken to persuade those concerned to conform has been inappropriate.

Failure by the headteacher to take timely and appropriate action in matters of staff conduct and capability can lead not only to unnecessary tension in the classroom but may result in:

- union intervention
- governor involvement
- LEA intervention
- legal action.

External intervention may, of course, occur where the headteacher has taken appropriate action, in which case his/her position is likely to be strengthened. The headteacher who displays a lack of judgement and attempts to resolve a staff disciplinary matter without reference to the principles of natural justice and LEA rules and procedures may ultimately be placed in an untenable position before an industrial tribunal. The consequences of this are innumerable, but it may be predicted that the event will:

- bring unwelcome publicity to the school;
- disrupt the conduct of school affairs;
- undermine the authority and status of the headteacher;
- provoke the displeasure of senior colleages and LEA officers;
- possibly result in disciplinary action being taken against the headteacher.

The headteacher will, therefore, wish to consider very carefully the appropriate action to take in matters of staff discipline, and here the LEA rules and procedures applying to staff conduct are a crucial and first point of reference.

While implementing disciplinary action against a member of the school adult community is not in itself a difficult process, the context in which this occurs can be extremely complex. To a greater or lesser extent, the headteacher is likely to be faced with the following features:

- where his or her authority is called into question with increasing frequency and where at the same time there is a lack of specificity of roles and responsibilities between LEA officers, inspectors/advisers, governors and school;
- the management structure and responsibilities among staff of the school are not sufficiently articulated or accepted by colleagues;
- the headteacher lacks real experience of staff disciplinary matters;
- genuine disagreement about professional standards and professional judgement;
- a lack of formally recognised sanctions available to the headteacher.

It is against this background that attention is addressed in this chapter to some of the issues and pitfalls associated with the maintenance of staff rules and code of behaviour.

Staff rules and code of behaviour

Preliminary tasks

To ensure that staff disciplinary matters are dealt with expeditiously and fairly the headteacher will wish to give early consideration to the following issues:

- *LEA policy applying to staff discipline*
- *LEA staff disciplinary procedures*
- *review of the school's internal arrangements*
- *development and maintenance of a code of staff conduct.*

LEA policy

LEA policies towards school staff disciplinary matters tend to vary between formal written statements of policy, which are circulated to schools, and policies which are implicit and where knowledge of their existence comes through a process of osmosis.

The apparent reluctance of some LEAs to articulate clearly staff disciplinary policies stems from a number of sources, including administrative inertia and a belief that such explicit statements would serve to undermine existing professional relationships between officers and school staff. This view is hardly tenable since most LEAs now have formal staff disciplinary procedures which are a direct reflection of policies.

Whatever the reasons for the lack of a written policy which is known to all those concerned, it is a relatively simple matter to produce a succinct statement which conveys the LEA intentions. Consider the example below.

A staff disciplinary policy statement
Colleagues will appreciate that orderly staff arrangements are a crucial aspect of a well run school. The aim of the LEA, therefore, is to promote:

a set of staff rules which are essential and clearly understood by all those concerned;

a staff discipline procedure and system of appeal to facilitate the handling of breaches of the staff code;

a process of review to ensure the continuing relevance of the rules and procedures.

This model could hardly be described as an administrative burden or a threat to existing relationships. It simply conveys the essence of the LEA aims which is all that is required in such policy statements.

LEA staff disciplinary procedures

While many LEAs continue to operate (with some minor modifications) the staff disciplinary procedure devised at national level, others have developed their own procedures in the light of their particular circumstances. Hence there is variation both in the substance and the way(s) in which they apply staff disciplinary procedures.

Readers are advised to refer to the chapter on employment law for the legal implications arising from staff disciplinary matters. Suffice to state here that a disciplinary procedure should:

- *be in writing, specify to whom it applies, and provide for effective and swift operation;*
- *provide for a disciplinary hearing;*
- *indicate the range of disciplinary sanctions and attendant lines of authority to impose them;*
- *specify the system of appeal and the individual's right to appeal against the decision;*
- *provide for the individual to be informed of the complaint against him/her and the opportunity to state his/her case before a decision is reached;*
- *state the right of the individual to be accompanied by a representation or 'friend';*
- *indicate how the decision will be communicated to the individual.*

The utility of a staff disciplinary procedure which does not accommodate the processes indicated in the list above must remain in doubt. Moreover, while the LEA may have taken great care in drawing up a disciplinary procedure it will be to no avail if the headteacher chooses to ignore its existence or fails to follow the procedure consistently and correctly.

While differences exist in the way(s) LEAs administer staff disciplinary procedures, the convention is to adopt the following processes:

- verbal warning
- written warning
- final written warning
- dismissal.

A verbal warning would normally apply for an act of minor misconduct. In the absence of an improvement in behaviour it is customary to move through the next stages of procedure which may ultimately lead to dismissal. In circumstances of gross misconduct, dismissal may be the appropriate sanction.

Systems of appeal

Fundamental to any disciplinary procedure is the right of the person concerned to appeal to a higher and independent body if they disagree with the finding of the disciplinary hearing or with the sanction applied. Consequently:

- *No member of the appeal body should have been previously involved in the case; this equally applies to members of governing bodies.*
- *The conduct of the appeal hearing should proceed with judicial impartiality.*
- *The verdict should be fair and seen to be fair.*

It is important that at every stage in the operation of the disciplinary procedure the person concerned is informed of his/her right of appeal and to whom the appeal should be made. This should always be done in writing and should include a time limit within which the appeal should be made, usually within ten working days. An appeal can be made on one or more of these counts:

- *status of charge or complaint*
- *decision of disciplinary hearing*
- *sanctions imposed*
- *conduct of the meeting.*

In a case of dismissal, the individual concerned may, of course, decide to pursue the matter through an industrial tribunal. This is less likely to occur where the internal arrangements for dealing with staff disciplinary issues are satisfactory and where the formal procedure is fair and has been applied correctly. It will have been noted in the chapter on employment law that these aspects have sometimes proved inadequate with all that entails for the position of the LEA and headteacher.

School internal arrangements

The headteacher will wish to ensure that staff are aware of the LEA disciplinary policy and procedure, especially because of the codification of rules required by employment law and legal processes.

The maintenance of staff rules and code of behaviour also calls for considerable skill and judgement. To identify accurately a particular issue, to determine when a situation is reached such that the headteacher passes from a helping counselling role into formal disciplinary procedure, and to decide which action will unite staff and which might divide them, are all cases in point.

Code of professional conduct

It is generally accepted that one of the characteristics of the professions is their capacity to set and maintain standards through self-regulation. The maintenance of standards, through the creation of rules and regulations is, however, not inconsistent with the exercise of considerable personal autonomy and professional integrity. Staff in the school are in this way bound together on a basis upon which they mutually accept and share common standards which they themselves have chosen to observe and maintain.

It is important that this capacity for self-regulation is recognised in the school situation and, as far as it is feasible, staff should be involved in the development of the staff rules and code of conduct appropriate to the circumstances of the individual school. This is necessary to gain a consistent understanding and acceptance of the rules. It can also work for a better and more appropriate code of conduct in the light of changes in the ways the school operates.

The headteacher's responsibility for developing the staff rules is limited to those rules which need to be formulated and codified at the level of the school and will be concerned mainly with the working arrangements and practices concerning that school. These, however, have to be seen in relation to the contract of employment, which defines the basis of employment relationships, and collective union/employer agreements which supplement it, together with relevant LEA regulations and procedures.

The extent to which rules should be codified and written always presents a dilemma for the headteacher. On the one hand it is neither possible nor even desirable to write rules to cover every situation or circumstances. On the other hand, a complete absence of written rules and regulations makes it difficult for staff to know or remember what is expected of them and how to deal with things when out-of-the-ordinary matters arise. When developing and codifying the staff rules and regulations, the headteacher should be concerned to include only those rules that are absolutely necessary for the organisation and administration of the school and to state the possible consequences of not complying with them.

Consider these examples taken from the handbook of one school:

> On no account should a pupil be allowed to drop a subject or to change subjects without the written permission of the deputy head.

> All staff must consult the 'Today Noticeboard' in the staffroom and check their pigeon holes each day.

> All staff will ensure pupils obey the school rules at all times.

> The duty house tutor will complete the 'Yard Duty Reminder' to staff the week preceding the duty.

> Teachers will at all times act on the medical note on pupils brought up to date each September by house tutors, paying regard to the confidentiality of the information.

> Staff will at all times follow the outline relating to liaison with parents as set out in the staff Handbook, particularly where pupils may have caused serious disruption to lessons.

> Staff organising extracurricular activities will do so by specific reference to the ECA booklet.

> Staff will be on the school premises by 8.50 a.m. each school day.

The school handbook from which this sample of rules was taken is extremely comprehensive about most aspects of school life; it allows staff to see exactly where they are, and runs to 137 pages.

In formulating rules applying to staff the headteacher will wish to be assured that they are:

- *necessary*
- *reasonable*
- *easily understood*
- *known to staff*
- *capable of enforcement*
- *consistently applied*
- *known by governors and LEA.*

In practice, rules of which a breach is serious enough to merit suspension, or summary dismissal, should be separated from those which are more appropriately dealt with through a procedure which provides an opportunity for the person concerned to rectify a lapse in standards.

Guidance on offences which may warrant suspension or summary dismissal is given in the DES Administration Memorandum 6/82 and include:

- *sexual offences and violence involving children*
- *other serious kinds of violence*
- *misappropriation of school monies*
- *fake claims of a gravely deceptive nature as to qualifications*
- *repeated misconduct or multiple convictions of a minor kind.*

This is not an exhaustive list and is included for purposes of illustration. Additional reference should be made to the LEA regulations and procedures.

Maintenance of staff discipline
In the light of the code of staff conduct in your school and the internal arrangements for dealing with such matters, consider the two incidents below:

The case of a member of staff who is persistently late, or improperly dressed.

A senior teacher who never manages to attend department meetings.

Where the responsibilities for staff conduct are ill-defined, or the members of staff concerned fail to take the appropriate action in cases of staff competence and misdemeanour, the disciplinary procedure is likely to prove ineffective. A fundamental requirement is that there shall be consistency in the approach to resolving such matters. This is very difficult to sustain where those ostensibly responsible are unclear about their respective role(s) and responsibilities. A job description may be helpful to clarify the duties of the staff concerned. Additional clarification may be forthcoming from the LEA regulations and articles of school government.

When being advised on how to discharge this responsibility, the staff concerned should be advised about good practice, as follows:

- *They must ensure that all the people for whom they are responsible know the rules and the procedure for applying them.*
- *They are to be firm and fair in ensuring that rules and regulations are observed.*
- *They must deal with incidents without delay and with objectivity.*
- *They must inform.*
- *They must record.*
- *They must endeavour to correct staff behaviour by their advice and decisions.*
- *They must advise a more senior colleague about the adequacy of any particular provision in the rules and regulations.*
- *They must recognise when a breach of rules is beyond the scope of their authority.*

The intention is to enable members of staff to overcome any difficulties in complying with the school's requirements. This will normally take place on a friendly and informal basis. However, if there are recurrent problems or difficulties which indicate lack of application or concern on the part of the member of staff, then the headteacher should be informed immediately so that he or she can take the necessary action to secure an improvement. In circumstances of gross misconduct by a member of staff, the headteacher will wish to be advised immediately in order to make an early investigation into the alleged incident.

Where a member of staff does not respond positively to advice and counselling in matters of professional competence, or fails to heed instructions to improve behaviour, the headteacher may have little option but to take steps to invoke the formal disciplinary procedure. Here it would be customary for the headteacher to alert the chairman of governors and to seek the advice of the appropriate LEA officer about the problem before formal action is instigated.

It cannot be stressed too strongly that the headteacher must endeavour to contact the person with the formal responsibility for handling matters of staff discipline within the LEA. Problems have arisen where the headteacher has received ill-conceived advice from doubtless well-meaning but inexperienced LEA personnel.

Before implementing the formal disciplinary procedure, the LEA will need to be satisfied that the professional standards and code of behaviour have been consistently applied in the school and that records have been kept of the matter in question, along with the action taken to date.

If, after consideration of the information supplied by the headteacher, a decision is made that the situation warrants a disciplinary hearing, then the appropriate stage of procedure should be invoked by those responsible. The stage of procedure adopted should relate to the gravity of the offence.

Consider these incidents:

1 A PE teacher 'fisted' a boy which prompted a complaint from the parents to the headteacher.

2 The head of department of Technology is not performing very well and the headteacher pressed him to be more imaginative in his leadership. This action was regarded by the head of department as unfounded criticism and he resisted the headteacher's suggestions.

3 I had a teacher of English with a gift for drama but he could not manage in a classroom: it seems he can only relate to small groups.

4 A caretaker physically assaulted the headteacher who had to receive hospital treatment.

These cases represent differences in substance and gravity of offence. The particular stage of the procedure invoked should be appropriate to the nature of the teacher's misdemeanour.

Review of the incidents presented

Incident 1

Here those responsible would need to address attention to the following issues:

- Were there any witnesses to the incident and, if so, is their evidence corroborative?
- The nature of the alleged assault, i.e. did the teacher actually strike the pupil with his fist?

- Was the teacher acting in self-defence? Did the pupil receive first aid and/or attend a doctor?
- Was the teacher receiving medical treatment, e.g. for stress?
- Has the teacher been involved in an act of violence against a pupil previously?

Incident 2
Issues to be addressed here include the following:

- What criteria is being used to judge the performance of the head of department? Is he aware of the criteria?
- What was the head of department actually asked to do in order to improve his/her performance?
- Was any support offered to the head of department to assist him/her to improve performance? What was the nature of the support?
- Are there any mitigating reasons, e.g. health, that could help to explain the head of department's poor performance?
- Was this the first occasion the headteacher has suggested to the head of department that he/she is not performing very well? How long has the head of department been in the post?
- Did the headteacher inform the head of department in writing of his/her shortcomings and what the future expectations about performance were? If so, when did this occur?
- Has the head of department been given a job description?

Incident 3
Issues that merit discussion here include:

- Does '. . . could not manage in the classroom . . .' refer to the maintenance of order and discipline of pupils in the classroom or is it a question of presentation of the lesson?
- Was the teacher given any assistance in order to improve his/her performance and, if so, what was the nature of the help and over what time period?
- Are there any mitigating circumstances which may help to explain the deficiencies of the teacher, e.g. personal health problems or a high proportion of pupils with serious personal problems?

Incident 4
In cases of violence against a person, the caretaker committing the assault would be suspended pending an enquiry by the appropriate LEA officer. In the absence of extreme provocation, and no medical evidence in support of the caretaker, such gross misconduct may warrant summary dismissal.

Gross negligence or gross misconduct
In dealing with a charge of gross negligence or gross misconduct, the headteacher's principal task will be to conduct an investigation. The headteacher does not have the legal power to dismiss staff; that lies with the employer, the education committee or, in the case of voluntary aided schools, with the board of governors.

The headteacher, however, does have the power to suspend on full pay any member of staff, and this sanction can be used in cases that would warrant summary dismissal. Although the headteacher (as agent) has power to suspend, he or she does not have the power to reinstate. If an incident of this level of severity occurs, the headteacher should consult the Chairman of governors and LEA officers about whether the person concerned should be suspended on full pay, pending an investigation and the convening of a disciplinary hearing. The headteacher should then inform the person concerned that he is being suspended on full pay, pending a disciplinary hearing, and to leave the school premises. This should be confirmed in a letter.

Certain offences, such as those listed on page 186 can warrant summary dismissal, that is without going through all the stages of the procedure.

Staff conduct, competence and capability

While gross misconduct is easily identified, there are often real difficulties in deciding whether an individual is incapable of carrying out the properly assigned tasks (for medical reasons, among others), or is incompetent because of the lack of training or unsuitability for the job. Both are matters of staff conduct but the approach to dealing with the problem will usually be quite different.

Consider these incidents:

> A teacher was judged by the headteacher to be an incompetent teacher. On the advice of the headteacher the LEA redeployed her to another school. Shortly after the transfer she had a nervous breakdown. It subsequently emerged that she had a history of stress-related illness.

> A head of department was regularly absent from school and when he did attend he was invariably late. He was given a verbal warning as to his conduct by the head-teacher, but offered no explanation. A colleague subsequently informed the head-teacher that the wife of the head of department was very ill.

In the former case the teacher resumed her duties after medical treatment and her teaching performance proved satisfactory. Her former headteacher said that he would not have recommended her transfer if he had known about her medical circumstances. His original diagnosis of her teaching performance was based exclusively on professional criteria.

In the latter case, the head of department was incapable of fulfilling his contractual obligations because of his domestic circumstances. On being informed of his problem the LEA granted the head of department compassionate leave and put him in touch with the social services department. After a short absence he was able to resume his normal duties. The individual concerned was fortunate that a colleague reported his circumstances to the headteacher. In the absence of such information the headteacher would be justified in approaching the LEA with a view to invoking the formal disciplinary procedure.

It is obviously not possible to cover all eventualities, but the headteacher should ensure that:

- *senior members of staff monitor and report cases of incompetent teaching;*
- *LEA advice is sought where there seems to be any doubt about the teacher's health or personal circumstances;*
- *an LEA adviser/inspector conducts an assessment of the level of competence of a teacher who seems to be having difficulties with teaching;*
- *systematic counselling and in-service training is provided for the 'ineffective' teacher.*

The fact remains that the division between conduct and capability is not always a clear-cut one, and a keen sense of judgement is crucial in such cases. Here, the timing of the decision to move from the process of counselling and generally supporting a teacher to invoking the disciplinary procedure is extremely important.

The headteacher who unsuccessfully persists with counselling and support for an incompetent teacher may find it difficult to justify disciplinary action (because it has gone on too long). Equally, in circumstances of relatively limited support, the headteacher may find that it would be seen as unreasonable to invoke the disciplinary procedure because insufficient help was given.

When assessing the teaching performance of a member of staff it is important that the criteria used are credible. The fact that a headteacher identified a weak teacher in the school is not necessarily a sufficient reason in itself for stating that the teacher is incompetent. A teacher may be deemed to be weak in comparison with his/her immediate colleagues, but may be considered satisfactory in relation to peers in another school.

Where an individual is dismissed on the grounds of incompetence and pursues a claim for unfair dismissal, it is likely that the industrial tribunal would require the criteria used in the assessment to be produced.

Breaches of the staff code: a check list

Before taking any disciplinary action the prudent headteacher will check the following:

- *He/she will clarify in precise terms the nature of the offence. Is it misconduct, poor performance in the job or a combination of poor performance and misconduct?*
- *He/she will write down all the facts which can be substantiated if challenged. Are they suspicions rather than facts? Is the evidence circumstantial rather than proven facts?*
- *In the case of misconduct, the headteacher will establish what happened, when and where it happened and whether the individual concerned gave any reason for his/her conduct at the time.*
- *In the case of poor performance, he/she will refer to a job description and/or record of the assessment made of the individual including the nature and duration of the assessment.*
- *He/she will be confident that the individual concerned will be aware of the expected standards of conduct and/or performance.*
- *He/she will assemble all relevant documents including the individual's personal file, a copy of the school rules and disciplinary procedures, copies of relevant letters, contract, LEA rules, and memoranda which would have a bearing on the case.*

Support staff

Disciplinary procedures applying to school caretaking, catering staff and so forth are common to all manual occupational groups in the employment of the local authority. This practice raises a number of implications for the conduct of staff management in the school.

With the exception of voluntary aided schools (where practice varies considerably) school governors would not usually be involved in the processes of adjudication where an individual is charged to be incompetent or who apparently committed an act of misconduct, though in such cases the headteacher may wish to seek the advice of the chairman.

In such circumstances, the headteacher will wish to avoid undermining the formal disciplinary procedure and indeed the authority of the immediate supervisor concerned, especially where he or she is an integral part of the disciplinary process. This requires not only knowledge about the procedure but also demands on occasion considerable tact and skill on the part of the headteacher.

The headteacher has traditionally been seen by caretakers and their peers to be the appropriate authority within the school to assist them in resolving any problems they may be having, including employment relations issues. In most instances the headteacher will cope with incidents of misconduct adroitly, but there are some headteachers who, with the best possible motives, have got themselves into difficulties by their actions and those of the school supervisors.

Thus, where a supervisor complains to the headteacher about (say) the conduct of a member of their staff, he or she will wish to consider very carefully the most appropriate action to take. A reprimand to the individual concerned may have the desired outcome, but equally it may be entirely inappropriate in the light of the local authority regulations or in the absence of the full facts of the case.

In these circumstances the headteacher's decision to issue a reprimand may effectively prevent or inhibit further action being taken under the formal disciplinary procedure, because in simple terms it is against the tenets of natural justice to be 'punished' twice for the same offence. Moreover, the headteacher's intervention may serve to undermine the status of the formal procedure, in particular the personnel responsible for its application, since the headteacher is not usually a party to the formal disciplinary process.

This cautionary note is included merely to alert the headteacher to potential pitfalls which are best avoided. Where the headteacher is confident that an informal 'ticking off' is comensurate with the offence, then this approach has much to commend it, if only to ensure the preservation of good interpersonal relationships.

Dual reporting system

In recent years there is a growing tendency for LEAs to appoint personnel to the Authority who have supervisory responsibilities for school support staff. Here, a particular difficulty can arise when (say) the caretaker is at the centre of a disciplinary issue.

Consider the incident below:

> The headteacher issued a reasonable instruction to the caretaker who refused to obey on the grounds that he took his orders from the LEA supervisor.

This sort of incident points to an inherent weakness of any system of dual reporting and supervision, particularly when the parties concerned are geographically separated which can give rise to communication problems. In such circumstances the headteacher should clarify with the LEA his or her position *vis-à-vis* the management of support staff in the school.

Many of the sorts of problems illustrated above may be avoided where the headteacher has established close communication links with the LEA supervisors. Issues can be swiftly dealt with before attitudes harden and relationships sour beyond recovery. Moreover, where a supervisor in the school is apparently in breach of the rules, it is likely that the central or area supervisor will be responsible for making the initial decision as to whether the alleged offence merits the application of the formal disciplinary procedure. In the absence of an established relationship with such personnel, the headteacher may find it difficult to press for action to be taken against individuals who are a disruptive influence on the work of the school.

Competence and misconduct

Reference was made earlier to the need to make a distinction between competence and misconduct. This observation also applies to support staff. Assessment of competence can present very real difficulties for the headteacher, primarily because he or she is unlikely (in many instances) to have the necessary expertise to make an informed judgement as to whether an individual is failing to meet the required standards of the job, though it is sometimes difficult to avoid the temptation.

For support staff generally, it is the responsibility of their immediate supervisors to ensure that their staff demonstrate a satisfactory level of performance in their allotted tasks. However, as indicated above, the headteacher continues to remain the first point of reference for perhaps the majority of school supervisors when they are faced with a problem.

In the circumstances the headteacher will need to be satisfied that the complaint about an individual's level of competence is genuine and not inspired by personality differences. If the former appears to be the case, the supervisor concerned should be advised to contact the LEA supervisor responsible.

Where there appears to be some doubt about the work performance of a school supervisor, the headteacher will invariably conduct a preliminary investigation in an endeavour to ascertain what might be the cause of the individual's apparent lapse in standards. Of course, it may be that the supervisor in question was an unfortunate appointment who was unable to attain the level of performance required from the moment he or she entered the school. Either way, it is important that the headteacher should not be seen to condone the apparent ineffectiveness of an individual through lack of action, and the assistance of the LEA should be sought to resolve the issue.

It is not simply that inertia on the part of the headteacher may serve to reinforce latent frustrations and tensions among both teaching and non-teaching staff, though this merits serious consideration. Where an individual is allowed to fall short of the necessary levels of performance for any length of time, it is likely to become progressively more difficult to bring about an improvement in his or her effectiveness. Furthermore, in the event that the dismissal of the person concerned was felt necessary, the Authority may have some difficulty in convincing an industrial tribunal of the merits of their decision (assuming it went that far).

Finally, it should be acknowledged that most members of the school adult community conduct themselves in accordance with the expectations of the headteacher, pupils and the wider community. They demonstrate a high level of commitment to the school, observe the rules and are proficient in their work.

However, it is a fortunate headteacher who has never had to deal with a member of teaching or support staff who has transgressed the school rules, or failed to demonstrate the level of competence necessary to carry out his/her duties effectively. Such incidents are generally quickly resolved, but there are those headteachers who have cause to reflect ruefully about a particular case that was mishandled. The guidance offered in this chapter is designed to assist the headteacher to minimise the possibility of taking inappropriate action when confronted with cases of misconduct or incompetence.

The incident which follows is included as an example of the sorts of issues explored in the complementary set of training materials.

Incident: The moonlighting groundsman

The deputy head, returning from a moderating panel during normal working hours, pulled into a local garage for some petrol. It was the school groundsman who came to serve him. When he returned to school he informed the headteacher.

The school is one of the few still to retain its own groundsman. Most schools in the LEA are now subject to the local authority grass-cutting service.

Trainer's guidelines: issues for consideration
The groundsman is almost certainly in breach of contract and therefore subject to disciplinary action.

What would you advise the headteacher to do in this case? Should he:

- turn a blind eye;
- have a quiet word with the groundsman;
- establish the facts, e.g. how often and at what times did the groundsman work at the garage;
- clarify who is responsible for supervising the groundsman;
- inform the LEA;
- other actions?

When such incidents arise, the headteacher will wish to consider the implications of setting a precedent which other members of staff may refer to in the future; the alienation or possible loss of a valued member of the school community; and the reaction of the LEA in the event that the episode is subsequently brought to their attention.

Index